# THE CATHOLIC BIBLICAL QUARTERLY

## MONOGRAPH SERIES

## 16

## ENOCH AND THE GROWTH OF AN APOCALYPTIC TRADITION

by
### James C. VanderKam

# ENOCH AND THE GROWTH OF AN APOCALYPTIC TRADITION

by

## James C. VanderKam

The Catholic Biblical Association of America
Washington, DC 20064
1984

All biblical citations, unless otherwise indicated, are from the Revised Standard Version of the Bible (RSV), copyrighted 1946, 1952 © 1971, 1973.

ENOCH AND THE GROWTH OF AN APOCALYPTIC TRADITION
by James C. VanderKam

©1984 The Catholic Biblical Association of America
Washington, DC 20064

PRODUCED IN THE UNITED STATES

**Library of Congress Cataloging in Publication Data**

VanderKam, James C.
  Enoch and the growth of an apocalyptic tradition.

  (The Catholic Biblical quarterly. Monograph series; 16)
  Bibliography: p.
  Includes index.
    1. Enoch.   2. Apocalyptic literature—History and criticism.   3. Ethiopic
book of Enoch—Criticism, interpretation, etc.   I. Title.   II. Series.
BS580.E6V36   1984      229'.913      83-10134
ISBN 0-915170-15-9

# TABLE OF CONTENTS

Jan/8

## PREFACE

The sheer number of recent publications relating to Jewish apocalyptic literature and thought indicates a lively interest today in these subjects. Students of early Judaism and biblical scholars have often devoted some attention to the relevant documents, but now one sees many experts examining them not only as background information for, say, New Testament studies, but also as worthy objects of research in themselves. The results have been new editions and translations of texts, historical and theological insights, etc.; but despite the welter of publications, some old problems remain to challenge the student of Jewish apocalyptic phenomena. Among these is the issue of isolating the sources and influences which, in conjunction with creative minds, produced or at least encouraged apocalyptic ways of thinking. Foreign influences—notably Persian ones—have long been recognized, but within the complex of early Judaism itself some scholars have seen prophecy as the dominant source, while others have pointed to wisdom. The entire discussion has been plagued by use of vague terms such as "prophecy," "wisdom," and "apocalyptic" and by the widespread tendency to treat each as though it were a unitary phenomenon. Given this background, it seemed that there would be some value in narrowing the question of sources by focusing upon one early and central figure in the apocalyptic texts—Enoch— and in scrutinizing the traditions that were associated with him for clues regarding the evolution of at least this particular apocalyptic strand. Enoch is an especially good candidate for the role because he figures as a seer in a relatively large number of early texts and because new data from Qumrân about the earliest of these texts are now available. It is not being suggested that just one movement with distinctive views that its adherents sustained over several centuries penned the Enochic texts; these texts which share a hero are being used only as sources of information about whom their authors thought Enoch was and the influences that led them to regard him as an apocalyptic seer.

During the preparation of this book I have received assistance and encouragement from several institutions and individuals, and it is a pleasure to register my gratitude to them here. The National Endowment for the Humanities has supported my research through a summer seminar directed by Professor Jack Sasson (1979) and a summer stipend (1980). North Carolina State University has contributed in many ways to expediting the work. The D. H. Hill Library has been generous in its purchasing policies, and the staff of the Interlibrary Loan Department has been relentless in tracking down a number of non-bestsellers. Robert S. Bryan, Head of the Department of Philosophy and Religion, has managed to create conditions that are conducive to research in an undergraduate department with its inevitable heavy teaching demands. His encouragement and support have meant much to me during my years at the University. The reader will quickly realize the magnitude of the debt that I owe Mrs. Ann Rives who typed most of the manuscript and did so with miraculous accuracy and inexplicable good cheer.

During my pursuit of Enochic traditions I have sought and received comments from experts on several points. My colleague, Professor Ronald H. Sack, has proved to be a valuable guide in Assyriological matters and was kind enough to read and critique chap. III. I have also reaped the benefits of comments from two of the grand gentlemen of scholarship on the Ancient Near East. Matthew Black, former Principal of St. Mary's College, the University of St. Andrews—who introduced me to Enoch studies during my Fulbright year at St. Mary's (1971–72)—read a draft of chaps. I and II when I taught at St. Mary's during the Candlemas and Whitsunday terms of 1981. Professor Otto Neugebauer of Brown University, master of the field of ancient science, read chap. IV and offered comments about it. Black and Neugebauer also permitted me to use their new commentary on *1 Enoch* 72–82 before it was published. To these scholars I offer my hearty thanks though it is, as always, necessary to add that, for better or worse, the views expressed in the book are my own.

I wanted this book to be published in the CBQMS because of the excellent reputation that the series, its editors, and its editorial board have among biblical scholars. The former and present editors—the Rev. Bruce Vawter and the Rev. Robert Karris—and the anonymous readers have certainly continued this tradition through their kindly and expeditious labors that have brought the manuscript so smoothly through the stages of evaluation and publication.

I have also had no lack of support on the home front. Words of wit and wisdom from Walt and Mary Penn Sherlin have both spurred me on and cast a world of perspective on Enochic studies. My daughter Laura, who was born around the time when I began systematic work on this monograph, has served as a reminder, as her birthdays have passed by in swift succession, of how long the project has taken. My son Jeffrey and I have spent many pleasant hours reading and discussing classical myths. His encyclopedic knowledge of and enthusiasm for these stories have proved most helpful on several occasions.

The one to whom I owe the most, though, and for whom words of thanks are inadequate is my wife Mary. Her love, wisdom, insight, and encouragement while I was writing this manuscript and throughout our married life have been priceless treasures. This book is rightly dedicated to her.

# I

## THE PROBLEMS TO BE CONSIDERED

The chapters in this book offer a detailed study of the origins, development, and functions of the earliest Jewish traditions about Enoch, the legendary seventh antediluvian patriarch. It should be emphasized at the outset that the primary concern is not to investigate all aspects of the literature that bore this man's name in antiquity; the focus of the investigation is rather the traditions about the man himself. The study begins with Gen 5:21-24, the most ancient passage about him, and then follows the evolution of Enochic lore until approximately the middle of the second pre-Christian century. By that time a substantial corpus of literature had accumulated about his name, and it gives evidence that, for whatever reasons, the roles which Enoch fills had evolved in distinctive ways. The larger intention of the present investigation is to use traditions about Enoch himself, which are met so frequently in Jewish literature of the early Hellenistic age, as a means for approaching some fundamental questions about the origins and nature of apocalyptic literature and, if possible, about the groups whose views are expressed in those extraordinary works. It is now evident that some of the earliest apocalyptic writings circulated under Enoch's name; the prominent roles that he plays in many such compositions suggest that a careful study of traditions about him may cast some light on larger literary and sociological problems in this period of second–temple Judaism.

### A. Debates About the Antecedents of Apocalyptic Literature

In the last 150 years specialists have debated at great length the difficult and complex problem of the source(s) from which Jewish apocalyptic thinking and literature evolved.[1] As is well known, the two leading candidates in

---

[1] The most elaborate account of research in the field in general is Johann M. Schmidt, *Die jüdische Apokalyptik: die Geschichte ihrer Erforschung von den Anfängen bis zu den Textfunden von Qumran* (2nd ed.; Neukirchen-Vluyn: Neukirchener, 1976). Briefer surveys can be found in a number of places, among which one could mention Klaus Koch, *The Rediscovery of Apocalyptic* (SBT 2/22; Naperville, Allenson, 1970) 36–111; and Paul D. Hanson, "Prolegomena to the Study of Jewish Apocalyptic" in *Magnalia Dei: The Mighty Acts of God* (ed. F. M. Cross, W. E. Lemke, and P. D. Miller; Garden City: Doubleday, 1976) 389–401.

contemporary scholarship are biblical prophecy and biblical wisdom, though advocates of each theory concede that neither in itself adequately explains the variegated apocalyptic phenomenon. One of the principal difficulties that has plagued the discussion about apocalyptic roots has been what Michael Stone calls "a semantic confusion of the first order."[2] Frequent use of such hopelessly vague terms as *apocalyptic* has produced uncertainty about precisely what it is whose origins are being sought—a literary genre, a theological outlook, or the contents of books that are normally called apocalyptic. Recently Paul Hanson has introduced greater clarity into the discussion by distinguishing between three separate but often related entities.[3]

1. *Apocalypse* refers to a literary form or genre which is one of several that appear in apocalyptic literature. An example of this sort of revelatory narrative is Daniel 7, where in a dream or vision the seer is shown a symbolic sequence having to do with the end of time. Its meaning is divulged to him by an angel, and the entire experience leaves Daniel virtually catatonic.

2. *Apocalyptic eschatology* is a religious perspective which in important respects represents a continuation of prophetic eschatology but which generally lacks the belief of Israel's classical prophets that divine plans would be effected in mundane history and through human agents. Rather, in apocalyptic eschatology deliverance from the present evil world to a new and different one is envisioned.[4]

3. *Apocalypticism* refers to the "symbolic universe" of a *group* in which apocalyptic eschatology has assumed the all-powerful role of an ideology.[5]

---

[2] "Lists of Revealed Things in the Apocalyptic Literature" in *Magnalia Dei*, 439. Cf. also Hans Dieter Betz, "Zum Problem des religionsgeschichtlichen Verständnisses der Apokalyptik," *ZTK* 63 (1966) 392–93.

[3] See his article "Apocalypticism," *IDBSup* 28–31. For a definition of the term *apocalypse* and an analysis of Jewish, Christian, Greek, Latin, and Persian apocalypses, see J. J. Collins, ed., *Apocalypse: The Morphology of a Genre* (*Semeia* 14; Missoula: Scholars, 1979). J. Carmignac ("Qu'est-ce que l'apocalyptique? Son emploi à Qumrân," RevQ 10 [1979] 3–33) arrives at a definition similar to Collins' but while Collins uses the term *apocalypse*, Carmignac employs *apocalyptique*.

[4] Hanson, *The Dawn of Apocalyptic: The Historical and Sociological Roots of Jewish Apocalyptic Eschatology* (Philadelphia: Fortress, 1975) 11–12. On this topic see also Collins, "Apocalyptic Eschatology as the Transcendence of Death," *CBQ* 36 (1974) 21–43.

[5] James Barr ("Jewish Apocalyptic in Recent Scholarly Study," *BJRL* 58 [1975] 9–35) surveys a number of English contributions to the field and distinguishes four levels on which one can approach the phenomenon (a minimal number in his view): (1) language use; (2) structure; (3) what is told; and (4) doctrine (see especially p. 16). While there is some overlap in these categories, the distinctions are valuable for dealing with the subject in a disciplined way. Regarding the term *apocalyptic*, Barr states: ". . . when we use the term apocalyptic we generally have in mind content and point of view rather than simply form: we think of a set of ideas and attitudes, which find typical expression in the apocalypse form more strictly so called but which are also found over a much wider range of literature" (18).

These distinctions, which are presupposed in this investigation, should permit a greater degree of precision in putting and facing the question of source(s).

It is self-evident that examples of the genre apocalypse resemble to some extent accounts of revelations to biblical prophets (e.g., those in Zechariah 1-6) and that apocalyptic eschatology has points of contact with the eschatology of the prophets. Hanson has investigated this latter relationship in his stimulating book *The Dawn of Apocalyptic*, in which he traces, primarily through analyses of Isaiah 56-66 and Zechariah 9-14, how the prophetic view developed into an apocalyptic one amid party struggles and pessimistic conditions within the post-exilic Jewish community in Palestine. Hanson's efforts, despite the fact that much remains hypothetical and uncertain, represent a more carefully delimited statement of the connection between prophetic and apocalyptic thought in this regard, but he quite properly makes no exclusive claim that this link explains all features of apocalyptic eschatology.[6]

The scholar whose name is most frequently associated with the theory that the *contents of apocalyptic books* are an outgrowth of Israelite wisdom is Gerhard von Rad.[7] Von Rad was not content to claim that wisdom elements played a role alongside prophecy in the development of apocalyptic material. He took a much more radical stand by excluding prophecy altogether from this process ("completely out of the question").

> The decisive factor, as I see it, is the incompatibility between apocalyptic literature's view of history and that of the prophets. The prophetic message is specifically rooted in the saving history, that is to say, it is rooted in definite election traditions. But there is no way which leads from this to the apocalyptic view of history, no more than there is any which leads to the idea that the last things were determined in a far-off past.[8]

---

[6] One important admixture that he perceives is Canaanite mythological traditions which had been preserved over the centuries in the royal cult at Jerusalem; see, for example, *The Dawn of Apocalyptic*, 22-31, etc.; "Apocalypticism," 30-34. The prophetic connection has, of course, been defended by many authors, among whom should be mentioned H. H. Rowley, *The Relevance of Apocalyptic* (2nd ed.; London/Redhill: Lutterworth, 1947) 11. Rowley, too, recognized other influences (e.g., p. 41).

[7] *Old Testament Theology* (2 vols.; Edinburgh: Oliver and Boyd, 1962, 1965) 2.301-15; *Wisdom in Israel* (Nashville/New York: Abingdon, 1972) 263-83. Von Rad was hardly the first to advocate a derivation from wisdom; see Schmidt, *Die jüdische Apokalyptik*, 13-14, 21, 31-32, etc.

[8] *Old Testament Theology*, 2.303. Von Rad has certainly overstated the contrast between prophecy and "apocalyptic," as P. von der Osten-Sacken (*Die Apokalyptik in ihrem Verhältnis zu Prophetie und Weisheit* [Theologische Existenz Heute 157; Munich: Kaiser, 1969] 10-34), among others, has shown. Von der Osten-Sacken's argument against von Rad's thesis regarding the derivation of "apocalyptic" from wisdom does not, however, touch upon mantic wisdom.

He saw the essence of apocalyptic thinking in a kind of knowledge that was unconnected with saving history—a trait which reveals close ties with wisdom as it is found in the Old Testament.[9] In this connection he noted the important place of knowledge in apocalyptic writings as evidenced by Enoch's extensive scientific concerns, Daniel's role as a wise man, and Ezra's scribal office.[10] "Probably all that is new is that at a specific point in history this branch of scholarship came out of the seclusion of the study with a preaching mission, and that it set itself to console men."[11] In his *Wisdom in Israel* he investigated a connection between the divine determination of times in wisdom and apocalyptic literature and the presence in works such as Sirach of the theory that history was moving toward a culmination. For him the inclusion of foreign materials (e.g., Iranian dualism) and a strong eschatological interest mark simply "the branching out of wisdom in the direction of widely varied intellectual spheres."[12] Though he does not develop the point, von Rad at least raised the issue of whether foretelling on the basis of dreams was a function of the wise man in Israel (Joseph and Daniel are examples).[13]

It may seem strange that a scholar of von Rad's eminence could defend the thesis that groups whose views and labors found expression in literature such as Proverbs could be related in fundamental, essential ways to those who wrote apocalyptic literature. But in fairness to him it should be observed that, in his view, Israel's sages performed more functions than formulating practical rules for safe and comfortable living. The literary deposits of those other efforts (prediction, etc.), if there ever were any, have unfortunately not survived. As a consequence of the lively discussion that his revival of the sapiential-connection theory evoked, von Rad thoroughly revised his treatment of the topic in the fourth edition of his *Theologie des Alten Testaments.* He dealt more fully with mantic aspects of wisdom and delimited his theory more sharply. He wrote:

> Glaubt man die Apokalyptik von den Traditionen der Weisheit her verstehen zu müssen, so wäre das wohl nur dahin einzugrenzen, dass sich in ihr bei all ihrer Stoffülle die Weisheit doch nicht in extenso fortsetzt, sondern nur einige ihrer Sektoren, also vor allem die alte Traumdeutungswissenschaft und die Wissenschaft von den Orakeln und den "Zeichen."[14]

Rather, he deals only with von Rad's unlikely claim that "apocalyptic" grew from the sorts of wisdom found in the Hebrew Bible.

[9] Ibid., 306.
[10] Ibid.
[11] Ibid., 307.
[12] *Wisdom in Israel*, 279–82. The quotation is from p. 279.
[13] Ibid., 280–82.
[14] *Theologie des Alten Testaments*: vol. 2: *Die Theologie der prophetischen Überlie-*

His understanding of the process by which the development from older forms of wisdom to the material now found in the apocalyptic books took place (the "eschatologizing of wisdom") did not, however, change in his last formulation from that reflected in the English translation. This exposed him to the justifiable charge that he did not distinguish sharply enough between an educational kind of wisdom and the less rational sort that found expression in divination.[15] Von Rad also did not pursue the mantic connection in the vast divinatory literature of the ancient Near East.

Among many others, two scholars have more recently thrown additional light on the subject of the relations between wisdom and the contents of apocalyptic writings, and both have done so in conversation with von Rad's suggestions. The first is Michael Stone who has adduced and analyzed the data most extensively in his essay "Lists of Revealed Things in the Apocalyptic Literature."[16] In it he deals with the fact that at crucial junctures in many *apocalypses*—at the point where the reader expects a description of the contents of the vision—there appear lists of revealed things (e.g., 2 Bar 59:5–11). These lists, which can assume either a declarative or an interrogative form, include items such as the number of raindrops, the breadth and length of the earth, the length and height of heaven, the number of the stars, etc. While they exhibit some points of similarity with lists in biblical sapiential books (Job 28 and 38, for instance), they are by no means the same.

> At the most, certain isolated cosmological elements are common to the apocalyptic lists and Job 38. Further, the apocalyptic lists are primarily of the declarative type, Job 38 and associated Wisdom materials are interrogative in formulation. The lists in the apocalypses are not merely inherited units of Wisdom material; they do comprise rather catalogues of actual subjects of speculative investigation, study, and perhaps even of the contents of ecstatic experiences of the apocalyptic authors. If they derive ultimately from Wisdom list materials then the elements included in them and their ordering appear to have been

*ferungen Israels* (Einführung in die evangelische Theologie 1; 5th ed.; Munich: Kaiser, 1968) 331 (cf. his statement about revising the chapter on "apocalyptic" in the foreword to the 4th ed. [p. 9]). See also *Wisdom in Israel*, 281.

[15] For his later statement, see *Theologie des Alten Testaments*, 329. For the criticism, see H. P. Müller, "Mantische Weisheit und Apokalyptik," *Congress Volume, Uppsala 1971* (VTSup 22; Leiden: Brill, 1972) 271 (on 268–71 he surveys other critiques of von Rad's thesis). Cf. also Collins, *The Apocalyptic Vision of the Book of Daniel* (HSM 16; Missoula: Scholars, 1977) 56–57.

[16] *Magnalia Dei*, 414–52. Cf. also Ithamar Gruenwald, *Apocalyptic and Merkavah Mysticism* (AGJU 14; Leiden/Cologne: Brill, 1980) 3–19; Collins, "Cosmos and Salvation: Jewish Wisdom and Apocalyptic in the Hellenistic Age," *HR* 17 (1977–78) 134–38 (Jewish wisdom of the Hellenistic period differs from biblical wisdom in its "emphasis on the role of the cosmos" [136]).

profoundly influenced by the actual speculative concerns and activity of the apocalyptic authors.[17]

Stone was unable to specify the source(s) from which the lists derived but rightly insisted that any account about the origin and character of the apocalypses take them into consideration, since these rather stereotyped enumerations of natural phenomena evidently possessed a marked importance for the authors of the apocalypses.

The second scholar whose contributions must be considered is H. P. Müller who in 1972 published his highly significant essay "Mantische Weisheit und Apokalyptik."[18] To von Rad's critics he concedes that the great theologian of the Old Testament should have delimited more carefully the type of wisdom that evolved into the material that is now found in apocalyptic books, but he also maintains that von Rad was pointing in the correct direction. It is Müller's thesis that neither the courtly-pedagogical kind of wisdom familiar from Israel's monarchical period nor its more democratic successors in the post-exilic age developed into the concerns that one finds in apocalyptic literature; rather, it was a phenomenon that he terms *mantic wisdom* which formed the background of the material in question.[19] That is, in his view, the arts and writings of the diviner lie at the base of apocalyptic literature. In defending his hypothesis, he explores biblical references to mantic wisdom and finds that virtually all of them (he believes that the Joseph stories are an exception) appear in exilic and post-exilic writings.[20] A natural inference from the dates of the relevant books is that biblical writers became more familiar with the techniques of diviners after B.C. 587 when Judean contact with Mesopotamia was, of course, immediate. In biblical narratives, Joseph is presented as a practitioner of mantic wisdom in that he interprets dreams, but he exercises other sapiential skills in the pharaoh's court as well. Daniel, however, is pictured exclusively, in the oldest stories about him, as a mantic sage.[21] It is of some interest, given the Mesopotamian connections of this sort of wisdom, that Daniel is a Jewish character who, in Müller's opinion and in that of many others, is modeled on the Canaanite *Dan²el*. However that may be, Müller holds that one can read from the book of Daniel the course that mantic wisdom took as it moved toward apocalyp-

[17] Ibid., 435–36.

[18] VTSup 22. 268–93.

[19] Ibid., 271. He does not, however, regard this as the only source from which the apocalyptic material evolved.

[20] Ibid., 274.

[21] Ibid., 274–77. Müller thinks that Dan 1 is later than the remaining stories about the Jewish hero in chaps. 2–6 and that in this chronologically later chapter alone there is an attempt to relate his brand of wisdom to courtly, educational wisdom (279).

tic concerns because the sage of the first few chapters becomes the seer who receives apocalyptic visions in chaps. 7–12.[22]

Müller claims that five important traits of apocalyptic literature can better be explained from his hypothesis that mantic wisdom was the central source for the apocalyptic books. They are: (1) their eschatological orientation; (2) their determinism; (3) the seers' claims to a special enlightenment or authorization; (4) the tendency to encode reality in symbols; and (5) possibly the pseudonymity so frequently found in this literature.[23] Regarding the historical circumstances that surrounded the movement from strictly mantic concerns to the form that they took in apocalyptic works, he hypothesizes that this sort of wisdom was a constant undercurrent in Israel but that it surfaced only occasionally and momentarily. However, during the second-century reaction against the rationalism of Hellenistic culture, various forms of native, Near Eastern religions reemerged and intermingled with one another. Among them was the thoroughly religious mantic wisdom that had continuously been practiced in Mesopotamia for millennia; its *vaticinia ex eventu* served as a welcome means of adding meaning to the difficult present for those who were reduced to being the spectators rather than the fashioners of history.[24]

Müller has undoubtedly paved the way for a more precise understanding of several constitutive elements in the apocalypses and apocalyptic literature in general. His efforts at delimiting the kinds of sapiential phenomena that lie at the base of apocalyptic concerns and writings have resulted in a more convincing version of the wisdom connection than von Rad had been able to formulate. He has not, however, exhausted the Jewish evidence that documents the intimate bond which unites the divinatory with the apocalyptic world; in fact, one could argue that he has failed to adduce the very best

---

[22] Ibid., 279–80. Cf., too, Collins, "The Court-Tales in Daniel and the Development of Apocalyptic," *JBL* 94 (1975) 229–34. He stresses that the view of revelation found in the mantic (1–6) and in the apocalyptic chapters (7–12) is the same and that there is an implied "self-identification of the *maśkîlîm* of Daniel 11 with those of Daniel 1" (233). The court tales of 1–6, in which prediction is made possible through revealed wisdom, were models on which the apocalyptic visionaries of 7–12, now removed from the courtly setting, based their predictive visions which were written in Palestine during the Antiochan persecution.

[23] Ibid., 280-90.

[24] Ibid., 290–91. Collins ("Cosmos and Salvation," 138) formulates the connection between wisdom and apocalyptic thought thus: "The conviction that the experience of God and even eschatology is mediated through the cosmic order constitutes the common ground of wisdom and apocalyptic." He does, however, note sharp divergences between the two as well (138-41). It is worth observing that his discussion of apocalyptic views of the world does not apply to compositions such as *1 Enoch* 72–79, 82 or *1 Enoch* 1–36, since in them order in the universe is presupposed and unchanging (cf. pp. 140–41).

example of this connection—Enoch. The associations that surround this character in the Jewish and antecedent Mesopotamian traditions and the functions that he performs in the earliest Jewish compositions that involve him confirm Müller's thesis in no uncertain terms. Although it means anticipating some of the major conclusions of this book, here it can be said that Enoch was a Jewish literary crystalization of Sumero-Akkadian lore about the seventh antediluvian king Enmeduranki. This mythical sovereign appears in texts as the founder of a guild of diviners—the *bārûs* (see chap. II). It is sufficiently clear that in Jewish literature Enoch bore divinatory associations (though they were modified by Jewish theology), and it is precisely this figure who appears as the seer in a number of the earliest apocalypses. Moreover, he also figures centrally in two works (the Astronomical Book and the Book of Watchers) that antedate the Enochic historical apocalypses (see chaps. IV and V) and that have a strong "scientific" interest. These two booklets display some traits that are later found in apocalypses, but it seems inappropriate to assign them to the same genre. In other words, it appears that at least one strand of Jewish apocalyptic literature developed within the context of associations that accompanied Enoch, while another cycle is linked to a different mantic—Daniel. Müller has investigated the Daniel material; here the problem will be approached *via* the figure of Enoch about whom a great deal more has been preserved. The procedure will be to analyze the relevant compositions and traditions in chronological order insofar as that is possible.

## B. Ancient Descriptions of Enoch and Modern Studies of Them

### 1. The Descriptions

Before proceeding to that investigation, however, it will be useful to give some indication of the directions in which Jewish lore about Enoch grew and of the most noteworthy scholarly studies of those traditions or parts of them. Regarding the evolution of Enochic traditions, the main problems to be solved, to put the matter briefly, are to explain the background of the intriguing but sketchy picture of Enoch in Gen 5:21–24 and then to show how and why Jewish writers expanded it into the full-blown and utterly extraordinary portraits of the later sources. Perhaps the question can be posed most graphically by juxtaposing two texts from opposite ends of the historical period that will be under consideration: Gen 5:18, 21–24 (perhaps from the sixth century, possibly from the fifth) and Jub 4:16–25 (from the mid-second century).[25] Each of these texts will be scrutinized in later chapters, but simply

---

[25] Gen 5:21–24 belongs to the priestly genealogy of the antediluvian patriarchs. Although J. T. Milik (*The Books of Enoch: Aramaic Fragments of Qumrân Cave 4* [Oxford: Clarendon, 1976] 8, 30–32) has maintained that *1 Enoch* 72–82 (less 81) and 6–19 are earlier than Genesis

quoting them here will illustrate succinctly many of the problems that will be discussed in this book.

*Genesis 5 (RSV)*

18. When Jared had lived a hundred and sixty-two years he became the Father of Enoch.

21. When Enoch had lived sixty-five years, he became the father of Methuselah.

*Jubilees 4*[26]

16. And in the eleventh jubilee Jared took to himself a wife . . ., and she bare him a son in the fifth week, in the fourth year of the jubilee, and he called his name Enoch.
17. And he was the first among men that are born on earth who learnt writing and knowledge and wisdom and who wrote down the signs of heaven according to the order of their months in a book, that men might know the seasons of the years according to the order of their separate months. 18. And he was the first to write a testimony, and he testified to the sons of men among the generations of the earth, and recounted the weeks of the jubilees, and made known to them the days of the years, and set in order the months and recounted the Sabbaths of the years as we made (them) known to him. 19. And what was and will be he saw in a vision of his sleep, as it will happen to the children of men throughout their generations until the day of judgment; he saw and understood everything, and wrote his testimony, and placed the testimony on earth for all the children of men and for their generations. 20. And in the twelfth jubilee, in the seventh week thereof, he took to himself a wife,

and are thus the oldest texts about Enoch, his case is thoroughly unconvincing, as will be shown in chaps. IV and V below. For the dating of Jubilees, see VanderKam, *Textual and Historical Studies in the Book of Jubilees* (HSM 14; Missoula: Scholars, 1977) 214–285.

[26] Translation of R. H. Charles, *The Book of Jubilees or the Little Genesis* (London: Black, 1902).

22. Enoch walked with God after the birth of Methuselah three hundred years, and he had other sons and daughters.

and her name was Ednî, the daughter of Dânêl . . ., and in the sixth year in this week she bare him a son and he called his name Methuselah. 21. And he was moreover with the angels of God these six jubilees of years, and they showed him everything which is on earth and in the heavens, the rule of the sun, and he wrote down everything. 22. And he testified to the Watchers, who had sinned with the daughters of men; for these had begun to unite themselves, so as to be defiled, with the daughters of men, and Enoch testified against (them) all.

23. Thus all the days of Enoch were three hundred and sixty-five years.
24. Enoch walked with God; and he was not, for God took him.

23. And he was taken from amongst the children of men, and we conducted him into the Garden of Eden in majesty and honour, and behold there he writes down the condemnation and judgment of the world, and all the wickedness of the children of men. 24. And on account of [him the waters of the flood did not come][27] upon all the land of Eden; for there he was set as a sign and that he should testify against all the children of men, that he should recount all the deeds of the generations until the day of condemnation. 25. And he burnt the incense of the sanctuary, (even) sweet spices acceptable before the Lord on the Mount.

---

[27] Charles' translation reflects his reading of *ʾamṣeʾa* (he brought) in his edition of Jubilees (*Maṣḥafa Kufālē or the Ethiopic Version of the Hebrew Book of Jubilees* [Anecdota Oxoniensia; Oxford: Clarendon, 1895]), but several of the new, unpublished MSS show that the correct reading is *ʾi-maṣʾa* ([the waters] did not come).

The much more elaborate account in Jubilees, which includes most but not all of the elements in Genesis, demonstrates both the dependence of the later tradition on the biblical text and the fecundity of speculations about Enoch in some Jewish circles, though even it does not include every feature of his portrait found in extra-biblical texts. From which source(s) did Jewish writers take their descriptions of this character? To what literary and theological uses did they put their remarkable stories about him? The present book addresses issues such as these.

### 2. Earlier Studies

Stories about Enoch continued to arouse interest—and apparently some suspicion—in Judaism during the Tannaitic and subsequent periods and in Christianity during the Patristic age. Yet only in more recent times have scholars begun to approach these traditions from a historical point of view. Continued use of long-available texts and the rediscovery of cuneiform literature have allowed scholars to place significant parts of the Jewish literary and traditional phenomenon into its larger setting in the ancient Near East and to see more clearly the ways in which Jewish writers reworked foreign myths and legends and pressed them into service in their theological compositions. Many writers during the last century have commented on the sources and development of Enochic lore, but three experts have written the most significant and detailed studies. Their contributions should now be surveyed.

a. Heinrich Zimmern, "Urkönige und Uroffenbarung" in Eberhard Schrader, *Die Keilinschriften und das Alte Testament* (2 vols. 3rd ed. ed. H. Zimmern and H. Winckler; Berlin: Reuther & Reichard, 1902-03) 2.530-43. These pages are the logical starting point for a survey of research on this topic for two reasons: in them Zimmern made readily available to commentators the most important cuneiform text for understanding the background of Jewish traditions about Enoch, and his comments about Enochic passages became highly influential and proved to be correct in most cases. Until fairly recently there had been no significant advance beyond the information and analysis that Zimmern provided. Since many of the topics that he treated will be examined in more detail below, his positions can be sketched briefly here.

Zimmern discussed the biblical and to a lesser extent the apocryphal and pseudepigraphical accounts about Enoch in the context of his comparison between the list of pre-flood kings enumerated by Berossus (a Babylonian priest who in ca. B.C. 280 wrote a Greek account of his people's myths and history) and the genealogy of patriarchs in Genesis 5. He identified biblical Enoch, the seventh of ten antediluvian patriarchs in Genesis 5, with King Euedoranchos, the seventh of ten pre-diluvian kings in Berossus. Once he had established the relationship between the two—an association which a

number of scholars had defended previously—he furnished a German translation of K 2486 + K 4364. This cuneiform text traces the origins of the
*bārû*-diviners back to King Enmeduranki (= the Euedoranchos of Berossus)
of Sippar. The text will be quoted and discussed in chap. II, but here it
should be said that it pictures Shamash, the Babylonian sun-god of whose
cult city Enmeduranki was king, and Adad summoning the king into their
presence where they teach him the divinatory techniques that became the
mark of this sort of professional. Enmeduranki then conveyed these secrets
to various leaders of other cities. The text also makes provision for transmitting such classified information from father to son.

   Zimmern, who thought that Berossus' king list and the list of fathers in
Genesis 5 were largely identical, drew attention to the remarkable agree-
ments between the biblical pericope about Enoch and traditions about Enmeduranki. The particulars that he noted were: (1) like Enmeduranki Enoch
was especially blessed by God; (2) Enoch's removal to God corresponds to
Enmeduranki's entry into the fellowship of Shamash and Adad and his
initiation by these gods into the secrets of heaven and earth; and (3) Enoch's
365 years are related to the fact that Enmeduranki was affiliated with the cult
of the sun god (540).

   Turning to extra-biblical developments of the Enochic portrait, he made
this important observation:

> Es ist übrigens wahrscheinlich, dass der ausgedehnte Sagenkreis, der sich im
> späteren Judentum an die Person Henochs als Begründer der Astrologie, Astro-
> nomie, Schreiberkunst u.s.w. knupft (Buch Henoch u.s.w.), nicht lediglich aus
> der kurzen Notiz Gen. 5, 21–23 herausgesponnen ist. Vielmehr könnte sehr wol
> in dem, was im Spätjudentum von Henoch, dem 'Wunder des Wissens', ausge-
> sagt wird, ausser Gen. 5 auch noch direkt die Figur des babylonischen Enmedu-
> ranki nachgewirkt haben (540).

Finally he observed that the heavenly tablets from which Enoch read could
be related to the tablet that Enmeduranki received from the gods; that the
transmission of *bārû*-secrets from father to son was the same technique as
Enoch's relaying to his son what had been revealed to him; and that Enoch's
scribal role resembled that of the god Nabu (541; cf. 404–05).

   Zimmern's labors were confined chiefly to highlighting parallels between
Genesis and various Mesopotamian traditions, and in that respect his work
remains valuable though dated. Yet, while he performed an essential service
in making Assyriological evidence accessible to students of the Bible and of
pseudepigraphical literature, he by no means conducted a detailed survey of
the diverse sources and portraits of Enoch in post-biblical Jewish literature.
Perhaps this shortcoming is to be attributed to the nature of the publication
in which he wrote, but it remains the case that he barely skimmed the

post-biblical Enochic material. The next work that will be summarized and evaluated focused directly on some of this neglected literature.

b. H. Ludin Jansen, *Die Henochgestalt: Eine vergleichende religionsgeschichtliche Untersuchung* (Norske Videnskaps-Akademi i Oslo II. Hist.-Filos. Klasse, 1; Oslo: Dybwad, 1939). Jansen's book may be the most elaborate study of Enochic traditions in print. His concerns were to characterize Enoch on the basis of the descriptions of him in *1 Enoch*, to ascertain the sources of this material (that is, whether it was native/Jewish or foreign), and to determine how and why it was incorporated into the composite picture of the man (4). He divided the miscellaneous data about him into descriptions of Enoch as an earthly figure and as a heavenly or superhuman one. He found that when Enoch was depicted as a human agent he functioned as a prophet and wise man, similar in some respects to Old Testament models but a unique combination nevertheless. As prophet, Enoch declares judgment (1–5; 92; 94–105) and salvation (cf. 90:29–30; 93; 91:12–17; 92:3–5), focuses attention on the final judgment, receives revelations from an angel who has derived some of the disclosed information from heavenly tablets, and delivers his message, which serves as a means of salvation, to a select group rather than to the entire nation. While these latter elements show advances beyond virtually all instances of biblical prophecy, the truly novel factor in the Enochic portrait is the combination of prophecy with his special type of wisdom. As a sage, Enoch reveals information about the *Urzeit* during which he lived, periodizes history, learns and teaches astronomical lore, and divulges the cosmological details that he has discovered on his remarkable journeys. He is, then, in some ways a Jewish prophet, but "sobald er von Zeitperioden spricht, von Himmelsweisheit, die er auf kosmischen Reisen erlangt hat, oder Sternlehre gibt, hat er den einheimischen Boden verlassen" (12). When Enoch is pictured as a divine figure, he appears as the one who in effect saves Noah from the flood by disclosing salvific information to him, as Ea did to Utnapishtim, the Babylonian flood-hero. In the passages in which he assumes a superhuman role, Enoch serves as a mediator between God and man or God and the world (13). Naturally there is no precedent for this characterization of him in extant Jewish literature prior to *1 Enoch*.

Thus, for Jansen some aspects of the portrait of Enoch as prophet-sage and the entire picture of him as a heavenly being pointed to non-Jewish sources for their inspiration. Of the various foreign possibilities, he rejected outright influence from Greek traditions (10) and felt compelled to limit use of Persian sources because of the familiar problems with dating them. He believed that the book's astronomical and cosmological lore and the descriptions of Enoch as a heavenly character who was closely associated with the flood suggested Babylon as the place of origin for the non-native portions of the Enochic figure (13). On the basis of his characterizations of Enoch and his researches into comparative traditions, Jansen formulated and defended two theses that are relevant to the present study:

1. Der überirdische Henoch im Henochbuche ist jüdischer Niederschlag der babylonisch-chaldäischen Vorstellung von Ea-Oannes.
2. Der irdische Henoch des Henochbuches ist ein Prophet und Weiser, der die Tätigkeit eines einheimischen Gerichts- und Heilspropheten und Gelehrten und die Wirksamkeit eines chaldäischen Weisen und Apokalyptikers in sich vereinigt (13, where they are italicized).

An important issue that must be confronted in a historical investigation of this sort is the medium through which ancient Babylonian mythical traditions were communicated to Hellenistic Jewish scholars. Jansen argued that the Chaldeans (the professional, not the ethnic, group) filled this role and adduced evidence that by the Hellenistic period they had spread into the entire eastern Mediterranean region and beyond where they enthusiastically propagated their views. He also maintained that Ea was the god who was in particular proclaimed by this religion of wisdom and that Berossus for one embodied its missionary concerns (cf. p. 18).

Jansen, as noted above, observed that Enoch had accumulated some traits that the sources associated with the god Ea. His understanding of Ea's roles was colored somewhat by the fact that he considered Ea and Oannes (the name that Berossus gave to the creature—half man and half fish—who brought all aspects of culture to the first humans) to be identical for all practical purposes. Indeed, he entertained the suggestion that the word *Oannes* was somehow derived from the word *Ea* (though he realized that this could not be demonstrated). Consequently for Jansen, Ea was a divine sage and bringer of culture and was therefore to be compared with Enoch (27). An examination of the differing versions of the flood story disclosed that in each one Ea performed the function of saving the hero by disclosing information about the impending deluge. Jewish scholars would have encountered the god Ea, then, in Chaldean religious propaganda, both in connection with the flood story and throughout the teachings of this system (32).

Ea-Oannes did not, however, possess all of the characteristics that parts of *1 Enoch* attribute to the superhuman Enoch; these additional traits often find their prototype in traditions about Babylonian sages or heroes of primeval times. Examples would be Gilgamesh who had experienced much and was a city-builder (cf. Gen 4:17); Utnapishtim, the flood-hero, who was removed from earthly society by the gods and transferred to the ends of the earth; and Adapa, who ascended to heaven. Jansen stressed that all of these characters were closely affiliated with Ea and claims that in point of fact they were earthly representatives of the Ea figure (37). The superhuman Enoch inherited traits of both the divine and quasi-human sides of this complex figure. Jansen argued that *1 Enoch*, in its accounts about the flood (65:1-67:3; 106-107; 6-11), actually stood nearer to Babylonian versions of the story than did Genesis 6-9: whereas Genesis took from its source just one of the two principal characters (the flood-hero, not the divine being who is other than the sender of the flood and who communicates a means of salvation to the hero), *1 Enoch* took both in the form of Noah and Enoch (chaps. 6-11 are an exception), though Enoch resembles both Ea and his earthly counterparts—the sages of old.

In defense and elaboration of his second thesis, Jansen noted that the earthly Enoch was, to be sure, a prophet of judgment and salvation, but the distinctively new element in his character was the combination of prophecy with astronomical teachings. Enoch fortified his prophetic message by contrasting human transgression against divine law with the obedience of heavenly luminaries to the laws that were designed for them. As a wise man, Enoch manifested some of the characteristics of late Jewish wisdom—as the theodicy of chap. 103 shows—but his precise astronomical knowledge (especially chaps. 72-82) betrayed his kinship with the Chaldean sages. Chap. 80 indicated that understanding of celestial laws was essential for recognizing the disturbances that were to precede the judgment. The many cosmological details (particularly in chaps. 17-36), another Chaldean specialty, likewise served a theological end in *1 Enoch*: to grasp the greatness of God one must be familiar with the universe that he created (71). Astronomy and cosmology, then, were interrelated with theological concerns and were borrowed from the Chaldeans who also associated the two in their compositions.

Jansen found additional links between the earthly Enoch and Chaldeans in their apocalyptic division of history into three parts, the first two of which climax in a deluge and in a fiery judgment that is at times described in flood imagery. Berossus used this threefold schema (which differs from the twofold division in the book of Daniel) and wedged Babylonian history into it. He provided the model for the Enochic survey of history (chaps. 83-91), though the cyclic view expressed by Berossus is lacking in *1 Enoch* (78).

According to Jansen, then, the Enochic figure looked thoroughly Jewish when described as a prophet of weal and woe and as a wise man, but native connections were inadequate for explaining his role as astronomer, cosmologist, and apocalypticist (81). The Enoch figure was created in order to teach the elect how to escape disaster and to comfort them in difficult times. In those times the pre-flood conditions appeared to be repeating themselves; thus, Enoch, who had lived in the general vicinity of the first judgment (the flood), brings the flood story as a gospel for the elect, while the Torah plays virtually no part in his message (83). The circles which gave rise to the Enochic literature were syncretistic; they refused to limit themselves to native traditions as they struggled to find answers to perplexing concerns. Jansen did not exclude the possibility that Enoch was the product of a Jewish affiliation of some sort with a Chaldean school in Palestine that was similar to the one that Berossus operated on the island of Cos (84–85).

Jansen's book certainly represented a major attempt to explain a baffling phenomenon, and he appears to have left few stones unturned in his search for sources. Nevertheless, despite his industry, Jansen's theories suffer from a number of shortcomings. First, though his contemporaries were commonly defending the thesis that *1 Enoch* consisted of at least five originally independent sources that had been only loosely joined into one book, Jansen largely ignores the literary situation and tends to blend material from all parts of *1 Enoch* into one *Henochgestalt*. As a result, he fails to treat the portrait of Enoch as it appears in each section of the book and does not deal with their relationships; in this way he forfeited the chance to evaluate inner–Jewish developments of Enochic lore. A second and strange problem with the book is that he ignores almost totally the Enmeduranki–Enoch parallels that several scholars (e.g., Zimmern) had defended in detail (cf. the slighting reference on p. 3). He mentions the books and views of these writers (p. 2) but in the remaining parts of his discussion he neglects these data completely. Third, he attributes a substantial role in the westward transmission of ancient Mesopotamian lore to the Chaldeans and regards Berossus as a propagandist for this "religion of wisdom." He thought that the Chaldeans attached their cosmological and astronomical teaching to the old myths and legends such as the Epic of Gilgamesh. It may be that the Enochic figure was created under inspiration of Chaldean teachings (and Jewish traditions), but some caution is needed when dealing with Jansen's description of Chaldean religion. He considered Ea the special god of these people, Oannes as Ea's double, and several primeval heroes as his counterparts on earth. It is now known on the basis of new evidence that he was wrong about the relationship between Ea and Oannes; moreover, that Ea held a central place in Chaldean religion is far from clear. An objection which is related to his extensive reliance on a theory involving Chaldean propaganda is that he failed to consider the possibility that the relevant Mesopotamian stories and teachings had been familiar in Israel long before the Hellenistic age. His view is that the flood story, for instance, was obviously known in Israel in the biblical period but that the different form of it in Enochic literature is to be explained by a fresh incursion of Mesopotamian influences (through the Chaldeans) at a much later time. He may be correct, but there are other possibilities, since biblical literature probably did not record all such traditions that were known through the centuries in Israel. In other words, Jansen did not seriously consider the possibility that the *Henochgestalt* of *1 Enoch* was much older than the various pieces of literature that present it.

Other objections could surely be brought against Jansen's conclusions and the ways in which he handled the material (e.g., he does not treat the question of why Enoch, not Noah, experiences the transfer to the ends of the earth that the flood hero had enjoyed in all Mesopotamian versions of the deluge), but perhaps enough has been said at this point to show that his book, while valuable, is to be used with caution.

c. Pierre Grelot, "La légende d'Hénoch dans les apocryphes et dans la Bible: origine et signification," *RSR* 46 (1958) 5–26, 181–210. Grelot's long article, which was written without the benefit of Jansen's book (see p. 6, n. 1), evidences the author's very serious concern not to confuse the effort of amassing parallels or antecedents with a careful study of Jewish stories about Enoch. A substantial part of his paper is devoted to an attempt to discern the ultimate significance of the Enochic legend in the Bible and in subsequent Jewish thought in contrast to the meaning of the parallels in their respective Mesopotamian contexts (6). Grelot, unlike Jansen, did not limit himself to the data of *1 Enoch* but included the evidence of Jub 4:17–24 as a convenient summary of material that is more widely dispersed in *1 Enoch*. Moreover, he treats Gen 5:21–24 in considerable detail and sees in it more of the evolved Enochic legend than do many other scholars. Note should be taken of his method because it is important for this last point: he begins his analysis with the fully elaborated descriptions of Enoch in *Jubilees* and *1 Enoch* and then moves in the reverse of chronological order to the biblical text in order to ascertain how much of the full legend is there presupposed and expressed (5, 191–93). One may well ask, given how much he sees in Gen 5:21–24, whether his method has not unduly influenced his results on this question.

Grelot observes that scholars have regularly sought the origins of the elaborate portrait of Enoch in traditions about two primeval heroes—Enmeduranki and the hero of the flood. He reviews the evidence for this hypothesis, making extensive use of Berossus' *Babyloniaca* (6–13), and concludes that Jewish tradition has indeed focused traits of these two characters upon Enoch: (1) from Enmeduranki it has derived Enoch's role as the originator of civilization, as the one who has received celestial, encyclopedic revelations of a profoundly religious character (17, 20); (2) from Berossus' flood-hero comes Enoch's function as the transmitter of antediluvian wisdom to posterity by means of his books (the only ones to survive the deluge). This latter role was not assigned to the biblical flood-hero because the scriptural account did not record a removal of Noah from the society of his children immediately after the flood (17, 23–24). Since he remained with them and thus could teach them by other means, the device of books preserved from before the flood was unnecessary. In other words, he maintains that the actions which Berossus credited to Xisouthros have been divided into two in *Jubi-*

*lees*: his role as preserver of the human race is assigned to Noah, while his
function of transmitting antediluvian wisdom becomes Enoch's prerogative
(17–18). Grelot even claims that, though Berossus' phrase "the beginnings
and the middles and the ends of all writings" (used of the books that Xisouthros preserved) may simply be idiomatic for *everything*, the contents of
*1 Enoch* do in fact show him teaching about creation (geography, calendar),
the middle of history (angelic sin and the flood), and its end (the apocalyptic
sections [20]). A further point of contact between the flood-hero and Enoch
is geographical, since both of them are removed along the same path to a
paradise located in the northwest (22–23). He believes that the most plausible hypothesis for explaining these parallels is ". . . une référence immédiate
de l'Hénoch juif à ses modèles mésopotamiens," (25) and that the composite
Enochic figure was the product of a school in the Babylonian diaspora,
perhaps after the Jewish restoration to Palestine or possibly earlier (25).

Grelot then proceeds to the difficult task of determining how much of
this developed Enochic legend is presupposed and reflected in Sir 44:16 and
Gen 5:21–24. The reference in Sirach shows a more evolved form of the
Enoch figure than does the sparse notice in Genesis; it is analogous to the
one found more fully in *1 Enoch* and *Jubilees* in that it reflects awareness of
his esoteric knowledge and his role as witness (181–83). Grelot claims that
Gen 5:21–24, too, evidences much of the developed legend and argues his
case by stressing three points: (1) P draws attention to him by using the
genealogical device of switching Enoch from third position in the earlier
J list (Gen 4:17) to the suggestive seventh position in his list (the place
occupied by Enmeduranki in some versions of the antediluvian king list);
(2) the author may be playing on the connection between the seventh person
in the list and wisdom through use of the name *ḥănôk*, the root of which
refers to *understanding, wisdom* (whereas in 4:17 he is the *dedicator* of a
city); and (3) while the trait of "walking with God" does not connect Enoch
with traditions about Enmeduranki, his 365 years do bring him into contact
with this royal devotee of Shamash, the sun-god. Enoch thus may be presented in Genesis as the founder of the priestly calendar (184–88). As a
result, it is probable that the pseudepigraphical books (*1 Enoch, Jubilees*)
merely develop and incorporate traditional materials that date in their essen-
tials from the time of the exile (189). Respect for the biblical fact that Noah
had not been removed (J) led P to transfer the traits of removal and walking
with God to the only other prominent member of the antediluvian genealogy, viz. Enoch. Thus, Gen 5:21–24 seems to be referring laconically to a
longer and well known story. By the time of the priestly edition of Genesis,
the Enochic legend has assumed its definitive form (192), although at a later
time it was enriched especially in an apocalyptic direction that corresponds
to no parallel in Mesopotamian literature (192, n. 87). Grelot does not,

therefore, posit fresh contact with foreign traditions *at the times when 1 Enoch and Jubilees were written*; rather, the story that was preserved around this biblical core was the source of the evolved legend. The context of the Babylonian captivity provides the most plausible *Sitz im Leben* for the borrowing or contact (195).

To his credit, Grelot tries to find the deeper significance that the Enochic legend assumed in P and later in the evolution of Jewish thought. He views the development of this legend as a priestly way of helping Jews better to resist the lure of pagan cults in Babylon by incorporating (but definitely modifying) mythological traditions of Mesopotamia into Jewish antiquities. Through modification, these traditions were made to serve biblical ends (197–98). He perceives in the biblical Enochic legend a profound theological significance: the removal of Enoch (*lqh* in a technical sense) is a cryptic reference to his transfer, like that of Utnapishtim, to the garden of life. ". . . Hénoch, transféré au Paradis, est entré dans la vie éternelle, sort qu'il partage avec les anges. Pour lui, contrairement à tous les hommes pécheurs, le dessein originel de Dieu s'est realisé" (205). Thus Enoch's special destiny is a type of that which God intends and keeps for all his people in sharp contrast to the deep-seated pessimism of the Epic of Gilgamesh which stresses that eternal life is denied to mankind and enjoyed by Utnapishtim alone as an unrepeatable exception (199–210).

Grelot's essay will come under discussion at several places in this book, but here some general issues relating to his work should be raised. First, he has surely concentrated on far more convincing traditio-historical antecedents for the Jewish Enochic legends than Jansen did; in this respect his conclusions more nearly resemble those of Zimmern. With Zimmern he makes much of the transparent affinities between Enmeduranki and Enoch, but also, as did Zimmern, he fails to elicit the full value from the parallels. Specifically, both scholars neglected to explore possible lines of connection between Enmeduranki's divinatory character and the roles (including that of apocalyptic seer) that Enoch plays in Jewish literature. Second, Grelot quite properly regards Gen 5:21–24 as a cryptic reference to wider cycles of Enoch material, but in some cases (e.g., his suggestion that the name *hănôk* signifies the sapiential associations of this character) he has discerned more there than the text warrants (see chap. II). This seems to be a product of his chronologically backwards approach to the texts. A third noteworthy shortcoming of Grelot's essay is the absence of a compelling explanation for the fact that Enoch, not Noah, enjoys a removal to the divine realm, though this was the reward of the flood-hero in various Mesopotamian versions of the deluge. Did P ascribe this trait to Enoch merely because the text of J which lay before him indicated no such reward for the biblical survivor of the flood? There is some reason to believe that there is more to the problem than

Grelot thinks as will become clear in chap. VI. Fourth, Grelot, with Zimmern and Jansen, operates as though there were just one Enochic legend or portrait in Jewish sources; due attention is not paid to the fact (with which each of these writers was familiar) that there are several independent sources of varying dates that transmit different pictures of him. It is simply not proper to take the *Jubilees* pericope as a summary of all other versions of the Enoch figure. And finally, however commendable it is that he tried, it seems unlikely that Grelot has discovered the ultimate theological meaning of the biblical words about Enoch (see further chap. II).

Now that the efforts of Zimmern, Jansen, and Grelot have been summarized and assessed, it is only fair to acknowledge that each man, in his own way, has made solid contributions to understanding some of the problems raised by Jewish traditions about Enoch. They have explored likely (and occasionally unlikely) antecedents and adduced a wealth of data that relate in one way or another to the subject. The extent to which the present work is indebted to their labors will become apparent in the pages that follow. The major lines of investigation have been drawn most clearly by Zimmern and, with more detail, by Grelot, viz. that Enoch embodies traditions about the seventh antediluvian king and, to a lesser degree, about the flood-hero.

### C. A New Study

It now seems wise, despite the excellent work that has been done, to approach the matter afresh and that for several reasons. One is, and it has already been suggested above, that neither Zimmern nor Grelot has extracted from the traditions about Enmeduranki in particular their full value for explaining some of the directions in which Enochic lore evolved. The seventh king's intimate association with divination is the major gap in their treatment. It appears to have great significance for the Enochic material, but neither of these scholars has developed this point. A second fundamental reason for a new study is that none of the three authors whose views were surveyed above has reckoned seriously with variation and growth within pseudepigraphic portraits of Enoch. The tendency of all three has been to lump every statement about him in works such as *1 Enoch* or *Jubilees* into a single, composite description. Such a procedure ignores the universally recognized fact that *1 Enoch* itself consists of at least five originally independent booklets, all dating from different periods and written to serve distinguishable ends; it also overlooks the fact that the pericope about Enoch in *Jubilees* does not simply summarize statements that are scattered throughout *1 Enoch* but makes its own contribution and serves the purposes of yet another author. Given the diversity of the material, every effort should be made to honor variation and nuance in Enochic traditions. Only then can one gain a broader understanding of and appreciation for each account. Thus, in this book, the several descriptions of Enoch will be examined separately and in chronological order insofar as that is possible.

A third impetus for renewed study has been the recent publication of several previously unavailable texts that have a direct bearing on the subject at hand. Pride of place in this category must go to J. T. Milik's *The Books of Enoch: Aramaic Fragments of Qumrân Cave 4*, in which he has edited nearly all fragments of the 11 Aramaic MSS of *1 Enoch* that were discovered in Cave 4 at Qumran.[28] Though the existence of these fragments was announced quite some time ago, only a few had been made available for scholarly perusal before 1976. Grelot, writing in 1958, could use only the two small scraps that Milik published that same year; Zimmern and Jansen wrote, of course, well before discovery of the first Qumran scrolls. As a result, none of the major studies of Jewish traditions about Enoch has been based on the Aramaic texts to any large extent. These MSS, written in the original language of *1 Enoch*, have enlarged and greatly strengthened the textual foundation for studies of *1 Enoch*, despite their generally poor state of preservation. As will be seen in the chapters that follow, they have in some cases necessitated drastic upward revision in the dates that experts had generally assigned to the different sections of *1 Enoch*. Some of these booklets are now recognized as being far older than had been thought before the 4Q MSS came to light, and greater confidence can be lodged in the new datings than in the old because they are the results of paleographical analysis—a more precise tool for dating purposes than the literary-critical methods or vague historical allusions that scholars had been reduced to using, when they lacked sufficiently early textual evidence. While discussing new textual material for *1 Enoch* mention should be made, too, of Michael Knibb's recent edition of the Ethiopic text of *1 Enoch*.[29] In it he has assembled a wider range of Ethiopic evidence than had been available in the older edition of R. H. Charles. The Qumran caves have yielded, in addition to the MSS of *1 Enoch*, a number of fragments of the original Hebrew version of the *Book of Jubilees*[30] and several columns of the Aramaic Genesis Apocryphon.[31] Both of these works offer important descriptions of Enoch.

[28] Oxford: Clarendon, 1976.

[29] *The Ethiopic Book of Enoch: A new edition in the light of the Aramaic Dead Sea Fragments* (2 vols.; Oxford: Clarendon, 1978).

[30] All of the published fragments are presented and analyzed in VanderKam, *Textual and Historical Studies in the Book of Jubilees*, 18–95.

[31] N. Avigad/ Y. Yadin, *A Genesis Apocryphon: A Scroll From the Wilderness of Judaea* (Jerusalem: Magnes/ Heikhal ha-Sefer, 1956); J. Fitzmyer, *The Genesis Apocryphon of Qumran Cave 1: A Commentary* (BibOr 18A; Rome: Biblical Institute, 1971).

On the Mesopotamian side, developments have also been swift and noteworthy. In an essay dated to 1967, W. Lambert published in improved and often expanded form the texts that relate to the seventh antediluvian king Enmeduranki.[32] Other new texts have illuminated the larger context within which Enmeduranki is most frequently mentioned—the "Sumerian" King List. The most significant document in this respect is the Uruk Apkallū List which pairs antediluvian kings with their sages (called *apkallūs*).[33] The latter figures may eventually supply valuable comparative material for some aspects of the later Jewish portraits of Enoch. In fact the Assyriologist R. Borger has recently published an essay in which he argued that the theme of Enoch's ascension was borrowed precisely from Mesopotamian tales about Utuʾabzu, the sage who was active during Enmeduranki's legendary reign (see chap. II for an analysis of his argument).[34] Finally, the Akkadian prophecies have opened new possibilities for explaining the evolution of apocalyptic literature in Mesopotamia and Judea.[35]

The facts that the contributions of older evidence have not been exhausted and that much new material is available are, then, major reasons why the present investigation has been undertaken. But the most significant aim of this book is to show that the traditions about Enoch may indeed be the most useful avenue for exploring the origins and early development of Jewish apocalyptic literature and concerns. The last decades have witnessed extensive discussion of apocalypses and apocalyptic books, but there has been no thorough analysis of the contributions which the Enochic lore can make to this field. The chapters that follow represent an attempt to fill that void.

[32] "Enmeduranki and Related Matters," *JCS* 21 (1967) 126–38.

[33] J. van Dijk, "Die Inschriftenfunde" in Heinrich J. Lenzen, *XVIII. vorläufiger Bericht über die von dem Deutschen Archäologischen Institut und der Deutschen Orientgesellschaft aus Mitteln der Deutschen Forschungsgemeinschaft unternommenen Ausgrabungen in Uruk-Warka* (Berlin: Mann, 1962) 44–45.

[34] "Die Beschwörungsserie BĪT MĒSERI und die Himmelfahrt Henochs," *JNES* 33 (1974) 183–96.

[35] For the bibliography on these texts, see chap. III.

# II

## BIBLICAL MATERIAL ABOUT ENOCH[1]

### A. The Priestly Genealogy of Genesis 5

The immediate context for the major biblical pericope about Enoch (Gen 5:21–24) is the priestly genealogy of Genesis 5 in which the editor lists the ten heads of humanity beginning with Adam, continuing through his (first?)[2] son Seth, and ending with Noah in the tenth generation. Before he begins the genealogy itself, P sets the stage for this line of humanity by echoing the words of the creation and blessing of humankind in Gen 1:27–28; later, within the Adam section of the list, he refers to Seth's creation in the image of Adam as Adam had been fashioned in the divine likeness (5:1, 3; cf. Gen 1:27). Though the motif of the divine image does not appear in the genealogy after v 3, it seems that P wished to convey that the Sethite line was the one in which God's blessing and likeness were transmitted, in contrast to J's Cainite genealogy (4:17–24) in which a curse appears to have resided (see 4:11; cf. v 24).[3]

The segments of the Sethite genealogy follow a regular pattern: the compiler notes that a patriarch at a certain age fathered a son (who is named), that he lived a certain number of years after the birth of this son during which time he continued to beget sons and daughters, that at his death he had attained a certain age, and that he died. The editor fleshes out this skeletal framework to varying degrees at just three points in the ten-member list: 1. Adam (vv 3–5, where the outline is expanded only by the words *bidmûtô kĕṣalmô* ["in his own likeness, after his image"] in v 3); 7. Enoch (vv 21–24, where several substitutions are made in the expected

---

[1] The name Enoch, spelled either *ḥănōk* or *ḥănôk*, appears in several OT passages besides Genesis 4 and 5: 1 Chr 1:3 (= the Enoch of Genesis 5); Gen 25:4 (= a son of Midian [= 1 Chr 1:33]); and Gen 46:9; Exod 6:14; 1 Chr 5:3 (= a son of Reuben). Cf. also Num 26:5 where the name of Reuben's son and a gentilic from it are found.

[2] The genealogical form of chap. 5 suggests that for Adam as for the others in the list the son who occupies this position is the first-born.

[3] C. Westermann, *Genesis* (BK I/1; Neukirchen-Vluyn: Neukirchener, 1974) 471; Robert R. Wilson, *Genealogy and History in the Biblical World* (Yale Near Eastern Researches 7; New Haven/London: Yale University, 1977) 155–56, 164–65.

pattern—see below); and 10. Noah (the genealogical clichés appear at 5:28-29a,[4] 32; 9:28-29; the flood narratives have been wedged between these brackets). It seems reasonable to surmise that by means of these changes in the pattern the editor wished to call attention to patriarchs one, seven, and ten.

While these alterations break the monotony of the highly schematic genealogy and thus focus attention on the first, seventh, and tenth patriarchs (especially the later two), comparison of the priestly Sethite genealogy with J's Cainite list in 4:17-24 (especially vv 17-18) uncovers an additional attempt by P to underscore the unusual Enochic section. The relationship that obtains between these two genealogies has been debated extensively. Several recent studies have clarified to some extent the traditions which they mirror (see below),[5] but the striking similarities between them indicate that, as one would have expected, P has revised J here as elsewhere. The names in the two lists are these:[6]

---

[4] 5:28-29a is actually part of the Lamech genealogical section though it relates to his first-born Noah. Verse 29b, a J passage that has been retained in the priestly genealogy, offers an etymology of *Noah* (*zeh yĕnaḥămēnû mimmaʿăśēnû ûmēʿiṣṣĕbôn yādênû* ["this one shall bring us relief from our work and from the toil of our hands"]) that is related to the postdiluvian story of Noah's viticulture (cf. J. Skinner, *Genesis* [2nd ed.; ICC; Edinburgh: Clark, 1930] 133-34).

[5] Both Skinner (*Genesis*, 138-39) and H. Gunkel (*Genesis* [9th ed. = 3rd ed.; Göttingen: Vandenhoeck & Ruprecht, 1977 (1910)] 132) saw a relationship between the two lists but realized that the issue was more complex than simply a priestly revision of the Yahwist's genealogy. For a thorough study of the origins, relationship, and purposes of the two lists, see Wilson, *Genealogy*, 138-66. Several Assyriologists have recently revived the hypothesis, first proposed by H. Zimmern (in E. Schrader, *Die Keilinschriften und das Alte Testament* [ed. H. Zimmern and H. Winckler; 3rd ed.; Berlin: Reuther & Reichard, 1903] 542), that behind J's seven-member list lie Mesopotamian traditions about the seven antediluvian *apkallū* (= sages [See pp. 45-50 below]); cf. J. J. Finkelstein, "The Antediluvian Kings: A University of California Tablet," *JCS* 17 (1963) 50 n. 41; W. W. Hallo, "Antediluvian Cities," *JCS* 23 (1970) 63-65 (who sees reflections of some Mesopotamian city names in Gen 4:17-24). Finkelstein's additional suggestion—that similarities in names between the J and P genealogies may be related to the fact that "some of these sages [i.e., *apkallū*] bear names that are in some instances strikingly similar to those of the kings in whose reigns they appeared . . ."—fails to explain the correspondences in Hebrew traditions since the names in the two biblical lists appear neither to have been borrowed from names in *apkallū* and king lists nor to have been translated from them. The hypothesis that P used the names in J but modeled the form of his genealogy on an exemplar of the Mesopotamian king list provides the most economical explanation of the evidence.

[6] In commentaries on Genesis one often finds a table in which these two lists are compared (e.g., Skinner, *Genesis*, 138), but the juxtaposition is regularly done in an artificial way in that J's Adam is aligned with P's Enosh—a procedure that is supposedly justified by the fact that both mean *man*. The obvious correlation is Adam—Adam in the two genealogies. The table in Wilson, *Genealogy*, 161, sets out the evidence more objectively and is the basis for the list above.

|  |  |  |
|---|---|---|
| *J* | | *P* |

| | | |
|---|---|---|
| (ʾādām) | 1. (ādām) | 1. ʾādām |
| (šēt) | 2. qayin | 2. šēt |
| (ʾĕnôš)[7] | 3. ḥănôk | 3. ʾĕnôš |
| | 4. ʿîrād | 4. qênān |
| | 5. mĕḥûyāʾēl | 5. mahălalʾēl |
| | 6. mĕtûšāʾēl | 6. yered |
| | 7. lemek | 7. ḥănôk |
| | yābāl yûbāl tûbal-qayin | 8. mĕtûšelaḥ |
| | | 9. lemek |
| | | 10. nōăḥ |
| | | šēm ḥām yepet[8] |

There are unmistakable similarities between names in several instances
(*qayin/qênān*; ʿîrād/yered;[9] *mehûyāʾēl* rather remotely with *mahălalʾēl*;
*mĕtûšāʾēl/mĕtûšelaḥ*),[10] and in two cases the spellings are identical (*ḥănôk*;
*lemek*). Nevertheless, within the parallel section that includes nos.
2–7 in J and 4–9 in P, the priestly list shows two names in an order different than J's,
and, assuming that P revised J's list, these variations in all likelihood betray
P's concern that the two names occupy specific positions that were not those
which J has assigned to them. A single change in order involved switching
the names *ḥănôk* and *mĕḥûyāʾēl/mahălalʾēl* so that *ḥănôk* moves from the
third position in J to the seventh place in P, whereas one would have expected
his name in the fifth slot. Jack M. Sasson has recently assembled evidence to
show that one genealogical convention which was followed at times by

[7] These three names are drawn from the Yahwist's abbreviated Sethite genealogy in
4:25–26. The priestly editor thus had before him in J all ten names which appear in his list (note
J's etymology of *Noah* in 5:29b); cf. Westermann, *Genesis*, 473, 476–77. He has revised J's order
and perhaps changed the spelling of a name or two, though such differences may have arisen
independently.

[8] There is no need to discuss here the function(s) of each genealogy in its present setting
(for this, cf. Wilson, *Genealogy*, 148–58, 163–66), but the last entries in each list, three sons (and
in J one daughter) of one man—the first time in either enumeration that more than one son was
mentioned by name—show an obvious difference in function between them. In J these three are
the creators of various cultural forms, whereas in P they become the heads of humanity in the
postdiluvian world.

[9] Jack M. Sasson ("A Genealogical 'Convention' in Biblical Chronography?" *ZAW* 90
[1978] 174) thinks that the difference in spelling between the two names is due to J's "parasonan-
tic pun" which "allowed Enoch, builder of cities (ʿîr) to be the father of ʿîrād." W. F. Albright
("The Babylonian Matter in the Predeuteronomic Primeval History [JE] in Gen 1–11," *JBL* 58
[1939] 96), however, attributes the spelling ʿîrād to a corruption of *yered* by vertical dittography
with ʿîr.

[10] In the LXX both names are spelled *Methousala*.

Hebrew chronographers was that "minimal alterations were made in inherited lists of ancestors in order to place individuals deemed worthy of attention in the seventh . . . position of a genealogical tree."[11]

Once the names *ḥănôk* and *mĕḥûyā ʾēl/mahălalʾēl* were switched, the result was that *ʿîrād/yered*, who was *ḥănôk*'s son in J, becomes his father in P. Whether P attached any significance to this revised relationship can no longer be determined, but, as is well known, later expositors seized upon the meaning of the root *yrd* (to go down) and claimed that the divine beings of Gen 6:1–4 descended to the earth in his time. It is not impossible that P knew of this tradition, but it was apparently not of sufficient importance for him to violate genealogical form in order to include it. The significant fact for the present study is, however, that in P's list Enoch has assumed the symbolic seventh position. Thus, in addition to the unusual elements in the Enochic pericope itself, its location also calls attention to him.

In the literature on Genesis 5 there is a well established tradition which holds that P modeled his pre-flood genealogy on a Mesopotamian list of antediluvian kings, the so-called Sumerian King List. Even before a cuneiform text containing such a king list had been published, scholars had hypothesized a connection on the basis of the testimony of Berossus, a priest of Marduk who in ca. B.C. 280, wrote *Babyloniaca* in order to make the culture and antiquities of his Babylonian people available to Greek readers.[12] The Berossian evidence was considered relevant because, despite the comparatively late date of his book, he claimed to have based his presentation on very ancient sources—a claim that has been substantiated frequently in the last

---

[11] "A Genealogical 'Convention'?" 171-72, 175; his article "Generation, Seventh," *IDBSup* 354-56; and P. Grelot, "La légende," 183-85. Wilson (*Genealogy*, 161–63) attributes this variation in order to what he terms "genealogical fluidity" which is often found in the middle sections of genealogies and thinks that names involved in such shifts have lost their "genealogical function." This is, however, an inadequate explanation for the transfer of Enoch's name from third (= fifth in P) to seventh position—as Wilson himself seems aware (162 n. 66). J. T. Milik (*The Books of Enoch*, 31) has suggested rather implausibly that *1 Enoch* 6–19, which he believes is earlier than P, still reflects the order Enoch–Irad of J.

[12] P. Schnabel (*Berossos und die babylonisch-hellenistische Literatur* [Leipzig/Berlin: Teubner, 1923; reprinted Hildesheim: Olms, 1968]) has collected all ancient citations of the *Babyloniaca* and has provided extensive studies of the book's contents and textual vicissitudes. More recently the remains of *Babyloniaca* have been assembled by F. Jacoby, *Die Fragmente der griechischen Historiker* (Part 3C, vol. 1; Leiden: Brill, 1958) 364-97. Berossus himself provided a fairly narrow framework for dating the book by dedicating it to Antiochus I Soter (Schnabel's frg. 51 from King Juba of Mauretania) who was co-regent with his father Seleucus I from 293-80 and sole ruler from 280-61. Schnabel dated *Babyloniaca* to the years of Antiochus' co-regency (pp. 7–10), as does S. Burstein, *The* Babyloniaca *of Berossus* (Sources and Monographs, Sources from the Ancient Near East I, 5; Malibu: Undena, 1978) 4, with Appendix 2.

century.[13] Berossus listed 10 kings who ruled the entire 432,000 years from the beginning of kingship until the flood, the hero of which—*Xisouthros*—was the tenth king.[14] The similarities *in form* with Genesis 5 are immediately evident: 10 long-lived members in a list that covers the pre-flood period, and the tenth member was the hero of the flood. For a time it was also thought possible to relate names in the two lists with one another on the basis of their meanings in their respective languages. For example, the name of Berossus' third king—*amēlōn*—appeared to be the Akkadian word *amēlu* = man, while the name of the third member in Genesis 5—*ʾĕnôš*—means *man* in Hebrew.[15] Now that several cuneiform copies of the antediluvian section of the king list are available, it has become apparent that such alleged parallels in meaning do not exist.[16] Most scholars have, nevertheless, continued to see some connection between the king-list tradition and the Sethite genealogy, but Westermann has now maintained, it seems, that there is no parallel between

---

[13] Berossus' *Babyloniaca* has not been preserved, nor has the writing of any ancient author who quoted directly from it. Therefore, all citations from or references to it are at best third-hand and in many cases even more distant (see the charts in Schnabel, *Berossos*, 110, 168, 171). His list of 10 antediluvian kings (see the chart, below p. 36-37) has survived in Eusebius's *Chronicle*, in which the church historian cites it from Alexander Polyhistor's abridgement of *Babyloniaca* and from Abydenus. Since the Greek text of the *Chronicle* has also not survived, one is reduced to using the Armenian translation of it. Nevertheless, the Greek form of the names is known because the Byzantine chronographer George Syncellus quoted this information from the Greek text of the *Chronicle* which was still extant in his time. Despite the prohibitive odds posed by the textual history of these and other excerpts from *Babyloniaca*, cuneiform texts have often verified both the antiquity of Berossus' traditions and the accuracy with which even the spellings of names have been preserved in the surviving excerpts. On this see G. Komoróczy, "Berosos and the Mesopotamian Literature," *Acta Antiqua* 21 (1973) 125-52.

[14] See Schnabel, *Berossos*, 261-263 (frgs. 29-30); Jacoby, *Die Fragmente*, F 3 (pp. 374-77). Berossus' spelling of the tenth king's name—*xisouthros* in Syncellus (from Polyhistor-Eusebius; variant *sisouthros* from Abydenus-Eusebius; in Armenian: *Xisuthros*)—reflects that of the flood-hero in the Sumerian Flood Story—Zi-u-sud-ra.

[15] Zimmern (*Die Keilinschriften und das Alte Testament*, 531-32, 539-40) associated Berossus's third king *Amēlōn* with *amēlu* and biblical Enosh; his fourth king *Ammenōn* with Akkadian *ummānu* (*Werkmeister*) and biblical Kenan (a smith); and his eighth king *Amempsinos* with Akkadian *amēl-Sin* (man of Sin [the moon god]) and biblical Methuselah (man of Shelah [a god's name]). That is, each had the form "man of" plus a divine name. These connections were accepted by Gunkel (*Genesis*, 132) and Skinner (Skinner, *Genesis*, 137) and employed as significant parts of their arguments that Genesis 5 was based on a version of the king list.

[16] The names proved to be Sumerian, not Semitic as earlier scholars had mistakenly assumed. Thus *Amēlōn* represents *Ammeluanna* (<*Enmeluanna*), *Ammenōn* perhaps *Enmenunna* (but see Thorkild Jacobsen, *The Sumerian King List* [Oriental Institute of the University of Chicago, Assyriological Studies 11; Chicago: University of Chicago, 1939] 73 n. 18), and *Amempsinos Ensipazianna* (see the chart, p. 37). Cf. also Westermann, *Genesis*, 473-76.

them.[17] It is true that efforts to correlate the meanings of names in the two lists have ended in failure, but this does not entail that one should abandon the king-list tradition as P's model in a *formal* sense. The number of 10 antediluvian kings is attested in cuneiform (WB 62) as well as in Berossus, and the tenth member in these two versions is the flood hero, while in others he continues to be the last, of course, though not the tenth. Furthermore, there is evidence relating to the seventh member in both lists which goes far to demonstrate P's dependence upon a form of the king list. Therefore, in the following paragraphs, Gen 5:21–24 will be examined and then the unique information derived from it will be compared with Mesopotamian traditions about the seventh antediluvian king.

## B. Enoch in Gen 5:21–24

It should be observed that the traditions about a patriarch named *Enoch* (*ḥănôk*) are different in J and P. It may be that J regarded him as a city-builder who named his city after his son *ʿîrād*; at least this is one possible interpretation of the strange word-order in 4:17 (*wattēled ʾet-ḥănôk wayhî bōneh ʿîr wayyiqrāʾ šēm hāʿîr kěšēm běnô ḥănôk* ["and she conceived and bore Enoch; and he built a city, and called the name of the city after the name of his son, Enoch."]).[18] W. W. Hallo, who opts for this understanding of the verse, has suggested that *ʿîrād* reflects the name of the famous antediluvian city Eridu.[19] If this is the correct interpretation of 4:17, then J's Enoch embodies a tradition that has nothing in common with P's portrait of him other than the name.

---

[17] *Genesis*, 470–77, 485–86 (note: "Mann wird dann nicht mehr die altbabylonische Liste der Urkönige als Parallele zu Gn 5 ansehen können" [476]). For another negative verdict, see Thomas C. Hartman, "Some thoughts on the Sumerian King List and Genesis 5 and 11B," *JBL* 91 (1972) 25–32. Hartman argued that the purposes of the two genealogies are different and that the ten-generation structure of Genesis 5 is "more closely tied to this West Semitic (Amorite) penchant for a ten-generation pattern than it is to inspiration arising from the Sumerian King List . . ." (30) For ten-generation genealogies he bases himself on A. Malamat, "King Lists of the Old Babylonian Period and Biblical Genealogies," *JAOS* 88 (1968) 163–73. Wilson ("The Old Testament Genealogies in Recent Research," *JBL* 94 [1975] 175–88) has, however, effectively disposed of this supposed ten-generation penchant in Amorite genealogies. Cf. also Lambert, "A New Look at the Babylonian Background of Genesis," *JTS* 16 (1965) 291–93, 298–99; "Babylonien und Israel," *Theologische Realenzyklopädie* (ed. G. Krause/ G. Müller; New York; Berlin: DeGruyter, 1977– ), 5.73–77.

[18] In 4:17 the name that immediately precedes *wayhî bōneh* ("and he became a builder") is *ḥănôk*. A problem with this interpretation is, though, that the second use of *ḥănôk*, if it is the subject of *wayyiqrāʾ* ("and he called, named"), is in an awkward location.

[19] "Antediluvian Cities," 64, following U. Cassuto, *A Commentary on the Book of Genesis*, part 1: *From Adam to Noah* (Jerusalem: Magnes, 1961) 228–30. Cassuto argued from the parallel syntax in 4:1–2 that in 4:17 also the name of the son should be the subject of the following verb. For a discussion of this entire problem, see Wilson, *Genealogy*, 139–41.

Mention of the name *ḥănôk* raises the question of its meaning, and here, too, J and P may differ to some extent. It would not be unreasonable to suppose that, if J's Enoch was the first city-builder, the Yahwist understood the name as related to the familiar Hebrew verb *ḥānak* which means "to dedicate." This verb is used elsewhere in the Hebrew Bible for dedications of places and buildings (e.g., Deut 20:5; 1 Kgs 8:63//2 Chr 7:5).[20] But it would be hasty to assume that P, if he attached any special meaning to the name at all, understood it in the same etymological sense because, as was noted above, there is no hint in 5:21–24 that P's Enoch was the builder of a city. Grelot[21] has proposed that the priestly editor saw in the name the notion of *wisdom* or *understanding*. In Arabic *ḥunk/ḥink* (biblical Hebrew cognate *ḥēk* ‹ *ḥink*) means "worldly experience, worldly wisdom gained through experience, sophistication,"[22] while the Ethiopic verb *ḥanaka* (I,1) means "intelligere, percipere."[23] If the editor thought of the name *ḥănôk* in connection with words from this semantic range, then he was implying that Enoch was a man of knowledge rather than a dedicator or one who was dedicated, although it must be admitted that both would fit well with what is known elsewhere about the seventh man in the pre-flood genealogy. Later writers such as Ben Sira (44:16) associated great knowledge with Enoch, and it may be that they based this connection in part on his name.[24] Nevertheless, however alluring Grelot's hypothesis may be, it seems unlikely that the Hebrew name *Enoch* awakened such thoughts in readers' minds, as no Hebrew word that is related to the root *ḥnk* embodies this meaning. Furthermore, the type of knowledge that the Arabic evidence envisages is practical, derived from experience—a kind that does not tally at all with the revealed knowledge of Enoch found in later sources. If, therefore, the meaning of *Enoch* has any significance, it is safer to derive it from *ḥnk* = to dedicate.

[20] BDB 335 under *ḥnk* II.

[21] See Grelot, "La légende," 186; cf. G. Beer, "Das Buch Henoch" in *Die Apokryphen und Pseudepigraphen des Alten Testaments* (2 vols.; ed. E. Kautzsch; Tübingen: Freiburg/Leipzig: Mohr, 1900), 2.217.

[22] H. Wehr, *A Dictionary of Modern Written Arabic* (ed. J. M. Cowan; 3rd ed. Ithaca: Spoken Language Services, 1976) 210. Hebrew *ḥēk* means "palate, roof of mouth, gums" (BDB 335).

[23] A. Dillmann, *Lexicon Linguae Aethiopicae* (reprinted New York: Ungar, 1955) 108–09.

[24] Albright ("The Babylonian Matter," 96) relates the name to Canaanite *ḥanaku*, "retainer," (cf. Gen 14:14 *ḥănîkîm*; the word is ultimately of Egyptian origin) which appears in early second millennium Egyptian texts and suggests that *wayyithallēk ʾet hāʾĕlōhîm*, which he renders "and he associated constantly with God," "reflects an old aetiological explanation of the name as the 'retainer (of God).' There is no need to bring in Enmeduranki of Sippar. . . ." Precisely how this conclusion follows from the proposed etymology of the word is not clear. See also Thomas O. Lambdin, "Egyptian Loan Words in the Old Testament," *JAOS* 73 (1953) 150; he follows Albright in accepting an Egyptian origin for *ḥănîkîm* in Gen 14:14 (Egyptian *ḥnk.w*).

Now that the pictures of Enoch in J and P have been contrasted and the meaning of the name discussed, Gen 5:21-24 should be examined. If one compares these verses with the standard items of the Sethite genealogy, the following prove to be unusual features:

1. the second instance of the verb *wayhî* ("and he lived") is replaced by the phrase *wayyithallēk ḥănôk ʾet hāʾĕlōhîm* ("And Enoch walked with God") (v 22).

2. the sum of his years—365—is far and away the lowest in the list (v 23).

3. the customary *wayyāmōt* ("and he died") is replaced by *wayyithallēk ḥănôk ʾet hāʾĕlōhîm wĕʾênennû kî lāqaḥ ʾōtô ʾĕlōhîm.* ("And Enoch walked with God, and he was not for God took him") (v 24).

Each of these features should now be studied and then compared with Meso-potamian traditions about the seventh king.

1. The second instance of the verb *wayhî* is replaced by the phrase *wayyithallēk ḥănôk ʾet hāʾĕlōhîm* (v 22). In contrast to all other patriarchs in Genesis 5, Enoch is said not merely to have lived a certain number of years between the time when his first son was born and the end of his earthly life but to have "walked with God" (as the phrase is usually rendered) for 300 years. Only Enoch and Noah, of all the characters in the Bible, enjoyed this kind of relationship with the deity or this quality of life (5:22, 24; 6:9),[25] though others, such as Abram, are associated with walking *before* him (Gen 17:1; 24:20; 48:15; Mal 2:6 says about Levi *hālak ʾittî* ["he walked with me"]—the suffix refers to God—where only the conjugation of the verb distinguishes it from the present phrase). It may be that P furnishes some details of the way in which he used the expression in the words that imme-diately precede it in 6:9: *nōăḥ ʾîš ṣaddîq tāmîm hāyāh bĕdōrōtāyw* ("Noah was a righteous man, blameless in his generation")—words that indicate fault-lessness in cultic, ethical, and legal senses.[26] But there is reason to believe that P meant to add something new with this phrase and that he did not use it simply to say that Enoch and Noah lived lives that were pleasing to God.[27]

---

[25] Sasson ("Word-Play in Gen 6:8-9," *CBQ* 37 [1975] 166) observes that the editor of Genesis 6 has furnished a link between the two who are said to have walked with God in that the last three consonants of Gen 6:9 form the name *ḥănôk* in reverse (*hithallek nōaḥ*).

[26] For a discussion of this issue, see F. J. Helfmeyer, "*Hālakh,*" *TDOT* 3.394.

[27] Cf. Helfmeyer, ibid. The LXX translates *wayyithallēk ḥănôk ʾet hāʾĕlōhîm* as *euērestēsen de Enōch tǭ theǭ* in 5:22 and uses the same words in v 24 with the exception that *kai* precedes the entire clause and *de* is therefore omitted. This rendering is reflected in other Greek texts: Wisd Sol 4:10, 14; Sir 44:16; Heb 11:5-6. Armin Schmitt ("Die Angaben über Henoch Gen 5, 21-24 in der LXX," in *Wort, Lied und Gottesspruch: Beiträge zur Septuaginta* [Fest-

The *hitpaʿēl* of *hālak* occurs more than 60 times in the Hebrew Bible and is often used to indicate habitual or ongoing association. F. J. Helfmeyer writes that the phrase in question means "'intimate companionship'. . . with God, like that expressed in the divine revelations to Noah and perhaps to Enoch."[28] As it does elsewhere, the verb denotes that two parties are in continual contact (cf. 1 Sam 25:15 where the same verb and preposition appear but *God* is not the object of the preposition). Or, as Westermann puts it, "Die Wendung meinte in der alten Tradition, dass Henoch mit Gott in einer direkten, unmittelbaren Verbindung stand . . . und so auch mit Gottes Plänen und Absichten vertraut war. Dies ist der Ansatzpunkt für die Bedeutung, die die Gestalt Henoch in einer schon früh einsetzenden, aber erst in der apoka-, lyptischen Literatur zutage kommenden Tradition bekam."[29]

Two other notes should be appended to this discussion of the phrase *wayyithallēk ḥănôk ʾet hāʾĕlōhîm*. First, the clause occurs both at v 22 (during Enoch's earthly life) and at v 24 as part of the expanded replacement for *wayyāmōt*. The second occurrence of the expression implies that his familiar concourse with *hāʾĕlōhîm* did not, according to P, end with his translation. Second, the article before *ʾĕlōhîm* is unusual in P. Skinner, after noting this fact, commented that the definite form must have been borrowed from P's source and "may retain an unobserved trace of the original polytheism ('with the gods')."[30] This is not to say, of course, that the priestly editor meant *hāʾĕlōhîm* as a reference to several gods; the suggestion is merely that P did not succeed in removing all hints of the foreign source from which he borrowed for his portrait of Enoch. Also, later interpreters developed this definite plural as a reference to angels among whom they pictured Enoch as living both during and after his 365 years. As a matter of fact, *ʾĕlōhîm* does mean *angels* at times in the Hebrew Bible (cf. Ps 97:8 [English v 7; LXX: 96:7 *angeloi*]) and it may be that P in Gen 5:22, 24 has suggested this by the definite article in the two occurrences of the phrase in contrast to the anarthrous *ʾĕlōhîm* at the end of v 24.[31]

2. The sum of Enoch's years—365—is far and away the lowest in the list (v 23). Both the relative brevity of his life and the associations of the number

schrift für Joseph Ziegler; ed. Josef Schreiner; Forschung zur Bibel 1; Würzburg: Echter, 1972] 164) attributes this rendering to a "spiritualisierende Tendenz der LXX."

28 Helfmeyer, "Hālakh," 394.

29 *Genesis*, 485.

30 *Genesis*, 131.

31 BDB 43 under *ʾĕlōhîm* l.c. Other examples include Ps 8:6 (LXX *angelous*); 82:1, 6; 138:1 (LXX 137:1 *angelōn*). See the material adduced by D. Dimant, "The 'Fallen Angels' in the Dead Sea Scrolls and in the Apocryphal and Pseudepigraphic Books Related to Them"(Unpublished Ph.D. dissertation, Hebrew University, Jerusalem, 1974 [Hebrew]) 30-32.

365 underscore the significance of this feature in the Enochic pericope. In the MT Enoch's 365 years are 412 fewer than the 777 of Lamech, the next shortest-lived patriarch, the number of whose years seems conditioned by some unexplained association of his name with the number seven both in J and in P.[32] Apart from Lamech, whose life span has a special significance, the eight other members of the Sethite list died at ages that exceed Enoch's by at least 530 and as much as 604 years. In other words, Enoch's age at the end of his earthly life—a life tucked between the two longest-lived patriarchs— Jered (962) and Methuselah (969)—is completely out of line with the others in Genesis 5 and begs for attention and explanation.[33]

Commentators usually point out that Enoch's age was meant to suggest the days in a solar year.[34] In all versions the number is constant so that there is no question about its textual status. As will be argued below, the number 365 does appear to be a muffled way in which P expresses the solar associations of the model on whom he has fashioned his Enochic portrait,[35] but it may be that the priestly editor has derived the number from another source because there is some slight evidence that for him and other sacerdotal writers and editors of the Hebrew Bible the solar year had only 364 days. Certainly in later sources Enoch does become intimately associated with the 364-day cultic calendar (*1 Enoch* 72–82; cf. *Jub.* 4:17-18 and 6:32-38).[36]

3. The customary *wayyāmōt* is replaced by *wayyithallēk ḥănôk ʾet hāʾĕ-lōhîm weʾênennû kî lāqaḥ ʾōtô ʾĕlōhîm* (v 24). The first clause requires no further discussion; it presumably embodies the same meaning here as in v 22, though in this context it relates to the end of his earthly sojourn. P is claiming thus that Enoch's intimacy with *hāʾĕlōhîm*, however he meant that word, did not cease with his removal.[37] This reading of the expression surfaces in later literature as an interpretation of Gen 5:24.

[32] See Sasson, "A Genealogical 'Convention'?" 173.

[33] In the LXX and in the SP, with which *Jubilees* agrees for the ages of the antediluvian patriarchs, several of the year totals differ from those in the MT (cf. the convenient table in Skinner, *Genesis*, 134). In each version, nevertheless, Enoch's 365 years are by far the fewest.

[34] E.g., Skinner, *Genesis*, 132; Gunkel, *Genesis*, 135-36; E. Speiser, *Genesis* (AB 1; 2nd ed.; Garden City: Doubleday, 1964) 43.

[35] Westermann (*Genesis*, 485) prefers not to see a reference to a solar deity in the life-span of Enoch but relates it to his removal: "Dieser Entrückung zu Gott entspricht es, dass die Lebenszeit des Henoch eine volle, runde, ganzheitliche Zeit war. Diese runde Zahl konnte eine kurze sein, weil sie ja nicht mit dem Tode endete." His misunderstanding of this phenomenon is a product of his failure to see both Enoch and the entire genealogy of Genesis 5 against their proper background in the king list tradition.

[36] For a summary of the evidence and diverging views about it, see VanderKam, "The Origin, Character, and Early History of the 364-Day Calendar: A Reassessment of Jaubert's Hypotheses," *CBQ* 41 (1979) 390-411.

[37] The author of *Jubilees*, who describes Enoch as alive and busy in the garden of Eden

The negative particle *ʾayin* with suffix and the explanatory clause *kî lāqaḥ ʾōtô ʾĕlōhîm* (note that there is no article on *ʾĕlōhîm*) are too brief and enigmatic to be comprehensible in and of themselves. In view of the preceding *wayyithallēk ḥănôk ʾet hāʾĕlōhîm* it seems unlikely that *ʾênennû* expresses an absolute denial of his existence; rather, the meaning is that "he was not there, was not present."[38] The words which follow also support the interpretation that Enoch was removed to another location; they explain why he was not found in the customary places.[39] The clause as it stands is marvelously laconic and open-ended, leaving questions such as the location of Enoch's new home unanswered, but the verb *lāqaḥ* can in some contexts express more than the simple notion of taking. In some passages it is employed to describe removal to the divine presence: there are two instances in the story of Elijah's removal (2 Kgs 2:9 [*ʾellāqaḥ*] and v 10 [*luqqaḥ*]).[40] But it must be admitted that evidence from the Hebrew Bible alone leaves one with many questions about the precise referents of this and several other phrases and words in the entire Enochic pericope. In commenting on the verb *lāqaḥ* von Rad articulated a thought that could characterize one's reaction to these four verses as a whole: "The passage, to be sure, gives the impression of being only a brief reference to a much more extensive tradition. It is an open question, therefore, whether much of the apocalyptic Enoch tradition is not really very old and precedes in time (not follows) the Priestly narrative."[41]

## C. Mesopotamian Antecedents of Genesis 5

### 1. The "Sumerian" King List

Scholars have been aware for a long time that adequate explanations for the unique elements in Gen 5:21–24 could not be derived from biblical literature alone and, in their quest for parallel material from which to elucidate these enigmatic phrases, they have regularly turned to the so-called

---

after his translation (4:23–24), commits a strange *lapsus calami* at 7:39 where he mentions the day of Enoch's *death*.

[38] BDB 34 under *ʾayin* 2.b. Cf. Josephus, *Ant.* 1.3, 4 § 85. John Bowker (*The Targums and Rabbinic Literature* [Cambridge: Cambridge University, 1969] 143-50) has assembled many of the early Jewish and Christian comments on this passage. *Tg. Onq.* Gen 5:24 says that the Lord killed Enoch.

[39] The LXX renders with *kai ouch hēurisketo*. Schmitt ("Die Angaben," 164–66) notes that the motif of not being found is a standard element in Greek stories about the removal of a famous individual.

[40] See von Rad, (*Genesis*, 70) who refers to Ps 49:15 as well. The LXX uses *metethēken*, on which see Schmitt, "Die Angaben," 166–68. Cf. also 4 Esdr 14:49.

[41] *Genesis*, 70; Grelot ("La légende," 192–95) believes that by the time that the priestly editor composed his work, the Enochic tradition had already taken on what he calls "son alluré definitive" (192).

Sumerian King List.[42] At a time when it was fashionable to think that not only the form but also some of the names in the two lists—Genesis 5 and the king list—corresponded with one another, experts naturally looked to the seventh member of the Mesopotamian list who, in Berossus' version, was named *euedōrachos* (*\*euedōranchos*).[43] Cuneiform copies of the antediluvian section of the king list give his name in the forms *enmenduranna*, *enmeduranna*, and *enmeduranki*,[44] the last of which is reflected in Berossus' spelling. As the chart on pp. 36–37 shows, the different copies of the list exhibit important variations regarding order of kings, which kings are included, the lengths of their reigns, and, in Berossus, the cities with which some kings are associated. Consequently, it can no longer be said that Enmeduranki is *the* seventh member of *the* Sumerian King List. He is, to be sure, seventh in some versions of it (Berossus: seventh of ten; WB 444: seventh of eight; W 20030, 7: seventh of seven); and in Jacobsen's edition he also occupies the seventh slot. But in other copies or versions he is sixth (UCBC 9-1819: of eight; Lambert: of nine) or eighth (WB 62: of ten).

In the king list, the following is said about him:[45]

> I drop (the topic) Larak[46]
> its kingship to Sippar
> was carried.

---

[42] Though Josephus (*Ant.* 1.3, 9 § §104-08) did not appeal to the king list in order to clarify the biblical data about Enoch, he did refer to Berossus as one foreign historian of most ancient times who attributed tremendous ages to the earliest people. Josephus did this to bolster the credibility of the remarkable longevity that Genesis 5 assigns to antediluvian patriarchs.

[43] Several spellings are attested. In Greek, *Euedōrachos* (in Syncellus-Eusebius-Polyhistor; Schnabel's frg. 29b); and *Euedōreschos* (in Syncellus-Eusebius-Abydenus; Schnabel's frg. 30a). The Armenian translation of Eusebius' *Chronicle* offers *Evedôranchos* and *Edoreschos* (Schnabel's frgs. 20 and 30) at these two places. The spelling *Evedôranchos* indicates that the underlying Greek was *Euedōranchos* (Schnabel, *Berossus*, 262 n. to 1. 41). See also Jacoby, *Die Fragmente*, F3 (p. 376).

[44] See the list below. Jacobsen (*The Sumerian King List*, 75 n. 28) defended *en–men–dur–anna* as the original spelling and proposed that the form ending in *-anki* arose through simple confusion of the cuneiform signs for *na* and *ki*—a confusion that was encouraged by the familiar name of the ziggurat in Nippur *Dur–an–ki*. Finkelstein ("The Antediluvian Kings," 42–43), however, cautioned against Jacobsen's conclusion, since the spelling in *-anki* is now attested for the Babylonian period in UCBC 9-1819. He preferred to attribute the variant spellings to "the relative absence of uniformity about the antediluvian traditions, which . . . is indicated on numerous other grounds" (43).

[45] Translation of Jacobsen, *The Sumerian King List*, 75. Cf. also *ANET*[3] 265.

[46] The precise meaning of the formula for change of dynasty in this part of the text— *ba–šub–bé–en*—is disputed. See Jacobsen, ibid., 61–62 n. 116; Finkelstein ("The Antediluvian Kings," 42) prefers "I will bring to an end (the ascendency of) . . ."

(In) Sippar En-men-dur-Anna (k)
became king and reigned 21,000 years.
  1 king
reigned its 21,000 years. (i. 24-29)

In cuneiform versions Enmeduranki is always king of Sippar and the only king of that city who is mentioned, but Berossus says that he ruled in the city *Pautibiblon* which is his spelling of Bad-tibira.[47] He has placed five kings in this city and has omitted Sippar altogether from the list, although it plays a prominent role in his version of the flood story. "The only explanation that suggests itself for this omission is to attribute it to the vagaries of the various transmittors (*sic*) of the Berossian fragments rather than to the work of Berossus himself."[48] If including Enmeduranki among the kings of Bad-tibira can be attributed to confusion at some point in the excruciating textual history of Berossus' *Babyloniaca*, then Berossus may well not be an exception to the rule that Enmeduranki is associated with Sippar.

The regnal years of Enmeduranki vary considerably from text to text, as they do for all other kings in the list: WB 444: 21,000 (second lowest total); WB 62: 72,000 (highest—with two others); UCBC 9-1819: 6,000 (lowest)[49]; Lambert: 54,600 (perhaps the highest); and Berossus: 64,800 (highest—with two others).

Evidence from the different versions of the antediluvian part of the king list, copies of which range in date from the beginning of the second millennium to B.C. 165, reveals that Enmeduranki, whom scholars have frequently regarded as the Mesopotamian model for biblical Enoch, was: (1) usually listed as the seventh antediluvian king, though in some versions he is sixth or eighth; (2) constantly (with the possible exception of Berossus) associated with the Sumerian city Sippar; and (3) considered, with the others, an exceedingly long-lived king, though the texts vary about the number of his regnal years.

---

[47] Jacobsen, ibid., 71–72 n. 17. Finkelstein (ibid., 46 n. 23) refers to a text in which Badtibira is spelled phonetically as Patibira which more nearly resembles the form in Berossus. This explanation of the name Pautibiblon is to be preferred to the attempts of Zimmern (*Die Keilinschriften und das Alte Testament*, 532) and Grelot ("La légende," 9) to interpret the second part of Pauti*biblon* as a Greek translation of Sippar as if it were related to the word *šipru* (cf. Hebrew *sēper*). Grelot also suggested that the initial part of the word, which Zimmern was unable to explain, should be *Panti-* (which is, he says, a less well attested variant; it is not in Schnabel's edition of Berossus, but see Jacoby, *Die Fragmente*, F3 [p. 375 n. to l. 21]) and that there was a connection between this name ("all the books") and Berossus' statement that antediluvian books were buried at Sippar and thus preserved despite the flood.

[48] Finkelstein, ibid., 46.

[49] Finkelstein, (ibid., 43, 49–50) suspects that scribal carelessness has caused this relatively low number of regnal years.

| *WB 62* | *WB 444* | *Ni. 3195* | *UCBC 9–1819* | *Lambert* | *Berossus* | *Uruk*[50] |
|---|---|---|---|---|---|---|
| *Eridu?* | *Eridu* | | *Eridu* | *[Eridu]* | *Babylon* | |
| 1. Alulim (67,200) | Alulim (28,000) | | [Alulim] (36,000) | [Alulim] | Aloros (36,000) | Aiālu |
| 2. Alalgar (72,000) | Alalgar (36,000) | | Alalgar (10,800) | [Alalgar] | Alaparos (10,800) | Alalgar |
| *Larsa* | *Bad-tibira* | | *Bad-tibira* | *Bad-tibira* | *Bad-tibira* | |
| 3. -kidunnu (72,000) | Enmenluanna (43,200) | | Ammeluanna (36,000) | [Enmeluanna] | Amelon (46,800) | Ammeluʾanna |
| 4. -alimma (21,600) | Enmengalanna (28,800) | Enmegalanna | Ensipazianna (43,200) | Enmegalanna (36,000/3,600) | Ammenon (43,200) | Ammegalanna |
| *Bad-tibira* | | Ensipazianna | | | | |
| 5. Dumuzi (28,800) | Dumuzi (36,000) | *Larak?* | Dumuzi (36,000) | Dumuzi | Megalaron (64,800) | Enmeʾušumgalanna |
| *Larak* | *Larak* | Dumuzi | | *Sippar* | | Dumuzi |
| 6. Enmenluanna (21,600) | Ensipazianna (28,800) | | | Enmeduranki (54,600) | Daonon (36,000) | |
| *Sippar* | *Sippar* | | *Sippar* | *Larak* | | |
| 7. Ensipazianna (36,000) | Enmenduranna (21,000) | | Enmeduranki (6,000) | Ensipazianna (37,200) | Euedoranchos (64,800) | Enmeduranki |
| | | | *Šuruppak* | | | |
| | | | Ubartutu | | | |

| Sippar | Šuruppak | | Šuruppak | Larak |
|---|---|---|---|---|
| 8. Enmeduranna (72,000) | Ubartutu (18,000) | [Ziusudra]? | Ubartutu | Amempsinos (36,000) |
| Šuruppak? | | | | |
| 9. Ubartutu (28,800) | | | Ziusudra | Otiartes (28,800) |
| 10. Ziusudra (36,000) | | | | Xisouthros (36,000) |

50 The evidence from WB 62 and 444 (= H. Weld-Blundell Collection in the Ashmolean Museum, Oxford) is cited from Jacobsen, *The Sumerian King List*, 70–77. Ni. 3195 was published by F. R. Kraus, "Zur Liste der älteren Könige von Babylonien," *ZA* 16 (1952) 31; and UCBC 9-1819 by Finkelstein, "The Antediluvian Kings," 40–41. All of these texts date from the first half of the second millennium B.C. The text in the column entitled *Lambert* was pieced together by W. G. Lambert from K 11624 (which Jacobsen had published in transcription in *The Sumerian King List*, 60), K 11261, K 12054, with K 8532 and published in "A New Fragment from a List of Antediluvian Kings and Marduk's Chariot" in *Symbolae Biblicae et Mesopotamicae Francisco Mario Theodoro de Liagre Böhl Dedicatae* (ed. M. A. Beek, A. A. Kampman, C. Nijland, J. Ryckmans; Leiden: Brill, 1973) 273–75. Since it comes from the libraries of Asshurbanipal, the text dates to the seventh century B.C. W 20030, 7 was published by J. van Dijk in "Die Inschriftenfunde," 44–45. It dates from B.C. 165 (R.S. 24: year 147 of the Seleucid era; see p. 45). The text ought not to be called a king list but rather an *apkallū/ummānu* list or genealogy (see 45–46, 52); therefore, it may be that the writer did not list all antediluvian kings, but only those who were associated with an *apkallū*.

The fact that both Enmeduranki and Enoch occupy seventh position in related antediluvian lists is noteworthy evidence for a connection between traditions about both, though it does not constitute proof. But commentators have also seized upon the possibility that Enoch's 365 years may relate in some way to the association of Sippar, Enmeduranki's city, with Shamash, the sun-god. Sippar was the city of Shamash, and there an ancient temple— Ebabbarra—was dedicated to his cult.[51] It is not at all impossible that the king list and Gen 5:21–24 are related on this point as well, though one would have to regard the connection as somewhat indirect. Enoch's 365 years are not directly related to the years of Enmeduranki's reign, just as those of the other patriarchs in Genesis 5—whose life-spans are geared to fit different chronological concerns—show no immediate correspondence with the other reigns. The number 365 was, then, either the invention of P or of his source, and probably derives from the seventh king's traditional association with Shamash. By using it, P's tradition expressed in a manner that was acceptable in a monotheism what the polytheistic tradition had declared about Enmeduranki.

If the different versions of the king list were the only evidence about Enmeduranki, the links between traditions about him and those about Enoch would be confined to those listed in the preceding paragraph. Additional information about him is, however, available, and it bolsters the case for the hypothesis that P's Enoch was modeled to some extent on the traditions about Enmeduranki.

2. Texts About Enmeduranki

Though the other two texts in which Enmeduranki figures have been

---

[51] Sippar, though not a particularly large city, was the locus of many ancient traditions. The Sumerian Flood Story (1. 96) says that the fourth city (Sippar) was given to Utu, the Sumerian sun-god. It continued to be associated with the solar deity whether under the Sumerian name Utu or the Semitic Shamash. The Erra Epic claims that it was spared at the time of the flood: in IV 50–51 Ishum accuses Erra thus:

As to Sippar the primeval city, through which the Lord
  of (all the) countries (= Enlil) did not let the deluge
  pass because she was the darling of his eyes,
You destroyed her wall against the will of Šamaš; you
  pulled down her rampart.

(translation of Luigi Cagni, *The Poem of Erra* [Sources and Monographs, Sources from the Ancient Near East 1, 3; Malibu: Undena, 1977]). Berossus recorded an otherwise unattested tradition that Cronus ordered Xisouthros, the flood hero, to bury "the beginnings and the middles and the ends [i.e., everything] of all writings in Sippar, the City of the Sun." (Burstein, *The Babyloniaca,* 20) These writings were then dug up after the flood and distributed. On Sippar, see also Hallo, "Antediluvian Cities," 65; and Lambert, "Enmeduranki and Related Matters," 127.

known for many years, W. G. Lambert[52] has recently published enlarged and improved versions of them on the basis of newly identified fragments. These two texts will now be examined but in the reverse order in which Lambert gives them, since his second text is the most important one and clarifies allusions in his first text.

a. K 2486 + 3646 + 4364; K 3357 + 9941; K 13307[53]

Lambert comments that the text which he reconstructs from these fragments found in the libraries of Asshurbanipal "combines elements of three categories: legend, ritual, and explanations of ritual."

1 en-me-dur-an-ki š[àr sippar$^{ki}$]$^{54}$
2 na-ra-am $^d$a-nim $^d$en-líl[ù $^d$é-a]
3 $^d$šamaš ina é-babbar-ra [. . .]
4 $^d$šamaš u $^d$adad ana puḫri-šú-nu [ú-še-ri-bu-šu-ma]$^{56}$
5 $^d$šamaš u $^d$adad [ú-kab-bi-tu-šu]
6 $^d$šamaš u $^d$adad ina $^{giš}$kussî ḫurāṣi rabî [$^i$ ú-še-ši-bu-šu]
7 šamna (ì x giš$^{meš}$) ina mê$^{meš}$ na-ṭa-lu ni-ṣir-ti $^d$a-nim [en-líl u $^d$é-a$^{57}$ú-ša] b-ru-šu
8 tup-pi ilāni $^{meš}$ ta-kal-ta$^{58}$ pi–riš-ti šamê$^e$ ù erṣetim$^{tim}$ [i] d-di-nu-šu

3. Šamaš in Ebabbarra [appointed]$^{55}$
1. Enmeduranki [king of Sippar],
2. the beloved of Anu, Enlil [and Ea].
4. Šamaš and Adad [brought him in] to their assembly,
5. Šamaš and Adad [honoured him],
6. Šamaš and Adad [set him] on a large throne of gold, 7. they showed him how to observe oil on water, a mystery of Anu, [Enlil and Ea], 8. they gave him the tablet of the gods, the liver, a secret of heaven and [underworld],

---

$^{52}$ "Enmeduranki and Related Matters," 126–38.

$^{53}$ Ibid., 132 (the quotation that follows appears on p. 127). Copies of K 3357 + 9941 and K 13307 are given on pp. 137 and 135 respectively. These are the only newly identified fragments, while the others have long been available. K 4364 was initially published in H. C. Rawlinson et al., The Cuneiform Inscriptions of Western Asia (vol. 2; London: Bowler, 1866) 58 no. 3. Zimmern later connected it with K 2486 and published the combined text in his Beiträge zur Kenntnis der babylonischen Religion: Die Beschwörungstafeln Šurpu, Ritualtafeln für den Wahrsager, Beschwörer und Sänger (Assyriologische Bibliothek 12; Leipzig: Hinrichs, 1901) no. 24 (pp. 116–21). Through his German translation of these two fragments in Die Keilinschriften und das Alte Testament, 533–34 (he published a few more lines of the text than does Lambert) the text entered the great Genesis commentaries that were written at the beginning of the century (e.g., Skinner, Gunkel). Zimmern had also published K 3646 as no. 25 (pp. 120–21) in his 1901 volume but did not recognize it as part of the same text as no. 24.

$^{54}$ L. 23 guarantees Lambert's restoration of the city name as do all other traditions about Enmeduranki.

$^{55}$ The verb in this line must remain uncertain, since there is no line that parallels it elsewhere in the text.

$^{56}$ The verbs which Lambert restores in ll. 4-7 are confirmed by those in the parallel section (ll. 12-13).

$^{57}$ The restoration of divine names is verified by the parallel in l. 13.

$^{58}$ Lambert (ibid., 133) notes that l. 8 raises several problems. He deduces that of its

9 giŝerēna na-ram ilānimeŝ rabûtimeŝ ú-še-eš-šu-ú qat-su

10 ù-šu-ú ki-m[a K]A?-šu-nu-ma
mārīmeŝ nippuriki

11 sippa[riki ù b]ābiliki ana pa-ni-šu

12 ú-še-rib-šu-nu-ti-ma ú-kab-bi-
su-nu-ti ina giŝkussî ma-[ḫar]-
š[u ú-š]eš-ib-šu-nu-ti

13 šamna (ì x giŝmeŝ) ina mêmeŝ
na-ṭa-lu ni-ṣir-ti da-nim
den-líl u dé-a ú-šab-ru-šu-nu-ti

14 tup-pi ilānimeŝ ta-kal-ta pi-
riš-ti šamêe u erṣetimtim id-
din(sì)-šu-nu-ti

15 giŝerēna na-ra-am ilānimeŝ rabûtimeŝ qat-su-nu ú-še-eš-ši

16 tup-pi ilānimeŝ uzutakālta (tun)
salniṣirti(urù) šamêe u
erṣetimtim

17 šamna(ì x giš) ina mêmeŝ na-ṭa-lu
pirišti (ad.ḫal) da-nim den-líl
u dé-[a]

18 ša KI ṣa-a-ti enūma(ud) anu
den-líl u arâ(a.rá)a šu-ta-bu-lu

19 lúummânu(um.me.a) mu-du-ú
na-ṣir pirišti (ad.ḫal)
ilānimeŝ rabûtimeŝ

20 a-píl-šu ša i-ram-mu ina
tup-pi u qanₓ (GI)-dup-pi

21 ina ma-ḫar dšamaš u dadad
ú-tam-ma-šu-ma

22 ú-šaḫ-ḫa-su e-nu-ma mār
lúbārî(ḫal)

23 apkal(NUN.ME) šamni(ì x giš)
zēru da-ru-ú pirʾi en-me-
dur-an-ki šàr sippariki

9. they put in his hand the cedar–
(rod), beloved of the great gods.

10. Then he, in accordance with
their [word(?)] brought

11. the men of Nippur, Sippar and
Babylon into his presence,

12. and he honoured them. He set them
on thrones before [him],

13. he showed them how to observe oil
on water, a mystery of Anu,
Enlil and Ea,

14. he gave them the tablet of the
gods, the liver, a secret of
heaven and underworld,

15. he put in their hands the cedar–
(rod), beloved of the great gods.

16. {The tablet of the gods, the liver,
a mystery of heaven and underworld;

17. how to observe oil on water, a
secret of Anu, Enlil and Ea;

18. 'that with commentary'; *When
Anu, Enlil*; and how to make
mathematical calculations.}

19. The learned savant, who
guards the secrets of the
great gods

20-21. will bind his son whom he
loves wth an oath before
Šamaš and Adad by tablet and
stylus and

22. will instruct him. When
a diviner,

23. an expert in oil, of
abiding descent, offspring
of Enmeduranki, king of Sippar.

---

possible meanings *takāltu* means *liver* here, since hepatoscopy—"the commonest technique of
obtaining omens, and . . . especially the concern of Šamaš"—is under consideration. He takes
*tuppi* as a singular, though he does not exclude the possibility of a plural spelled *tuppī*. "As a
singular it cannot refer to tablets of liver omens, due to the large number of these in all periods.
Perhaps an inscribed liver model is meant, and when the author lived there was one 'canonical'
type believed to have come ultimately from the gods." Cf. also 1.29 of the text.

24 mu-kin ᵍⁱˢmākalti(díli.       24. who set up the pure bowl and
    gal) elletᵉᵗᵉ na-šu-ú             held the cedar-(rod),
    ᵍⁱˢerēni
25 ka?-rib šarri sigbarê(síg.      25. a benediction priest of the king,
    bar)ᵉ ᵈšamaš                a long-haired priest of Šamaš,
26 bu-un-na-né-e ᵈnin-ḫur-sag-gá   26. as fashioned by Ninḫursagga,
27 re-ḫu-ut ˡúnišakki(nu.èš)     27. begotten by a *nišakku*-priest
    šá za-ru-šu ellu            of pure descent:
28 ù šu-ú ina gat-ti u ina       28. if he is without blemish in
    mináti(šid)ᵐᵉˢ-šu šuk-lu-lu     body and limbs
29 ana ma-ḫar ᵈšamaš u ᵈadad    29. he may approach the presence
    a-šar bi-ra u purussî(eš.bar)    of Šamaš and Adad where liver
    iṭeḫḫi(te)ᵇⁱ 59             inspection and oracle (take
                               place).

This text unmistakably leads one back into primeval times[60] and provides an origin myth for the techniques of the *bārûs* (11. 19-29). There can therefore be little or no doubt that the Enmeduranki, king of Sippar, whom it mentions twice (11. 1, 23), is the seventh monarch of the traditional king list. The text attributes to him the earthly origin of three divinely revealed divinatory techniques: observing oil on water, use of a liver tablet, and manipulation of the cedar-(rod-[11. 7-9]). The former two are familiar methods for obtaining omens,[61] but the third is "an oft-mentioned ritual appurtenance, the function of which is no longer understood."[62] These techniques the king transmitted to men from the three special cities Nippur, Sippar, and Babylon (11. 10-15); the words of this section largely repeat those of 11. 4-9. L1. 19-22 address the issue of the channel by which the secrets thus obtained could be handed down from generation to generation (father to son): the

[59] Zimmern (*Die Keilinschriften und das Alte Testament*, 534) published a translation of several more lines which describe a diviner who does not meet the qualifications detailed in 11. 23-29. He is not to be permitted use of the divinatory techniques described in this text.

[60] Cf. Zimmern, ibid.

[61] On omens and techniques for obtaining and understanding them, see the survey in A. Leo Oppenheim, *Ancient Mesopotamia: Portrait of a Dead Civilization* (rev. ed. completed by E. Reiner; Chicago/London: University of Chicago, 1977) 206-27 ("The Arts of the Diviner"); and H. W. F. Saggs, *The Greatness That Was Babylon* (New York/Scarborough: New American Library, 1968) 307-11; 331-32; cf. p. 352. It is of considerable interest for understanding the background of later descriptions of Enoch that Enmeduranki is thus inextricably linked with these means for determining the divine will and the future. *Bārû*-diviners were the ancient omen experts. It has been conjectured that this term (spelled *bārîm*) appeared in the original version of several OT passages but was subsequently corrupted into *baddîm* (see KB 146 where Isa 44:25; Jer 50:36; Hos 11:6 are listed as possibilities).

[62] Lambert, "Enmeduranki and Related Matters," 127; cf. Zimmern, *Die Keilinschriften und das Alte Testament*, 533 n. 5.

*ummânu*, who was charged with guarding such lore, was to place his son under oath and then instruct him in these methods for discerning the divine will. At the end of l. 22 the term *bārû* appears for the first time, although the entire text is concerned with the origin and transmission of the techniques which this elite group of diviners, the experts in omens, employed. Enmeduranki was regarded as the founder of the *bārû* guild and the intermediate revealer of its divinatory methods. As a result, all *bārûs* (literally: observers) were regarded as offspring in some sense of the antediluvian king who had sat in the very presence of Shamash and Adad, the former of whom was especially closely associated with omens.[63]

The text designates Enmeduranki the beloved (*narāmu*) of the three chief gods Anu, Enlil, and Ea (1.2), but more noteworthy for the present purposes is his relationship with Shamash, the sun-god, and Adad, the weather-god. They brought him into their assembly, honored him, placed him on a golden throne, and divulged to him the three divinatory techniques discussed above. These two deities stand in the same relationship to Enmeduranki in ll. 4-9 as Enmeduranki does to the men of Nippur, Sippar, and Babylon in ll. 10-15. In addition, if Lambert has furnished the correct verb in l. 3, the text claims that it was Shamash himself who appointed Enmeduranki king of Sippar in his temple Ebabbarra (= house of the rising sun).

b. K 4874;[64] Rm 255; K 2211 + 8636 + 9168; VAT 17051 (BE 33135);[65] BM 47805 + 48032 + 48035 + 48037 + 48046

From these many fragments belonging to four copies, Lambert has pieced together part of what appears to be a longer composition. The bilingual (Sumero-Akkadian) text begins with praise for Marduk (ll. 1-3) and continues with words of tribute to a king whom Marduk has exalted (ll.

---

[63] Jacobsen (*The Treasures of Darkness: A History of Mesopotamian Religion* [New Haven/London: Yale University, 1976] 134) uses the word *righteousness* as the quality with which Utu (the Sumerian name for the sun-god; Šamaš is his Semitic name) is related. He was considered judge of heaven and earth and protector of the weak and oppressed. In addition to his judicial functions, he was also uniquely associated with oracles through which he warned and guided humankind. For some texts which depict his character and functions, see "Prayer of Asshurbanipal to the Sun-God" and "Hymn to the Sun-God" (from Asshurbanipal's libraries) in *ANET*[3] 386-89. Oppenheim (*Ancient Mesopotamia*, 196) notes that "for unknown reasons, Adad in later periods became linked to Šamaš in the role of oracle-giver"—as the texts here under consideration show.

[64] This fragment was first published by S. Langdon, "An Assyrian Royal Inscription from a Series of Poems," *JRAS* (1932) 33-41. According to Lambert, it and the fragment labelled Rm 255 belong to the same tablet.

[65] This and the remaining fragments are from Babylon, while those listed before it are, of course, from Asshurbanipal's libraries (Lambert, "Enmeduranki and Related Matters," 126).

4–6). In 11. 7–14 this king, Nebuchadnezzar I (1124–1103),[66] expresses in the first person his views about his status and royal virtues. Within this section the lines that are relevant to Enmeduranki occur:[67]

| | |
|---|---|
| 8 li-i-pu ru-u-qu ša šar-ru-ú-t[i]z e-ru na-aṣ-ru ša la-am a-bu-bi | 8. Distant scion of kingship, seed preserved from before the flood, |
| 9 ṣi-it ᵈen-[me-dur-an-ki][68] šar si-ip-par mu-kin ma-kal-ti elletiᵗⁱ na-šu-ú e-ri-ni | 9. Offspring of Enmeduranki, king of Sippar, who set up the pure bowl and the cedar–wood (rod), |
| 10 a-šib ma-ḫar ᵈšamaš u ᵈadad ilāniᵐᵉˢ da-a-a-ni | 10. Who sat in the presence of Šamaš and Adad, the divine adjudicators, . . . |

Nebuchadnezzar, a native Babylonian king who assumed the throne after a period of foreign (Cassite) rule, here asserts an astonishing and thoroughly fictitious ancestry in order to enhance the greatness of his person. In the process, he shows that in the twelfth century the traits of Enmeduranki that were met in the preceding text of the seventh century had also been current: that he set up the pure bowl, held the cedar–wood (rod), and entered the presence of Shamash and Adad.

### 3. Enmeduranki and Enoch

These two texts disclose information that is of great value for clarifying P's efforts at shaping traditional materials in Gen 5:21–24 and for understanding later pseudepigraphic developments of the Enochic portrait. Confining oneself to the biblical Enoch for the moment, it seems reasonable to infer, first, that P or his source translated the intimate association of Shamash and Enmeduranki into an acceptable monotheistic idiom by attribut-

---

[66] Lambert (ibid., 126-27) had surmised from the contents of the text that the king who speaks here was Nebuchadnezzar I, though the place in 1. 7 where his name was presumably mentioned was missing. He had also concluded from the givens of 11. 9-10 that Enmeduranki was the king of Sippar who was named in a broken section of 1.9. R. Borger ("Die Beschwörungsserie," 184–85) later identified a fragment (K 6088) in the British Museum that belonged to this text and confirmed both suggestions that Lambert had made. The entire text with this additional fragment and several others Lambert subsequently published in "The Seed of Kingship" in *Le palais et la royauté: archéologie et civilisation* (XIXe Rencontre Assyriologique Internationale, 1971; Paris: Geuthner, 1974) 432 (translation of 11. 8-14) and 434–38 (full text). This more complete version is given above. The beginning of 1. 7 in Sumerian reads: ᵈna-b-i-um- ku₇-d[ur?-ri-ú-ṣur. His father's name ([ᵈnin–urta–na–din]–šu–me) is apparently to be read in 1. 11.

[67] The Sumerian version of the lines is omitted because they are damaged to a large extent, especially in 1. 10.

[68] The Sumerian here reads ᵈe[n]. me. dur. a[n. ki.

ing to Enoch an age of 365 years, the number of days in a solar year. There is really no other adequate explanation for this number which clashes so strongly with the other numbers in Genesis 5, while solar connections immediately suggest themselves. For the priestly editor, Enoch could not be a devotee of the sun-god who was one deity among many, but traditional associations appear to have been so strong that he gave them muted expression through the harmless but suggestive language of Enoch's unusual age.

Second, the background of the clause *wayyithallēk ḥănôk ʾet-hāʾĕlōhîm* receives, as almost all commentators have recognized, remarkable elucidation from the reports that Enmeduranki enjoyed the fellowship of Shamash and Adad who taught him methods for determining the divine will. In this expression the mythological *Vorlage* of P's Enoch still glimmers through, but he could not have used the word *hāʾĕlōhîm* in a polytheistic sense. Rather, he seems to have rendered the traditional motif of the seventh king's entry into the society of the gods by employing *hāʾĕlōhîm* to mean "the angels." Such a procedure is reflected elsewhere in biblical literature: theologians, when they had recourse to mythological language, would reduce the gods of other nations to the rank of angels in order to incorporate these traditions or motifs into their monotheistic system (e.g., the heavenly court in Isaiah 6, Daniel 7).[69] This hypothesis may also explain use of the definite article in both instances in which the expression occurs: P uses *hāʾĕlōhîm* to mean "the angels" in distinction from the anarthrous *ʾĕlōhîm* at the end of v 24 which refers to God himself.

Thus the limited amount of evidence about Enmeduranki that is now available provides very helpful comparative material for analysis of some unique expressions in Gen 5:21–24. Both the unusually short life-span that is assigned to Enoch and the expression *wayyithallēk ḥănôk ʾet-hāʾĕlōhîm* are sufficiently clarified by Enmeduranki traditions. Nevertheless, the texts that have been cited do not furnish explanations for either the fact that *wayyithallēk*, etc. appears twice, the second time in connection wth Enoch's removal apparently, or for the clause *weʾênennû kî lāqaḥ ʾōtô ʾĕlōhîm*. Absence of any indication in the literature that Enmeduranki was removed to the divine

---

[69] See, e.g., H. Wildberger, *Jesaja* (BK X/1; Neukirchen-Vluyn: Neukirchener, 1972) 237-38. As is well known, one form of borrowing in this area was the council of the Lord which is patterned on that of Canaanite *ʾĒl*; see the analysis of F. M. Cross, *Canaanite Myth and Hebrew Epic* (Cambridge: Harvard University, 1973) 186-94. P never uses the term *malʾāk* (angel) or a form of it (cf. S. R. Driver, *An Introduction to the Literature of the Old Testament* [New York: Meridian Books, 1957] 12); thus one would not expect him to use it here to designate angels. For a similar case regarding the identity of the *bĕnê hāʾĕlōhîm* of Gen 6:1, 2, 4, see M. Delcor, "Le mythe de la chute des anges et de l'origine des géants comme explication du mal dans le monde dans l'apocalyptique juive: Histoire des traditions," *RHR* 190 (1976) 5-8.

presence at the end of his life appears to have been influential in Westermann's decision to oppose the tradition among commentators on Genesis
that Enoch and this king were in some sense related.[70] In this regard, however, the Assyriologist R. Borger has recently advanced a proposal which in
his estimation may supply the crucial missing link between the two antediluvian heroes.[71] Since his suggestion has to do with Mesopotamian traditions
about the *apkallū*, it will be useful to describe these unusual characters
briefly in order to evaluate the proposal.

### 4. Enoch and the *Apkallū* Traditions

As long as scholars have been aware of Berossus' *Babyloniaca* they have
known that ancient mythographers drew some connection between antediluvian kings and certain fish–men who revealed the fundamental elements of
human culture during the primeval period. Berossus mentioned seven creatures of this kind, the most famous and first of whom he names Oannes
('Ὠάννης). After noting that in the earliest period humankind was living on a
lawless level similar to that of animals, Berossus is reported to have written
as follows:

> In the first year [i.e., of the first king's reign][72] a beast[73] named Oannes appeared
> from the Erythraean Sea in a place adjacent to Babylonia. Its entire body was
> that of a fish, but a human head had grown from beneath the head of the fish
> and human feet likewise had grown from the fish's tail. It also had a human
> voice. A picture of it is still preserved today. He [i.e., Berossus] says that this
> beast spent the days with men but ate no food. It gave to men knowledge of

---

[70] *Genesis*, 485–86.

[71] "Die Beschwörungsserie," 183–96.

[72] So Schnabel, *Berossos*, 91. He based his conclusion on the fact that Oannes is unmistakably depicted as operating at the earliest time before humankind began living in a manner
distinct from that of animals. Burstein (*The* Babyloniaca, 13 n. 6) accepts this identification of
the first year and adds that the association of Oannes and Aloros (in the Sumerian forms of
those names) has been confirmed by the Uruk Apkallu List (see below).

[73] Syncellus, citing Eusebius, calls Oannes *zōon aphrenon* (see Schnabel, *Berossos*, 253
frg 8). Schnabel (ibid., 156–57) believed that the *hapax legomenon aphrenon*, which should
mean "irrational," represents "eine gehässige Änderung" for *emphron* ("sensible, prudent,
shrewd") introduced into the text of Polyhistor (Eusebius' source) by a Jew or Christian who
wished to distort the Babylonian myths (Jacoby [*Die Fragmente*, Fl (p. 369)] places *aphrenon*
in smaller print). The Armenian version of Eusebius' *Chronicle* paraphrases with "ein furcht-
bares Untier." Given the textual transmission of the *Babyloniaca*, however, one wonders whether
it is necessary to posit Schnabel's (following Gutschmid) "gehässige Änderung," though it
should be noted that he includes this alleged alteration in a series of others which support his
argument that Eusebius used an interpolated text of Polyhistor (155–62). Moreover, "irrational" is utterly inappropriate as a description of Oannes. In his translation Burstein (*The*
Babyloniaca, 13) renders with "beast" and omits an adjective (see his explanation, p. 14 n. 11).

letters and sciences and crafts of all types. It also taught them how to found cities, establish temples, introduce laws and measure land. It also revealed to them seeds and the gathering of fruits, and in general it gave men everything which is connected with civilized life. From the time of that beast nothing further has been discovered. But when the sun set this beast Oannes plunged back into the sea and spent the nights in the deep, for it was amphibious. Later other beasts also appeared . . . Oannes wrote about birth and government and gave the following account to men.[74]

Berossus then puts the creation story (in a form strongly reminiscent of *Enuma Elish*) into Oannes' mouth. As he lists them, the kings and their beasts are aligned thus:

| | |
|---|---|
| 1. Alōros | Ōannēs |
| 3. Amillaros | Annēdōtos |
| 6. Daōnos | Euedokos |
| | Eneugamos |
| | Eneuboulos |
| | Anementos |
| 7. Euedōrachos | Anōdaphos[75] |

Berossus said regarding the last six that "these creatures all together explained in detail the things which had been spoken summarily by Oannes."[76] In other words, they expanded and exegeted Oannes' teaching about culture and civilization.

Publication of new cuneiform texts has focused renewed interest on Berossus' strange account about the nonhuman origin of civilization. The most important of these texts is the so-called Uruk Apkallu List which names one *apkallū* (= sage) for each of the (first?) seven antediluvian kings (with one more in the earliest postdiluvian period). The *apkallū* names in virtually every case have proven to be those which Berossus assigned to the

---

[74] Translation of Burstein, ibid., 13–14, as are all other English citations from Berossus in this book.

[75] There are four extant versions of Berossus' *apkallū* list, all of which show some variations. The one presented here is from the Syncellus-Eusebius-Abydenus tradition. All versions agree that Oannes appeared during the reign of the first king, that four Oannes-like creatures were active at the time of Da(ōn)os (= Dumuzi), and that the last labored in the period of Enmeduranki. The only noteworthy difference, aside from spelling, is that the Polyhistor-Eusebius tradition assigns the second beast (Idotion/Annēdōtos) to the reign of the fourth king Ammemōn, while the Abydenus-Eusebius text ascribes him to the period of the third king Amillaros/Amēlōn. See Schnabel, *Berossos*, 261–64, frgs. 29–30; Jacoby, *Die Fragmente*, F3 (pp. 374–77).

[76] Burstein, *The* Babyloniaca, 19; Schnabel, *Berossos*, 262 frgs. 29, 29b.

seven antediluvian fishmen.[77] The names of the kings in the Uruk list and the sages with whom they are aligned are:

| | |
|---|---|
| 1. Aiālu | U²an |
| 2. Alalgar | U²anduga |
| 3. Ammelu²anna | Enmeduga |
| 4. Ammegalanna | Enmegalamma |
| 5. Enme²ušumgalanna | Enmebulugga |
| 6. Dumuzi | Anenlilda |
| 7. Enmeduranki | Utu²abzu.[78] |

Berossus and the Uruk list agree that there were seven pre-flood *apkallū* and that the last appeared at the time of the seventh king. Moreover, they present them in the same order, but they correlate them differently with the first seven kings.[79] There is also a noticeable difference in their spelling of the name of Enmeduranki's *apkallū*: the Uruk text has *Utu²abzu* while Berossus offers either *ōdakōn* or *anōdaphos*.[80] Precisely how this considerable discre-

---

[77] A connection between Oannes and his successors in Berossus and the seven pre-flood *apkallūs* had been suspected by Zimmern (*Die Keilinschriften und das Alte Testament*, 537–38; "Die sieben Weisen Babyloniens," *ZA* 35 [1924] 151–54) and others (see J. J. A. van Dijk, *La sagesse suméro-accadienne* [Commentationes Orientales 1; Leiden: Brill, 1953] 19–21) [extensive older bibliography about the *apkallūs* 20 n. 56]) before confirmation came from cuneiform texts.

[78] van Dijk, "Die Inschriftenfunde," 44–47. The text at this point is simply a list, with each line taking the same form: [*ina tarṣī*] x *lugal* y *abgal* (at the time of x, the king, y was the *apkallū*). The fact that Oannes is now known to be a reflection of the Sumerian Uan excludes the view once entertained by some scholars that *Oannes* was a form of the name *Ea* (see Jansen, *Die Henochgestalt*, 30–31; Zimmern [*Die Keilinschriften und das Alte Testament*, 535] had spoken more cautiously of an identity of subject-matter, not of name).

[79] These statements about the material in Berossus and the Apkallu List appear to be more in harmony with the evidence than are those of van Dijk ("Die Inschriftenfunde," 47–49) who thinks that Berossus actually preserves eight names, contrary to all extant texts and evidence from other sources, and that Berossus' tradition has moved the *apkallū* who originally occupied second position (Ōdakōn) to eighth. His difficulties stem from his conclusion that Berossus' second beast has a name *Annēdōtos* which should reflect that of the second apkallū *Uanduga* but does not. It must be admitted that there is something strange about this word in Syncellus: it appears with *to deuteron* (neuter, therefore it is not be translated "the second Annēdōtos" as van Dijk supposes. Annēdōtos is masculine [cf. *ton annēdōton*]) and again during the reign of Daōnos where it is followed by the numeral *d* (= 4). There seems to be some confusion in this tradition, but the remaining versions of Berossus indicate that *Annēdōtos* is the name of a beast, not an appellative. Also, while there is certainly some discrepancy between the Greek and Sumerian spellings of the name, the ending -*dōtos* is a reasonable transcription of the Sumerian ending -*duga*; *g* and *t* have been confused, as they easily are in Greek majuscule script (ΔΩΓΟΣ → ΔΩΤΟΣ). In this respect the name that van Dijk believes once corresponded to Uanduga—Ōdakōn—is no closer. Furthermore, Ōdakōn is merely a variant of Anōdaphos (see n. 80 below).

[80] These two spellings must be variants of one another, not two separate names that have

pancy in spelling arose is not clear (though the textual transmission of the excerpts from *Babyloniaca* provides all too many possibilities for corruption), but the fact that both lists agree on the order of all the other sages and in ascribing the last to Enmeduranki, the seventh king, makes the hypothesis that they were originally equivalents the more likely one.

Because the *apkallū* traditions are potentially important for analysis of Jewish literature about Enoch it will be useful to gather here some other statements from Berossus and cuneiform literature about them. The *apkallū*, whose number is regularly seven, are constantly associated with wisdom (as their name indicates) which they convey to humankind.[81] Cuneiform texts have confirmed Berossus' picture of them as fishmen. E. Reiner, who published several lines from a text which proved to be part of Borger's *bīt mēseri* series, translated lines 5'-9' in her enumeration as: "They are the seven brilliant apkallu's *purādu*-fish of the sea, [sev]en apkallu's 'grown' in the river, who insure the correct functioning of the plans of heaven and earth."[82] These same mythological figures are mentioned twice by Marduk in the Erra Epic. There he remarks to Erra, after telling him about the flood and its effects, that he "dispatched those (renowned) *ummânū* (-sages) down into the Apsu; I did not ordain their coming up again." (I 147)[83] Later, in a series of rhetorical questions to Erra, Marduk asks: "Where are the seven [*ap*]*kallu* of the Apsu, pure *purādu* (-fishes) who, like Ea their lord, distinguish themselves by their sapiential skill, (and who) are appointed to the cleansing of [my] body?" (I 162) It will be worthwhile to bear in mind, especially as later Jewish developments of the Enochic portrait are examined, the range of arts

---

been preserved, with the former now being misplaced in the Greek version (as van Dijk argues; cf. the preceding note). Each figures as the name of the seventh sage who lived during the reign of the seventh king: *Ōdakōn* is the spelling in the Polyhistor–Eusebius tradition, *Anōdaphos* in the Abydenus–Eusebius line. *Ōdakōn* appears to represent the latter part of (An)ōdaphos (Ōdakōn/–ōdaphos), and perhaps only this much was the original spelling (cf. van Dijk, "Die Inschriftenfunde," 49). *Ōd*- probably is a transcription of Utu (*d* and *t* would easily interchange in cuneiform), while -*abzu* (spelled *apsu*) is reflected in the syllables -apho(s) (AΨO read as AΦO). Burstein (*The* Babyloniaca, 19 n. 42) also favors the identification of Utu²abzu with Ōdakōn.

[81] Cf. van Dijk, *La sagesse*, 19–21. An epithet that is applied to Uan—*adapu*—means *wise* and suggests interesting possibilities for understanding other references to Adapa in cuneiform literature. On this, see van Dijk, "Die Inschriftenfunde," 47–48; Lambert, "A Catalogue of Texts and Authors," *JCS* 16 (1962) 74; and Hallo, "On the Antiquity of Sumerian Literature," *JAOS* 83 (1963) 176.

[82] "The Etiological Myth of the 'Seven Sages'," *Or* 30 (1961) 4 (text on p. 2); cf. also Borger, "Die Beschwörungsserie," 192. This text is one of several that illustrate the apotropaic uses of *apkallū* figurines.

[83] Cagni, *The Poem of Erra*; see also his note on p. 33 n. 40. The translation (below) of I 162 is also from Cagni.

and sciences that, according to Berorrus, Oannes (=Uᵓan) and his successors taught humankind: letters (*grammatōn*), sciences (*mathēmatōn*), crafts of all kinds (*technōn pantodapōn*), city-building, temple founding, laws, land-measuring, various agricultural arts—in general, everything needed for civilized life. Other Berossian fragments add astronomy to the list.[84]

For the present purposes, however, the salient point is that a cuneiform text names Utuᵓabzu as the *apkallū* who functioned during Enmeduranki's long reign. Borger's suggestion about the literary background of Enoch's removal builds on this point. He has issued a preliminary report about what he calls "die Beschwörungsserie BĪT MĒSERI" in which there are several references to the *apkallū*, including Utuᵓabzu. In an excerpt from Tablet 3 appear words that Borger translates: "Utuabzu, der zum Himmel emporgestiegen ist."[85] This line, which occurs in three different enumerations of the *apkallū*, led him to conclude:

> Aus dem Umstand, dass nach gut bezeugter mesopotamischer Tradition der siebente und letzte vorsintflutliche Weise namens Utuabzu, Zeitgenosse des siebenten vorsintflutlichen Herrschers namens Enmeduranki, zum Himmel emporgestiegen ist, ergeben sich überraschende Perspektiven in Bezug auf die Gestalt des siebenten alttestamentlichen Patriarchen Henoch. Die Möglichkeit, dass Enmeduranki als Zukunftskundiger und als siebenter Herrscher der Urzeit Prototyp Henochs war, bekommt eine unerwartete Stütze. *Das Mythologem von der Himmelfahrt Henochs stammt jedoch von Enmedurankis Ratgeber, dem siebenten vorsintflutlichen Weisen namens Utuabzu her!*[86]

Has Borger found the missing connection between traditions about Enmeduranki and Enoch? He may have. After all, it is remarkable that an ascension is attested in closest proximity to the character whose traits explain so much about the biblical Enoch. Moreover, as will become apparent, there is strong evidence that, at least in later Jewish tradition, the figure of Enoch

---

[84] See Schnabel, *Berossos*, 253–54. Berossus reported that Oannes wrote an account about *geneas kai politeias* and gave it to humankind (frg. 8, p. 254; Jacoby, *Die Fragmente*, Fl [p. 370]). Thus he was considered the first author. Moreover, the six sages who followed him explained in detail what he had said in summary fashion (see Schnabel, ibid., 262 frgs. 29, 29b; Jacoby, ibid., F3 [p. 376]). Schnabel concurred in the judgment of some earlier scholars that Oannes and the other six were the *Offenbarungsbücher* of the Babylonians (173–75). He wrote: "Das des Oannes ist das älteste, die der anderen sind die Kommentare dazu" (175). Hallo ("On the Antiquity of Sumerian Literature," 175–76) has gathered evidence which shows that several of the *apkallū* names resemble *incipits* more than anything else. "In sum, it would not be surprising if all the *apkallu*-names turned out eventually to identify known cuneiform series" (176). See also the fragmentary text published by Lambert in "A Catalogue of Texts and Authors," 60–67.

[85] "Die Beschwörungsserie," 192.

[86] Ibid., 193; cf. p. 194.

attracted to itself traits that were obviously borrowed from characters other than Enmeduranki (e.g., the flood hero). Some caution is in order, however. First, it is not clear from the *bīt mēseri* evidence whether an ascension to heaven was the final event in Utu᾿abzu's life or merely an interlude in his earthly career. Moreover, it can hardly be disputed that later Jewish writers developed the motif of Enoch's removal, not in ways that recall *apkallū* traditions, but rather in language borrowed from accounts of the flood hero's translation. This last point does not mean, naturally, that the priestly editor of Genesis 5 understood Enoch's removal in the sense that is found in later literature, but the verb that he uses (*lāqaḥ*) suggests that he, too, was attributing to Enoch the final destiny of the Mesopotamian flood hero. This is the verb that is employed (as will be seen below) in the Akkadian versions of the flood story (*laqû*) and describes a different approach to the realm of the deity than an ascension: Enoch, like the flood hero, was taken; he did not ascend.[87]

The question whether Utu᾿abzu's ascension furnished the literary basis for Enoch's removal should perhaps remain open until more evidence is available, but it does seem unlikely that Borger's proposal is correct. Nevertheless, even if the seventh *apkallū*'s ascension is not the forebear of Enoch's removal, this need not imply that Enmeduranki was not the model for the priestly Enoch. The parallels between them are much too close to justify scepticism on this point. P did, however, exercise editorial independence as he drew on foreign traditions; his Enoch, though carefully modeled on the image of Enmeduranki, was in the final analysis his unique creation. He was neither king nor *bārû*, neither devotee of Shamash nor ruler of an *apkallū*. For P he was simply one remarkable member in a series of ten antediluvian patriarchs to whom the divine blessing was given and whose line survived the flood. His Enoch is not a mirror image of Enmeduranki but he is by no means independent of traditions about him. The biblical image of Enoch is based on the Mesopotamian picture of Enmeduranki.

In summary, one can say that the priestly editor of Gen 5:21–24 has expressed his acquaintance with a fairly broad range of Mesopotamian traditions in remarkably few words. Here, as in his creation and flood narratives, he betrays how extensively he has drawn from foreign mythology in order to paint a picture of the primordial age that suited his purposes. The Enoch whom he presents has the following traits: 1. he was associated with the solar year (his 365 years) as Enmeduranki was associated with the solar

---

[87] This issue will be discussed in the context of traditions about Enoch's final removal in *1 Enoch*; cf. Milik, *The Books of Enoch*, 33. See also Lambert's cautious comments about Borger's thesis ("Babylonien und Israel," 77).

god Shamash; 2. he was a companion of the angels (walked with the ʾĕlōhîm) both during and after his 365 years as Enmeduranki had enjoyed the company of Shamash and Adad; and 3. he was removed by God to some unspecified location as the Mesopotamian flood hero was taken by the god of the flood from human society. The priestly editor was, for whatever reason, content to drop the subject of Enoch at that point. Some scholars have maintained that his terse reference to Enoch's removal by God expressed in cryptic fashion his theological conviction that Enoch's ultimate destiny was held out to all God's people as his desire for them,[88] or at least that P entertained belief in a kind of immortality. There is no suggestion in Genesis 5, however, that the priestly editor viewed Enoch's destiny as anything but an experience unique to Enoch—just as in the flood stories the reward of the hero is for him and his immediate circle alone, not for anyone else. For this writer, Enoch was special, not typical.[89]

The preceding analysis of Gen 5:21-24 has shown that P was aware of a wider body of traditions about the seventh head of humanity than may be immediately evident. In the following chapters, the portraits of Enoch that appear in the earliest Jewish pseudepigrapha will be studied. It will become apparent that their authors drew upon Gen 5:21-24 but also that they knew more ancient traditions about him than are found explicitly in P. A problem, perhaps insoluble at present, is whether the later writers simply expressed more of the traditions of which P seems cognizant though he does not elaborate on them or whether they based their Enochic portrait on Genesis 5 and on renewed contact, in the postexilic period, with Mesopotamian traditions about the earliest times.

[88] So Grelot, "La légende," 199-210.
[89] Gunkel, *Genesis*, 136; Skinner, *Genesis*, 132.

## III

## DIVINATION AND APOCALYPTIC LITERATURE

In chap. I. attention was drawn to the fact that some scholars have recently proposed a connection between mantic wisdom and Jewish apocalypticism. The connection is now met frequently in the literature but is rarely elaborated in any detail. Since it is extremely important for the present investigation, it seemed appropriate and convenient to gather the pertinent material regarding the subject in one chapter and to place it at this point in the book before treatment of the major Enochic texts. Reference will be made throughout the remainder of the book to the evidence accumulated here.

### A. Mesopotamian Divination

### 1. General Description

The sheer mass of omen texts that have been unearthed at various sites in Mesopotamia indicates that divination was a prominent aspect of life in the civilizations of that region. The energy that was devoted to it and the confidence lodged in its conclusions may have varied with time and place, but it is an indisputable fact that mantic techniques were widely practiced and diviners frequently consulted. Divination seems to arise from humanity's innate anxiety about and interest in the future.

> Basically, divination represents a technique of communication with the supernatural forces that are supposed to shape the history of the individual as well as that of the group. It presupposes the belief that these powers are able and, at times, willing to communicate their intentions and that they are interested in the well-being of the individual or the group—in other words, that if evil is predicted or threatened, it can be averted through appropriate means.[1]

It was believed that the gods communicated something about the future in numerous ways, and proper interpretation of their signals demanded appropriate techniques and skills for each kind. Oppenheim distinguished

---

[1] A. Leo Oppenheim, *Ancient Mesopotamia*, 207.

two categories of divinatory techniques—the operational and the magical.[2] *Operational* techniques or methods are those through which the diviner induces the deity to answer by creating a proper context, i.e., by presenting materials that the god could then influence as he or she wished. Types that belong in this category are the practices of pouring oil on water (or vice versa) and reading the divine answer from the resulting configurations;[3] making smoke rise from a censer and interpreting the ascending patterns; and (rarely) casting lots and thus receiving a yes or no answer. *Magical* techniques are those that were applied in circumstances in which the gods, at their instigation, communicated through sundry natural phenomena. Acceptable media were astronomical or meteorological occurrences; the behavior of animals[4] and people; internal and external features of animals; unusual traits in new-born animals and people; and mantic dreams. Among the types within this category, the literature suggests that at different times extispicy (especially of the livers of sacrificed lambs)[5] and astronomical observation were extremely popular.

2. Divinatory Literature

The vast omen literature from Mesopotamia reveals that diviners began keeping records of their observations and predictions from a very early time, that such texts continued to be copied throughout the history of cuneiform writing, and that over the centuries the nature of this sort of writing evolved noticeably.

---

[2] Ibid., 207–08. Other writers distinguish differently. For example, M. Jastrow (*The Civilization of Babylonia and Assyria* [reprinted; New York: Blom, 1971] 255) spoke of omens that were sought and those that "obtruded" themselves on one's attention. Cf. also H. W. F. Saggs, *The Greatness That Was Babylon* (New York: New American Library, 1968). 307. While divination itself is attested for all periods of Mesopotamian civilization and some texts were written already in the Old Babylonian period, certain methods seem to have been favored more at one time than at others. For example, oil divination seems to have faded in importance while astronomical divination, which is attested at early times, became extremely popular in the first millennium. It is now known that divinatory texts continued to be copied in Seleucid times. For a historical survey of Mesopotamian divination, see J. Nougayrol, "La divination babylonienne," *La divination* (ed. A. Caquot and M. Leibovici; 2 vols.; Paris: Presses Universitaires de France, 1968), 1.25–30.

[3] See G. Pettinato, "Zur Überlieferungsgeschichte der aB-Ölomentexte und einige Erwägungun zur Stellung der Ölwahrsagung in der Religionsgeschichte" in *La divination en Mésopotamie ancienne et dans les régions voisines* (Rencontre assyriologique internationale 14; Bibliothèque des Centres d'Études supérieures spécialisés; Paris: Presses Universitaires de France, 1966) 95–107.

[4] An example, though it is unusual for Mesopotamia, is observing and interpreting the flight path of a bird; see E. Reiner, "Fortune-Telling in Mesopotamia," *JNES* 19 (1960) 23–35.

[5] See the account in Jastrow, *The Civilization*, 255–57.

They first made reports on specific events, then assembled observations of each kind in small collections. The purpose was clearly to record experiences for future reference and for the benefit of coming generations. Thus, written records were made of unusual acts of animals, unusual happenings in the sky, and similar occurrences, and divination moved from the realm of folklore to the level of scientific activity. The subsequent systematization of such collections represents high scholarly achievement.[6]

Oppenheim's references to "scientific activity" and "high scholarly achievement" are worth exploring in greater depth. A written omen consists of a protasis and an apodosis: if situation x prevails, then consequence y will follow. A well known example reads: "If a town is set on a hill, it will not be good for the dweller within that town."[7] Omens appear to have been written down already at very early times and were probably originally rather simple listings, but the standard omen collections, which are available only in relatively late copies, embody not only the observations actually made over several centuries but also evidence a movement toward greater comprehensiveness. That is, it seems that scribes eventually strove to record all possible ominous situations, regardless whether they had ever been witnessed, and attached standardized prognostications to them.[8] As a result, the "canonical" omen collections served as convenient reference works for interpreting all ominous signs and thus understandably attained tremendous size. Some of the more famous collections illustrate this last point: *Enūma Anu Enlil*— some 70 tablets for astronomical and meteorological omens;[9] *Šumma ālu*— at least 107 tablets of omens about the behavior of animals especially; *Šumma*

---

[6] Oppenheim, *Ancient Mesopotamia*, 210.

[7] Cited from Saggs, *The Greatness That Was Babylon*, 308. It is the first omen in the series *šumma ālu* whose title is derived from its first two words.

[8] Oppenheim, *Ancient Mesopotamia*, 211–12. See his description of omen lists in *The Interpretation of Dreams in the Ancient Near East, with a Translation of an Assyrian Dream-Book* (Transactions of the American Philosophical Society 46/3; Philadelphia: American Philosophical Society, 1956) 256–57.

[9] E. P. Weidner has dealt with the material in this large series in several essays: "Die astrologische Serie Enûma Anu Enlil," *AfO* 14 (1941–44) 172–95; 308–18; 17 (1954–56) 71–89; 22 (1968–69) 65–75. Weidner, who estimates that the series must once have contained approximately 6500–7000 omens, treated the first 50 tablets but did not edit a text of them (he does furnish a few photographs). Erica Reiner has undertaken the arduous task of editing the *Enūma Anu Enlil* material; see Reiner with David Pingree, *Babylonian Planetary Omens, Part One: Enūma Anu Enlil Tablet 63: The Venus Tablet of Ammiṣaduqa* (Bibliotheca Mesopotamica 2/1; Malibu: Undena, 1975).

*izbu*—at least 24 tablets of omens regarding births and deformities;[10] and
*dZiqīqu*—11 tablets of omens for dream interpretation.[11]

Clearly the omens were divinatory statements and therefore served superstitious purposes, but it would not be inappropriate to regard their *protases*
as incipient scientific descriptions because they display that concern to list
fully and to classify phenomena which is an essential ingredient of scientific
endeavor. For example, the normal form for most sections of omens in the
Venus Tablet (no. 63) of *Enūma Anu Enlil* is: "In month MN, day n, Venus
disappeared in the east/west; it remains invisible for n days, and became
visible in month $MN_2$, day n, in the west/east: apodosis."[12] Perhaps it would
be preferable to label such statements as proto–scientific—they are based on
observation and cannot be called mathematical astronomy—but at least one
can say that they are detailed and precise (where they can be interpreted
properly), though the reason for their composition was not in the first place
to serve what are today considered scientific ends.[13] It is the apodoses, however, that reflect and express the underlying religious principles of the system; in this respect, these prognostications belong to a category altogether
different from that of the protases. In the apodoses one sees the effects of the
belief that there is a direct, inevitable connection between observed sign and
future occurrence. It appears that the diviners and those who enlisted their
services conceived of the universe much as a vast tablet on which the gods
could inscribe announcements of their will for the future and from which
experts could read them.[14] The apodoses presuppose a kind of fate or pre–determinism—a belief that the gods had fixed the course of human events in
advance so that, if the need should arise, they could be predicted through
mutually intelligible signs. Nevertheless, the predestination of Mesopotam-

---

[10] These general characterizations of the material in *šumma ālu* and *šumma izbu* are
taken from Erle Leichty, "Teratological Omens," *La divination en Mésopotamie*, 136. Leichty
has prepared an edition of the *šumma izbu* material: *The Omen Series Šumma Izbu* (Texts from
Cuneiform Sources IV; Locust Valley; J. J. Augustin, 1970). According to him the series, as
found in Asshurbanipal's library, contains more than 2000 omens (2).

[11] The standard work on *dZiqīqu* is Oppenheim, *The Interpretation of Dreams*. In this
series only tablets II-IX contain omens (cf. p. 262), while I, X, and XI have rituals and incanta-
tions against the consequences which the apodoses predict for evil dreams. The series *šumma
ālu* shows a similar combination (295).

[12] Reiner/Pingree, *The Venus Tablet*, 9. For the pattern elsewhere in the tablet, see p. 10.

[13] Cf. Oppenheim, "Perspectives on Mesopotamian Divination," *La divination en Mésopotamie*, 40–42; idem, "Divination and Celestial Observation in the Latest Assyrian Empire,"
*Centaurus* 14 (1969) 125–26; Nougayrol, "Trente ans de recherches sur la divination babylonienne (1935–1965)," *La divination en Mésopotamie*, 10; and especially O. Neugebauer, *The
Exact Sciences in Antiquity* (2nd ed.; Providence: Brown, 1957) 99–103 for discussions of the
issues.

[14] See Nougayrol, "La divination babylonienne," 32–33.

ian divination was not absolute; while there was a direct, automatic relation between sign and future event, an imminent calamity could be avoided or averted by means of appropriate rituals.[15]

### 3. The *bārû*

The highly technical literature and the complicated rituals and observations of the diviner undoubtedly required experts, products of careful training, to execute the necessary functions. The texts mention various sorts of diviners, each of which apparently specialized to some extent in a particular type or in particular types of divination (e.g., the *šā'ilu/šā'iltu; mašmāšu*, etc.). One of the most frequently and prominently mentioned kinds is the *bārû*. This title is in form a participle of the verb *barû* which means "to see, observe." Thus a *bārû* is literally "one who sees/observes," and the object of his seeing is omens.[16] As H. Zimmern, who published most of the important texts that describe the roles of the *bārû*, put it: "Der *bārū* ist der Wahrsager *kat' exochēn*. Er wird in allen Fällen zu Rate gezogen, in denen man Aufschluss über die Zukunft erhalten, in denen man für die Vornahme einer bestimmten wichtigen Handlung sich Rats bei den Göttern holen will."[17] Virtually nothing specific is known about the formal or professional training that an aspiring *bārû* had to undergo, but one can safely surmise that some instruction in the reading and use of the standard omen compendia figured prominently in it.[18] There are some texts which demand genealogical and physical purity of the one who wishes to be a *bārû*. For example, K 2486.22–29 reads as follows:

> When a diviner (= *lúbārî* [*ḫal*]), 23. an expert in oil, of abiding descent, offspring of Enmeduranki, king of Sippar, 24. who set up the pure bowl and held the cedar-(rod), 25. a benediction priest of the king, a long–haired priest of Šamaš, 26. as fashioned by Ninḫursagga, 27. begotten by a *nišakku*-priest of pure descent: 28. if he is without blemish in body and limbs 29. he may approach the presence of Šamaš and Adad where liver inspection (=*bíra*) and oracle (take place).[19]

---

[15] These are the *namburbû* rituals. For brief treatments, see Oppenheim, *Ancient Mesopotamia*, 226; Saggs, *The Greatness That Was Babylon*, 307–08. If one received a negative omen, another could be sought. Also, it appears that an astrological omen could override the verdict of a liver omen (Nougayrol, ibid., 48).

[16] AHw 1.109 gives for *bārû* "Opferschau(priest)er," while CAD 2.121 translates with "diviner."

[17] *Beiträge*, 82.

[18] Oppenheim, *Ancient Mesopotamia*, 81-82; Nougayrol, "La divination babylonienne," 39.

[19] Translation of Lambert, "Enmeduranki and Related Matters," 132. The continuation of the text can be consulted in Zimmern, *Beiträge*, 118–19. Ll. 30-42 deal with the case of a *mār*

In the texts one meets the *bārû* most frequently as a haruspex, i.e., as a diviner who reads the gods' decision about an issue or their will from the features of an animal's internal organs. In particular, he was the acknowledged expert at deciphering divine messages from the livers of sacrified lambs. Preparation for liver divination involved elaborate rituals,[20] and once the liver had been extracted and was available for inspection the *bārû* had to be able to analyse its many parts and features in the prescribed ways in order to decode the announcement. Something of the detail that was involved in this sort of observation can be gathered from the clay liver models that have been unearthed in Mesopotamia and Canaan[21] as well as from the technical literature of extispicy.[22] The model livers show lines that divide the surfaces into intricate grids; favorable and unfavorable responses from the gods were supposed to be indicated in the small sections thus demarcated.[23]

While the *bārû* was preeminently, it appears, a haruspex, there is evidence that members of this guild practiced other divinatory skills as well. K 2486.17 and 23 mention observation of oil on water (lecanomancy);[24] elsewhere divining by reading omens from configurations of rising smoke (libanomancy) is noted as a function of the *bārû*.[25] Whatever the range of professional services that he rendered, it is apparent that the *bārû* was a very high-ranking kind of diviner, and it comes as no surprise that such people

---

*bārî* (= a *bārû* in effect; see CAD 2.125) who lacks the requisite pedigree and physical traits; he is not to be permitted to carry out the functions of a *bārû*. Cf. also Zimmern's text 1-20.4-6, 19 (pp. 96-99) and his summary of the evidence on the matter (p. 87).

[20] Several of the texts that Zimmern published in *Beiträge* describe or rather prescribe these preparations in minute detail (e.g., No. 1-20.29-126 [pp. 98-105]). A diviner could consult liver omens for different purposes: for an answer to specific questions or simply to search for any divine message which might be lodged there. On this, see Nougayrol, "La divination babylonienne," 42-43.

[21] Convenient photographs are found in *ANEP* nos. 594-95 (p. 196). For photographs and discussions, see M. Rutten, "Trente-deux modèles de foies in argile provenant de Tell-Hariri," *RA* 35 (1938) 36-70; and B. Landsberger and H. Tadmor, "Fragments of Clay Liver Models from Hazor," *IEJ* 14 (1964) 201-17. In Ezek 21:26 the king of Babylon consults a liver for an omen at a crossroad (*rā'â bakkābēd*).

[22] Nougayrol, "La divination babylonienne," 34-35, 39-45; C. J. Gadd, *Ideas of Divine Rule in the Ancient East* (Schweich Lectures 1945; London: Oxford, 1948) 56-57.

[23] Nougayrol, "La divination babylonienne," 34-35; Zimmern, *Beiträge*, 84.

[24] See CAD 2.122 for other references.

[25] See CAD 2.122. There is no evidence after the Old Babylonian period that a *bārû* practiced either lecanomancy or libanomancy (CAD 2.125). Zimmern (*Beiträge*, 85) raised the possibility that a *bārû* could actually practice all types of divination. Leichty (*The Omen Series Šumma Izbu*, 7-12) adduces evidence that *bārûs* employed this series for obtaining omens having to do with birth deformities.

often held important positions within the government.[26] As noted in chap. II above, the crucial text K 2486 relates that Enmeduranki of Sippar founded this guild of experts and instituted their mantic techniques. It is this Enmeduranki with whom the Jewish Enoch shows so many similarities.

As Enmeduranki is said to have learned the arts of the diviner from the two gods Shamash and Adad, so his successors ("his offspring") regularly sought their oracles from the same two deities, especially from Shamash. The two are called "lords of the oracle" (*bēlē bīri*) or, more commonly in the texts that Zimmern edited, Shamash is the "lord of the decision" (*bēl dīni*) and Adad is the "lord of the oracle/omen" (*bēl bīri*).[27]

Some of the phrases that are used in the texts to describe the labors of the *bārû* are also worth noting:

*bīra barû*: to divine, given an oracle
*bārûtu epēšu*: to exercise the office of a *bārû*
*dīna dānu*: to give a verdict
*arkātu parāsu*: to decide the future (cf. *ana lamāda arkāti*: for learning the future)
*amāta šakānu*: to make an utterance
*adanna nadānu*: to determine the time (for something; cf. *šikin adanni*: fixing the time).[28]

It is also of interest that the science of the *bārû* is brought into close relationship with the terms *tablet* and *secret* or *mystery*. He is labeled a learned scholar who guards the mystery of the great gods (K 2486.19: *[lú]ummânu mudû nāṣir pirišti ilāni[meš] rabûti[meš]*), and, through his craft, he was thought to have access to the secret of heaven and of the underworld (K 2486.14).[29]

### 4. Astronomical Divination

This abbreviated foray into the world of Mesopotamian divination should include some additional information about the two types of divina-

---

[26] Cf. CAD 2.123–25 for references. Some texts also picture the *bārû* accompanying armies.

[27] Zimmern, *Beiträge*, 89–90. The latter two titles are frequent in the texts that he published as an "Anhang zu den Ritualtafeln für den Wahrsager (*bārû*)." Though K 2486 attributes to Shamash and Adad the revelation given to Enmeduranki, Zimmern's text no. 1–20.11–12 says that the science of the *bārû* was disclosed by Ea (*niṣirti bārûti/ša ᵈEa imbu*). Ea is mentioned in K 2486 but not as the revealer. Zimmern (p. 87) noted that the attribution of the revelation to Ea would harmonize with the Oannes legend. Among the texts that document a connection between Shamash and omens, see the Shamash Hymn in Lambert, *Babylonian Wisdom Literature* (Oxford: Clarendon, 1960) 135 ll. 149–55. For a prayer to Shamash and Adad before rituals and extispicy, see Albrecht Goetze, "An Old Babylonian Prayer of the Divination Priest," *JCS* 22 (1968) 25–29.

[28] For the references, see Zimmern, *Beiträge*, 87–88.

[29] Ibid., 89.

tion that seem most directly relevant to the concerns of Jewish apocalyptic texts—astronomical divination and oneiromancy. For the former type, the great omen compendium is *Enūma Anu Enlil* which comprises some 70 tablets of various sorts. Weidner, who toiled through the textual witnesses to the first fifty tablets of this collection, tentatively dated composition of the series, which incorporates earlier, shorter works, to either the second half of the second or the beginning of the first millennium B.C.[30] The first 22 or 23 tablets of the compendium contain lunar omens, and these were followed by sections consisting of omens derived from the sun, meteorological phenomena (e.g., thunder, rain, hail, earthquakes), and the positions of the planets and fixed stars.[31] Judging from the extant material, astrological divination reached the summit of its popularity during the Sargonid period and continued in frequent use afterwards.

Although the *bārû* is not pictured in the texts as the expert who *specialized* in astrological divination, there is reason to believe that the subject may have fallen within his scholarly ambit. K 2486, the "constitution" of the *bārûtu* which was treated in chap. II, mentions the series *Enūma Anu Enlil* at 1. 18. Unfortunatly it does so in a context that defies precise interpretation. In Lambert's transcription the line reads: *šá KI ṣa-a-ti enūma (ud) anu* ᵈ*en-líl u arâ (a.rá)ᵃ šu-ta-bu-lu*. He translates (the line is part of a section which he brackets from the context): "'that with commentary'; *When Anu, Enlil*; and how to make mathematical calculations."[32] Whatever may be the meaning of this obscure line, it is at least indisputable that the "canonical" omen compendium *Enūma Anu Enlil* (and apparently calculations based upon it) is mentioned in this all-important text regarding the *bārû*—a fact which certainly raises the possibility that his expertise may have extended to this highly significant field of divination in addition to the other areas that were noted above.[33] It should also be added that in the Late Babylonian period experts in astrological omens were called *tupšar enūma Anu Enlil*. Use of such a cover term meant that a writer did not distinguish categories of these scholars. Thus, though it cannot be demonstrated, it may be that *bārûs* were included.

5. Oneiromancy
The remaining mantic art that is particularly relevant for the present

[30] "Die astrologische Serie," 176.

[31] See, e.g., Oppenheim, *Ancient Mesopotamia*, 225.

[32] "Enmeduranki and Related Matters," 132. Zimmern, (*Beiträge*, 119) had read *ki-ṣa-a-ti*, a word for which he suggested the meaning "omens" or something similar. Lambert (p. 133), however, rejects his proposal because no such word is known to exist. He also rejects two renderings of the line that are offered in CAD.

[33] Zimmern, *Beiträge*, 85.

study—oneiromancy—has been thoroughly and definitively studied by Oppenheim in his *The Interpretation of Dreams in the Ancient Near East*. The standard omen series for dreams was called $^d$*Ziqīqu* (*zaqīqu*) after one of the gods of dreams who is invoked in the first line of the text. It is of some interest that this Ziqīqu was considered a son of Shamash, the solar deity, and that the dream goddess Mamu was regarded as his daughter.[34] That is, the dream divinities belonged in the family of Shamash, and he himself retained direct control of dreams as a means of communication between gods and men.[35] Indeed Shamash himself used dreams as vehicles for announcing his verdicts and was credited with being the instructor of the dream–diviner who approached him.[36]

Dream omina assume the regular conditional form of Mesopotamian omens as the following examples from Tablet III of the Assyrian Dream-Book illustrate.

If a man in a dream makes a door: the "evil-demon" will head (for him).

If he makes a chair: the "evil-demon" will head (for him).[37]

Generally speaking, the *content* of dream omens seems to have little if anything in common with the *content* of dreams that Jewish apocalyptic seers recorded, but one sort of dream omen is more closely related than the others. In this category the dreamer either descends to the netherworld or rises to the heavens, and depending upon his experiences in either place, consequences are predicted. For example,

If he hears in heaven repeatedly rumors of accusations:
  he will have worries [      ] (1. 69).

If he *ditto* [i.e., descends to the netherworld] and a dead person
  blesses him: he will die through the collapse of a wall (1. 82).[38]

The presence of these omens in $^d$*Ziqīqu* means that reports about otherworldly travel—a widespread phenomenon in ancient literature and one which is prominent in Jewish apocalyptic texts—also falls within the vast province of divination.[39] It is clear, however, that in this category as in dream omina generally, the consequences and experiences are private or personal.[40]

---

[34] Oppenheim, *The Interpretation of Dreams*, 232–33.

[35] Ibid., 232.

[36] Ibid., 307. Oppenheim drew a parallel between the double role of Shamash and the dual functions of Daniel's God with regard to dreams: ". . . the enigmatic 'symbolic' dream as well as its explanation originate from the same source" (222).

[37] Ibid., 263.

[38] Ibid., 282–83. Oppenheim provisionally assigned this Tablet C to Tablet II of the series $^d$*Ziqīqu*.

[39] Cf. ibid., 214.

[40] Ibid., 239.

That is, they do not involve the nations and powers of the world, but usually only the person of the dreamer himself.

The Akkadian verb that expresses what is done when an expert handles a dream is *pašāru* (Sumerian *búr*). The root of the verb is the same as the one used in Daniel for interpretation of symbolic dreams (Aramaic noun *pĕšar* [e.g., 4:3] and verb *pĕšar* [5:12]) and also in Genesis for Joseph's explanations of dreams (Hebrew noun *pitrôn* [40:5] and verb *pātar* [41:13]). Oppenheim maintained, though, that the Akkadian verb had a wider range of meaning than simply "to interpret." The verb *pašāru* could be used for "(a) the reporting of one's dream to another person, (b) the interpreting of an enigmatic dream by that person, and (c) the dispelling or removing of the evil consequences of such a dream by magic means."[41]

A diviner who is often met in connection with the handling of symbolic dreams is the *šāʾilu/šāʾiltu* (cf. 1 Sam 28:6), although dreams were not the only professional concerns of these people.[42] Other experts are also mentioned in oneiromantic contexts, but it is questionable whether the *bārû* was associated with dream omina. Oppenheim does mention a Middle Assyrian political letter in which there occurs a line that couples exercise of the *bārûtu* with a dream, but he observed that ". . . the passage implies that the *bārû* was not interpreting dreams but seeking to contact the deity by means of incubation-dreams."[43] He also refers to KAR 44 which, he says, mentions among the books with which an aspiring *bārû* was to be familiar one entitled "to make evil dreams pleasant (i.e., to change them into pleasant ones [1.14])."[44] Once again it may be the case that the *bārû* was expected to know at least some of the literature of oneiromancy, though this seems not to have been a field of divination with which he was very closely associated.

The principal results of the preceding survey may be summarized as follows. Mesopotamian divination involved a fairly large number of methods for ascertaining what was to happen. It was predicated on the assumption that the gods would, under some circumstances, disclose the future beforehand through mutually accepted signs. Interpretation of these signs required the services of well trained professionals who, over the centuries, developed and consulted standard omen compendia in which were recorded in conditional form the signs observed and the consequences predicted. The *bārû* (a

[41] Ibid., 219.
[42] Ibid., 222-25. According to Oppenheim, the *šāʾiltu* seems to have belonged to a lower social level than some of the other diviners.
[43] Ibid., 223. Cf. Zimmern, *Beiträge*, 86.
[44] Ibid., 295. KAR refers to the texts published by E. Ebeling, *Keilschrifttexte aus Assur religiösen Inhalts* (Leipzig: Hinrichs, 1920). On the text, see Zimmern, "Zu den 'Keilschrifttexten aus Assur religiösen Inhalts'," *ZA* 30 (1915/16) 204-29.

member of the guild instituted by Enmeduranki) was a high–ranking diviner who usually appears as a haruspex but whose professional competence did extend to some other areas as well (possibly including astrological and dream divination, though there is no proof for it). The chief deity in the mantic realm was Shamash, the lord of the decision or verdict.

## B. *The Relation Between Divination and Jewish Apocalypticism*

In the following chapters specific details regarding the relations between divination and Jewish apocalypticism will be discussed, but here some general comments are in order. However similar Mesopotamian divination and Jewish apocalypticism may be in some respects, they certainly have not produced comparable literature. That is, authors of Jewish apocalyptic texts did not write omen collections. There is simply no counterpart to such mantic literature either in the Bible or in the post–biblical Jewish literature.[45] Quite obviously, then, the suggested connection between these two phenomena must be envisaged differently than as direct literary imitation of omen compendia on the part of Jewish writers of apocalyptic works.

The historical interplay of these two entities should rather be conceived on a more general level. To put it briefly, both are fundamentally and essentially concerned with learning the future now and the two resort to similar and in some cases the same media for doing so, namely, opaque signs from the divine side which require the ministrations of specially trained experts to interpret their meaning. Both are interpretative endeavors. In other words, communication from the supernatural about what is destined to occur— something which both assume is possible—takes place, not through a clear verbal announcement or revelation as was usually the case with Israel's prophets, but through signs which remained enigmatic to all but the diviner or seer. God or the gods did not declare the future in a straightforward fashion; they symbolized or encoded it, and the symbols or code had to be deciphered before they could be understood by their recipients. This structure, which is common to Mesopotamian divination and Jewish apocalypticism, separates them from biblical prophecy.

### 1. The Akkadian Prophecies

New possibilities for demonstrating and understanding connections between divination and apocalypticism have been opened by several Akkadian

---

[45] Cf. W. W. Hallo, "Akkadian Apocalypses," *IEJ* 16 (1966) 231. This is not to say, however, that the omen style has left no mark on Israelite literature. On this, see B. Long, "The Effect of Divination upon Israelite Literature," *JBL* 92 (1973) 489–97. Also, see the comments in the following chapter regarding *1 Enoch* 72-82.

texts which have recently enjoyed a fair amount of attention—the "Akkadian prophecies." These texts appear to be related in some ways to omen literature but also show greater similarities with apocalypses than do omen collections. Too little is currently known about the "prophecy" genre to draw large conclusions from it, but a solid case can be made that it is an expression of the sort of thought world in which writers of Jewish apocalypses were at home. Jewish sages, though familiar with and influenced by mantic arts and literature, seem to have made use of such material—to have revised it—so that it could be pressed into direct service toward the ends which they intended. In this they were anticipated by their Mesopotamian counterparts who also eventually employed aspects of the mantic world in new contexts. It may be, as noted above, that Babylonian science drew some of its data from the observations of astrological diviners as they were recorded in the protases of omens; but omen literature was a source that could be exploited in other directions as well. The Akkadian prophecies appear to have borrowed some of the language and ideas of omen apodoses.

According to the latest classification, there are now five texts which belong to this genre: three which are cast in the third person (the Dynastic Prophecy, Text A, and the Uruk Prophecy) and two which employ the first person (the Marduk Prophetic Speech and the Shulgi Prophetic Speech).[46] A. K. Grayson, who has worked most extensively with the texts, characterizes them as follows:

[46] A. K. Grayson and W. G. Lambert ("Akkadian Prophecies," *JCS* 18 [1964] 7-30) edited four texts which they considered examples of the genre "Akkadian prophecies." These they labeled Texts A, B, C, and D. Subsequent research has shown that some revision is needed in the classification. Text B, which has been reconstructed more fully by Robert D. Biggs ("More Babylonian 'Prophecies'," *Iraq* 29 [1967] 117-32) and which will be discussed below, is no longer called a prophecy. Borger ("Gott Marduk und Gott-König Šulgi als Propheten: Zwei prophetische Texte," *BO* 28 [1971] 3-24) was able to show that the text which Grayson and Lambert called C belongs to the Shulgi prophetic speech, while their Text D is part of the Marduk prophetic speech—both of which are segments of the same series. Borger was also able to piece these sections together so that a fairly continuous text was obtained. The important Dynastic prophecy has now been published, translated, and analyzed by Grayson, *Babylonian Historical-Literary Texts* (Toronto Semitic Texts and Studies 3; Toronto/Buffalo: University of Toronto, 1975) 24-37. For the Uruk prophecy, see H. Hunger in *XXVI/XXVII. vorläufiger Bericht über die von dem Deutschen Archäologischen Institut und der Deutschen Orientgesellschaft aus Mitteln der Deutschen Forschungsgemeinschaft unternommenen Ausgrabungen in Uruk-Warka* (Berlin: Mann, 1972) 87 and plate 25. For the list of texts, see Grayson, *Babylonian Historical-Literary Texts*, 14-15; and his essay "Assyria and Babylonia," *Or* 49 (1980) 183-84. All existing copies of the texts are from the Persian or Seleucid periods. Translations of parts of Text A, the Shulgi prophetic speech, and the Marduk prophetic speech are to be found in Walter Beyerlin, ed., *Near Eastern Religious Texts Relating to the Old Testament* (Old Testament Library, London: SCM, 1978) 119-22.

An Akkadian prophecy is a prose composition consisting in the main of a number of "predictions" of past events. It then concludes either with a "prediction" of phenomena in the writer's day or with a genuine attempt to forecast future events. The author, in other words, uses vaticinia ex eventu to establish his credibility and then proceeds to his real purpose, which might be to justify a current idea or institution or, as it appears in the Dynastic Prophecy, to forecast future doom for a hated enemy. There is some evidence that the genre has its roots in Sumerian literature. In the Hebrew scriptures parts of the Book of Daniel are strikingly similar to the form and rationale of Akkadian prophecy. Comparative material is also known from Egypt in the form of the admonitions of Ipu-Wer and the prophecy of Neferti.[47]

A well preserved section of Text A illustrates the cryptic way in which the author surveys what will happen; as Grayson notes, the predictions borrow from the phraseology of omen apodoses and in this text exhibit the frequent use of ideograms which is characteristic of such clauses:[48]

9. A prince will arise and rule for thirteen years.
10. There will be an Elamite attack on Akkad and
11. the *booty* of Akkad will be carried off.
12. The shrines of the great gods will be destroyed. Akkad will *suffer* a defeat.
13. There will be confusion, disturbance, and disorder in the land.
14. The nobility will lose prestige. Another man who is unknown will arise,
15. seize the throne as king, and put his grandees to the sword.[49]

Grayson comments that while historical events do indeed seem to be reflected, only a person who is well versed in the history of the period in question could identify the kings and events so described. Here he properly alludes to clear similarities with Dan 8:23–25 and with 11:3–45, in which unnamed kings of the north and south ascend the thrones of their realms and in which events are also chronicled in intentionally vague but decipherable terms.[50]

In an investigation into the Ancient Near Eastern environment in which Jewish apocalypticism developed, the recently published Dynastic prophecy should occupy a prominent place.[51] One reads in it an account of rising and

---

[47] *Babylonian Historical-Literary Texts*, 6–7.

[48] Ibid., 13.

[49] Translation of Grayson, "Akkadian Prophecies," 14.

[50] Ibid., 9–10; *Babylonian Historical-Literary Texts*, 20–22. Hallo ("Akkadian Apocalypses," 235–39) has maintained that in Text A kings of the second dynasty of Isin are under consideration, beginning with the sixth ruler in it—Marduk-nadin-aḫḫe.

[51] Grayson, *Babylonian Historical-Literary Texts*, 24–37.

falling world empires whose fortunes and vicissitudes are related through *vaticinia ex eventu*. The text is badly damaged, but the remaining parts suggest the following succession of dynasties: Assyria, Babylonia, Persia (called Elam), and the Macedonian/Hellenistic kingdoms.[52] It is possible that col. iv, the last in the text, concludes with an authentic effort at predicting the downfall of the Seleucid regime. If so, it would be evidence for a strongly anti–Seleucid feeling among some learned residents of Babylon[53]— a sentiment that is, of course, so powerful in parts of Daniel and in other contemporary Jewish literature. It is most unfortunate that the opening lines of the Dynastic prophecy are not available, since in them one would probably have learned from whom the predictions were supposed to have come as well as how and to whom they were divulged. The end of the text is also fragmentary, but enough has survived to indicate that provision is made for concealing its contents from the uninitiated.[54]

2. Some Similarities Between the Akkadian Prophecies and Jewish Apocalypses

Grayson and Hallo, among others, have signalled the extraordinary importance of the prophetic texts for understanding the evolution of apocalyptic literature in the ancient orient.[55] In fact, after Grayson and Lambert had published texts A-D, Hallo suggested that they should be called *apocalypses*, since their affinities were more with Jewish apocalyptic texts than with biblical prophetic literature. In support of his proposal he cited the five criteria by which R. H. Charles had distinguished Jewish "apocalyptic" from biblical prophecy and argued, with some necessary reservations, that by all

---

[52] So Grayson, ibid. 24–27. The first three seem clear enough, but the fourth empire is more of a problem in that it is called that of the *Hanaeans*—hardly the expected designation for Alexander and the Macedonians. Grayson (p. 26) says that *Hanaeans* was originally the name of an Amorite tribe but that in late sources it refers to residents of Thrace. Another problem arises with his interpretation of iii.17: "the overthrow of the army of the Hanaean he will [bring about]." If this is saying that Darius III defeated Alexander, it conflcts with what is known about their battles. Thus the proper understanding of the line remains in question.

[53] Grayson, ibid. 16–19. He advances the conclusion with appropriate reservations.

[54] iv.7–9: "a secret/taboo of the great gods/[You may show it to the initiated but to the uninitiat]ed you must not show (it)./[It is a secret/taboo of Marduk, lo]rd of the lands." Grayson, ibid. 37; cf. 21, 27.

[55] Grayson, "Akkadian Prophecies," 9–10; *Babylonian Historical–Literary Texts*, 7, 20–22; Hallo, "Akkadian Apocalypses," 240–42. Lambert ("History and the Gods: A Review Article," *Or* 39 [1970] 175–77) sees similarities but distinguishes the two and argues that there is no reason to suspect a connection between the two genres. Gerhard Hasel ("The Four World Empires of Daniel 2 Against Its Near Eastern Environment," *JSOT* 12 [1979] 17–30) has highlighted the close parallels between the Dynastic prophecy and Daniel 2 but doubts there is any direct literary connection.

five criteria the Akkadian "prophecies" were more akin to the apocalyptic than to the prophetic texts. According to Charles, "apocalyptic" differed from prophecy in its 1) eschatology, 2) treatment of unfulfilled prophecy, 3) temporal and spatial scope, 4) anonymity or pseudonymity, and 5) deterministic view of world history.[56] Hallo's argument is dated now because of the significant changes in the textual base for the comparison (to say nothing about the inadequacy of Charles' criteria), but, as these five areas can assist one in sharpening the comparison between the two entities, his analysis should be pursued in more detail. Leaving aside for a moment the first and fifth criteria, Hallo has shown noteworthy similarities in the others. Though unfulfilled prophecy appears not to have been the same difficulty in Babylon as it was in Israel, use in the "prophecies" of the language of omen apodoses shows the writers' concern to establish the reliability of their predictions. The spatial and temporal scope of the "prophecies" is on a scale as grand as in the Jewish texts: they range from the distant past to the future and include the perceived world of the writers and their contemporaries. The spatial dimension is now known to be more closely analogous than could have been seen in 1966 (the date of Hallo's article) because of the subsequent publication of the Dynastic prophecy. Also, though nothing could be said then about anonymity or pseudonymity in the "prophecies," the Marduk and Shulgi prophetic speeches now furnish clear examples of pseudonymity.[57]

The points at which Hallo's case breaks down and which have been criticized by other Assyriologists are the first and fifth. Regarding eschatology Hallo wrote:

> Although our text does not present any "messianic" portions, it espouses a cyclical view of history which may very well have culminated in a final, catastrophic time of troubles leading into a final and permanent *Heilzeit* under the aegis of a saviour-king. Certainly such concepts were not lacking in cuneiform literature, and it is hard to imagine what other conclusion the texts in question could have been driving at.[58]

There is, however, no reference in the texts—either the original four which Hallo treated or the present and more completely reconstructed five—to a

---

[56] Hallo, "Akkadian Apocalypses," 241–42. The five criteria are taken from Charles, *Eschatology: The Doctrine of a Future Life in Israel, Judaism, and Christianity: A Critical History* (reprinted; NY: Schocken, 1963) 173–206.

[57] Both, as noted above, are first-person narratives; in the one Marduk speaks and in the other Shulgi, the second king in the Third Dynasty of Ur (ca. 2094–2046). He claims to have received a revelation from Shamash and Ishtar (I 3–4). See Borger, "Gott Marduk," 14–22. For Hallo's discussion of Charles' criteria in relation to the Akkadian prophecies, see "Akkadian Apocalypses," 242.

[58] Ibid., 241.

"final and permanent *Heilzeit*" or to a "saviour-king." Absence of an eschatological dimension of this sort, which in a variety of forms is characteristic of works that are commonly acknowledged to be apocalypses, makes it advisable to call the Akkadian texts prophecies rather than apocalypses.[59] Hallo was also able to say little about the fifth criterion—a deterministic view of world history—other than to refer to Grayson's claim that the prophecies presupposed a cyclical view of history. Lambert and now Grayson as well have, however, come to the conclusion that there is no evidence for a cyclical view of history in cuneiform literature or for a historical determinism.[60] Nevertheless, the undeniable minimum that emerges from this discussion is that there are marked similarities in form and content between the Akkadian prophecies and the historical surveys that are found in some Jewish apocalypses. The fragmentary state of the prophecies leaves too many uncertainties about the principals and the media of their disclosures, but both the prophecies and the apocalypses resort to *vaticinia ex eventu* in their cryptic, allusive surveys of the histories of kings and nations, use the device of pseudonymity at least in some cases, and often make provision for concealing the prediction from those outside the inner circle. They differ noticeably in that the prophecies seem to lack the sort of eschatology that characterizes historical surveys in Jewish apocalypses. Opposition to the Seleucids which may find expression in the Dynastic prophecy is of great interest in this context because of the powerful effect that this sentiment had on the rise of the Jewish apocalypses.

### 3. The Prophecies, Omens Apodoses, Text B, and Apocalypses

Perhaps at the present stage of knowledge it would be inadvisable to lay great stress on the marked affinities between the language of omen apodoses and the predictions of the Akkadian prophetic texts, but a relationship of some kind is present. In their spatial and temporal scope and in their literary form the prophecies differ significantly from the then–clauses in omens; yet, for their prognostications the writers of the prophecies have borrowed from

---

[59] So Borger, "Gott Marduk," 24; Grayson, *Babylonian Historical-Literary Texts*, 22. The Marduk Prophetic Speech forecasts a time of bliss, but there is no indication that it is conceived as a final and permanent one.

[60] Though he spoke of a Babylonian cyclical view of history in "Akkadian Prophecies," 10, Grayson (*Babylonian Historical-Literary Texts*, 21 n. 34; cf. p. 4) subsequently retracted his statement and now holds that there is no evidence of such a view even in divinatory literature. Note his comment: "The underlying concept of divination does not, as I have come to realize through greater acquaintance with Babylonian omens, imply either a cyclical or deterministic view of history. Omens are nothing more than divine messages foretelling in a general way what the gods have decided to do. The gods themselves act freely." Cf. also Lambert, "History and the Gods," 175.

the language of omen apodoses.[61] That is, while other influences have also contributed to creation of the prophetic genre, omen apodoses, too, played a role. In this connection Text B, which Grayson and Lambert included among their original four prophetic compositions, should be considered because it raises the issue of omen influence in a more pointed fashion than the five prophecies. It shares a number of traits with the prophecies but appears to belong to another genre since, among other distinctions, it seems not to make the same use of *vaticinia ex eventu* to establish the author's credibility as a forecaster (though there are many predictions in it).[62] Understanding of Text B has been advanced by Robert Biggs' publication of a new fragment of it from Nippur.[63] Whereas the prophecies draw heavily from the phraseology of omen apodoses, Text B, Biggs maintains, not only raids this source but has taken over omen protases as well.[64] Due to the significance of the text for the present purposes, his summary of ll. 1–31 should be quoted in full.

> . . . (1-6) obscure, but seem to describe divine communications with the people (through celestial phenomena?), then communications between Enlil and Anu-rabû; (7-12) description of a *mīšaru*-act; (13-17) a king of Babylon is killed, a son comes to the throne, but the land revolts and he is killed in his palace, general enmity follows (described as brother against brother, friend against friend); (18) the major temples destroyed, citizens of Nippur killed; (19f.) the gods consult and restore the king's rule; booty is carried off from Iamutbal; (20ff.) a prince who is not considered an heir to the throne seizes the throne and

[61] Grayson ("Akkadian Prophecies," 7) noted the connection, as did Hallo ("Akkadian Apocalypses," 242) who regarded the similarities as a reflection of the authors' concern to establish these prophecies ". . . as a particularly infallible example of prediction." In *Babylonian Historical-Literary Texts*, Grayson seems more reserved about a connection; he largely repeats (p. 13) what he wrote about the subject in "Akkadian Prophecies," but he adds later that "there is no meaningful connection with omen literature" (22) and terms the relation "purely stylistic" (16). "What could be more natural for the authors of these texts than to draw upon their extensive scribal education in omen literature . . . for their 'predictions'" (16). The salient point remains, though, that there is some connection even if it is only stylistic. See also Grayson, "Divination and the Babylonian Chronicles" in *La divination en Mésopotamie*, 69–76. R. D. Biggs ("More Babylonian 'Prophecies,'" 117), however, considers these texts ". . . simply a peculiar part of the vast Mesopotamian omen tradition, from which the 'prophecies' appear to differ only because they lack protases. . . ."

[62] So Borger, "Gott Marduk," 23. Grayson (*Babylonian Historical-Literary Texts*, 15) calls attention to the facts that Text B, unlike the prophecies, has a mythological introduction and ties with astrological literature.

[63] "More Babylonian 'Prophecies,'" 117–28. The tablet (Oriental Institute museum no. A 32332) is written in a neo-Babylonian script. Biggs' fragment betrays, in the section which follows the main text, a strong connection with astrology (ll. 32–38).

[64] Ibid., 117–18; but see the strictures of Lambert, "History and the Gods," 176.

takes control of the temples, after which plague and famine come (as punishment?); the reign ends; (25f.) the king and his family are all killed; the feeling of the country changes and all take up arms; there is fighting among kingdoms; the gods consult, the king's reign is short (?); (27) Amorites attack, sanctuaries, king and people are destroyed; there is an omen relating to Ešnunna, and Ešnunna is reinhabited, and the land is secure; (29f.) destruction of Elam, there is [peace (?)] in the major cities[65]

Biggs thinks that the first six lines, which are too fragmentary to permit any firm conclusions, are to be understood as a long omen protasis (the tenses are preterite), while the remainder of the main text consists of a series of predictions which often take the form of omen apodoses that are attested elsewhere.[66] Thus, in his view, the composition begins with an expanded omen protasis and continues with a long series of omen apodoses which express the predictions. Whether all features of his analysis are correct remains to be seen, but at least a recognizable similarity with omens in language and often in form is evident. Note should also be taken of the mythological setting of 11. 1–6. Text B here offers some information regarding the context in which the prognostications about political events are placed. It appears from the broken text that a message from the gods is involved. Nothing is said, however, about who received the revelation.

From the five prophecy texts and from Text B one may justifiably conclude that omen literature played an important role in the evolution of these varieties of predictive literature. The language of the predictions demonstrates that omens were indeed *a* source from which the prophetic authors of Mesopotamia drew their inspiration.

## 4. Summary

The essential points of the preceding analysis may be formulated as follows. Though omens, which were recorded from a very early time, continued to be copied, created, and edited throughout the history of cuneiform literature, their contents were sufficiently useful for diversion into new areas. Their protases could be termed proto–scientific statements because they consist of organized, rather complete lists of observed phenomena (and apparently non-observed items in some cases) in different fields of mantic interest. They may have supplied some data for the more strictly scientific advances in disciplines such as astronomy which Babylonian scholars refined to an astonishing degree in the first millennium. Apodoses of omens clearly reflect a far different concern, but these predictive statements furnished material and language for the prognostications found in Akkadian prophe-

[65] "More Babylonian 'Prophecies,'" 119.
[66] Ibid., 118.

cies and in works such as Text B (if it is not to be included among the prophecies) that exhibit definite similarities with the Jewish apocalypses in which surveys of history figure.

These data about omen literature and its developments in new contexts appear to be of extraordinary value for explaining the evolution of Enochic lore in the early Hellenistic period. Enoch—the Jewish counterpart of Enmeduranki, the mythical founder of the powerful and widely competent guild of the *bārû*-diviners—was at first associated almost exclusively with pseudo-scientific pursuits and hardly at all with prediction (especially in the Astronomical Book [*1 Enoch* 72-82] and much of the book of Watchers [*1 Enoch* 1-36]). It seems, however, that under the impress of the religious and political crisis instigated by Antiochus IV (175-64), Enoch, the traditional recipient and revealer of "scientific" information, became for various authors the seer of apocalyptic visions in which *vaticinia ex eventu* abound as the past and future of the chosen nation are depicted and in which attention focuses upon the ultimate *dénouement* of historical injustices (the Apocalypse of Weeks [*1 Enoch* 93:1-10; 91:11-17] and the Book of Dreams [*1 Enoch* 83-90]). In other words, Enochic traditions reveal central features and developments which parallel very closely the twofold nature of omens and their evolution in scientific and predictive directions in Mesopotamia. It seems unlikely, given the traditional association of Enoch with Enmeduranki, that these developments occurred independently. It is far more reasonable to suppose that mantic traditions from Mesopotamia provided a considerable part of the context within which Jewish Enochic literature arose and grew. This sort of influence from Mesopotamia was possible over a long historical span and was directly possible from the exile onwards into the Hellenistic age. It is necessary to add, though, that the prominent role of a climactic eschatology in Enoch's apocalyptic dreams and visions distinguishes them from the Akkadian prophecies which, according to the published fragments, do not express a similar conviction that human history is moving toward a decisive culmination after which entirely new conditions will prevail. It is doubtful whether any cuneiform document offers an eschatology in this more restricted sense. In a fragment that Seneca attributes to Berossus but whose authenticity has been questioned, one reads of the belief that there will be a final cataclysm when the stars converge in Cancer. Yet, even here one does not find an expectation that after this event there will be a new, enduring life and world.[67] As a result, there is no reason to suppose that the

[67] See Lambert, "History and the Gods," 177. Jacoby (*Die Fragmente*, 397, no. 21) lists the passage from Seneca under "(Pseudo-) Berossos von Kos." Cf. also Lambert, "Berossus and Babylonian Eschatology," *Iraq* 38 (1974) 171-73. Burstein (*The* Babyloniaca, 31-32) argues for the authenticity of the fragment, as had Schnabel (*Berossos*, 17-19).

full eschatological component of Jewish apocalypses derives from Mesopotamian sources. It would, of course, have been virtually impossible for a traditional Jewish writer in the early Hellenistic period to lack an eschatology due to the undeniable influence of biblical prophecy. Biblical, prophetic eschatology does not prepare one fully for the flowering of apocalyptic eschatology but it provides an explanation for considerable portions of it. Perhaps other influences, such as those now recorded in texts which express Persian eschatologies, provided additional stimuli. This issue will be considered at a later point. Here it is sufficient to have established that divination, which was traditionally associated with the seventh man/king, contributed in a major fashion to the development of Enochic apocalyptic literature.

## C. Divination in the Old Testament

One of the major theses of this book is that mantic wisdom was an important contributory factor in the evolution of Jewish apocalypticism as exemplified by the early Enochic literature. One obstacle in the way of drawing this conclusion is the fact that several biblical passages picture divination and its practitioners in an overwhelmingly negative light. If the writers of Jewish apocalyptic literature had been wholesale innovators, there would be no difficulty here; but there is every reason to believe that in most respects they were traditionalists who were extremely well acquainted with the Scriptures and who attributed high authority to them. Since this circumstance may raise questions about a strong connection between mantic wisdom and apocalypticism, the evidence regarding divination in the OT should be sketched in order to set the issue within a larger context. The present concerns do not require that the topic be discussed in detail; only a few basic points need to be made.[68]

While there are negative references to divination elsewhere, it is especially in prophetic and prophetically influenced literature from approximately the exilic period that divination is frontally assaulted. Deut 18:9-22 is the principal passage: it not only bans various sorts of diviners and magicians but also locates this opposition within a theological context.

There shall not be found among you any one who burns his son or his daughter

---

[68] There are several recent but brief analyses of divination in Israel. The most valuable is A. Caquot, "La divination dans l'Ancient Israël," *La divination*, 1.83–113; see also O. Eissfeldt, "Wahrsagung im Alten Testament," *La divination en Mésopotamie*, 141–46; B. O. Long, "Divination," *IDBSup* 241–43 (cf. I. Mendelsohn, "Divination," *IBD* 1. 856–58); Long, "The Effect of Divination upon Israelite Literature," 489-97. For the prophetic literature, cf. G. Fohrer, "Prophetie und Magie," *ZAW* 78 (1966) 25–47.

as an offering, any one who practices divination (*qōsēm qĕsāmîn*),[69] a sooth-sayer (*mĕʿônēn*),[70] or an augurer (*mĕnaḥēš*),[71] or a sorcerer, or a charmer, or a medium, or a wizard, or a necromancer. For whoever does these things is an abomination to the Lord; and because of these abominable practices the Lord your God is driving them out before you. . . . For these nations, which you are about to dispossess, give heed to soothsayers (*mĕʿônĕnîm*) and to diviners (*qōsĕmîm*); but as for you, the Lord your God has not allowed you to do so.

The Lord your God will raise up for you a prophet like me from among you, from your brethren—him you shall heed . . . and I will put my words in his mouth, and he shall speak to them all that I command him (18:10-12, 14-15, 18b; cf. Isa 8:19-20).

The import of these lines is difficult to miss: The Lord of Israel has chosen to communicate with his people about the future (see vv 21-22) through words revealed to prophets, not through signs disclosed to diviners.

A similar contrast between the clear prophetic word and the opaque sign of the diviner appears in Deutero-Isaiah. Since he wrote within a neo-Babylonian setting, it is not surprising that he alludes to diviners including astrologers. He does so in a wholly negative way and contrasts their methods with the unmistakable and certain manner in which the Lord, the creator, divulges what is to occur:

(I am the Lord) who frustrates the omens (*ʾōtôt*) of
    liars,[72] and makes fools of diviners (*qōsĕmîm*);
Who turns wise men (*ḥăkāmîm*) back,
    and makes their knowledge (*daʿtām*) foolish;
Who confirms the word of his servant,
    and performs the counsel of his messengers . . . (44:25-26ab).

The prophet declares to the "virgin daughter of Babylon," (47:1) whose

---

[69] S. R. Driver (*Deuteronomy* [ICC; 3rd ed.; Edinburgh: Clark, 1902] 223) wrote that *qsm* "is the word most commonly used to express the idea of *divining* in general." In 1 Sam 6:2 it is used for Philistine diviners.

[70] The precise referent of this word remains unclear; see Driver, *Deuteronomy*, 224, and Caquot, "La divination dans l'Ancien Israël," 85, for some of the views that have been advanced.

[71] Driver (*Deuteronomy*, 225) suggests that a *mĕnaḥēš* may be one who divines from natural omens. This is the term used for Joseph's divining with a cup in Gen 44:5. It may be that, in enumerating these many ways of communication with the supernatural, the writer's aim was completeness and that not all of the terms refer to distinguishable experts and practices (so von Rad, *Deuteronomy* [Old Testament Library, Philadelphia: Westminster, 1966] 123).

[72] The term in the MT is *baddîm*; it is almost certainly to be emended to *bārîm* by the simple interchange of *d* and *r*. This is suggested by the parallel term in the next line—*qōsĕmîm*—as many commentators (e.g., C. Westermann, *Isaiah 40-66* [Old Testament Library, Philadelphia: Westminster, 1969] 152 n. a; cf. KB 146) have recognized. Thus, in this passage Deutero-Isaiah mentions *bārû*-diviners.

downfall he perceives so vividly, the weakness of her famous devices for attaining security:

> Stand fast in your enchantments
> and your many sorceries,
> with which you have laboured from your youth;
> perhaps you may be able to succeed,
> perhaps you may inspire terror.
> You are wearied with your many counsels;
> let them stand forth and save you,
> those who divide the heavens,
> who gaze at the stars (*haḥōzîm bakkôkābîm*),
> who at the new moons predict
> what shall befall you (47:12–13).

While the divinatory methods for ascertaining the future were found to fail, the Second Isaiah frequently asserts that what the Lord predicts will surely occur. Isa 46:9bc–11 makes the point eloquently:

> for I am God, and there is no other;
> I am God, and there is none like me,
> declaring the end from the beginning
> and from ancient times things not yet done,
> saying, "My counsel shall stand,
> and I will accomplish all my purpose,"
> calling a bird of prey from the east,
> the man of my counsel from a far country,
> I have spoken, and I will bring it to pass;
> I have purposed, and I will do it.[73]

The prophetic opposition to pagan divination shows, strangely, that Israel's religious thinkers accepted the fundamental tenet of the mantic arts: through communication with the deity, the future can be known. This is the central point: it is not the presuppositions of divination that prophetic writers oppose; rather, it was the improper, idolatrous religious system within which such divining occurred.[74]

The last proposition is consistent with the many biblical passages which

---

[73] On these passages from 2 Isaiah, see Wm. McKane, *Prophets and Wise Men* (SBT 1/44; London: SCM, 1965) 94–97.

[74] As Deut 18:10–11 shows, some methods per se were excluded. This ought not to be taken to mean, however, that all Israelite religious leaders at all times advocated a common policy vis-à-vis divination. Cf. the comments of Collins, *The Apocalyptic Vision of the Book of Daniel*, 32–33.

indicate that various sorts of divination not only were practiced in Israel[75] but in several cases enjoyed official priestly sanction as well. Two kinds of sacerdotal objects are rather familiar—the ephod, and the *ʾûrîm* and *tummîm*. Much energy has been devoted to the effort to identify the exact nature of these objects, but, regardless what they were, they functioned in mantic ways.[76] Sacred lots are also well attested for making choices (e.g., Jos 18:6); Joseph is said to have divined with his cup (Gen 44:5); and the Balaam stories contain several references to his (successful) mantic labors (Num 22:7; 23:23; 24:1).[77]

While several of these mantic techniques appear to have been removed from use at relatively early periods,[78] one sort of divination that survived and became popular was dream interpretation. There are several biblical references to enigmatic dreams that required expert decoding, the best known of which are found in the Joseph cycle and the Daniel stories. These stories also presuppose that the future can be known precisely and that Israel's God reveals it through means which require interpretation—such as symbolic dreams. In each of these stories there is criticism of Egyptian or Babylonian dream analysts, but in no case is this sort of divination per se called into question. Once again the point is that knowledge of what will happen comes only from Israel's God and that such esoteric knowledge he gives only to those who remain faithful to him (Gen 40:8; 41:16, 25, 28, 32, 39; Dan 2:19–23, 27–28 [these verses are especially apt: "Daniel answered the king, 'No wise men, enchanters, magicians, or astrologers can show to the king the mystery which the king has asked, but there is a God in heaven who reveals mysteries, and he has made known to King Nebuchadnezzar what will be in the latter days'"], 30, 45, 47; 4:9, 18).[79] The Danielic stories offer dreams that refer to

---

[75] There is no unmistakable reference to hepatoscopy by an Israelite in the OT; nevertheless, discovery of clay liver models at Hazor makes it likely that extispicy was no alien phenomenon in Israel (see Landsberger and Tadmor, "Fragments of Clay Liver Models From Hazor," 201–17).

[76] They gave yes or no answers in some fashion. For the ephod, see 1 Sam 23:9–12—one of several instances of its use in the story of David's rise—and, for the *ʾûrîm* and *tummîm*, cf. Num 27:21; Ezra 2:63 = Neh 7:65. They were, according to Exod 28:30 and Lev 8:8 to be placed in the high priests' breastpiece.

[77] The Balaam story exemplifies the theses being advanced here: he practices divination and receives divine messages but only from Israel's God (thus the repeated emphasis that he can speak only what God declares [e.g., 22:18–20]). The Balaam story has a particular importance for the portrait of Enoch, as *1 Enoch* 1:1–3a borrows heavily from these chapters to describe Enoch. See below, chap. V (cf. also 93:1, 3a; chap. VI below).

[78] See Caquot, "La divination dans l'Ancien Israël," 87–88 (regarding the *ʾûrîm* and *tummîm*).

[79] The stories include disparaging comments about Egyptian (Gen 40:8; 41:8, 15, 24) and

eschatological events (2:28), unlike the Joseph cycle. But in both the future is revealed by the true God through dreams given to foreigners—dreams that could be decoded only by God's messengers. Dream divination thus is placed in a new theological context.[80]

Revelation via dreams that required interpretation was found already in some late prophetic literature—especially Proto-Zechariah. There one meets a figure who becomes crucial in accounts of visions in apocalyptic works—the interpreting angel (Zech 1:9, 14; 1:19; 2:3; 4:5-7, 11-14; 5:3, 5-11; 6:4-8). Daniel as well needs assistance in order to understand the difficult visions/ dreams which he sees in the latter half of the book (7:16-18, 23-27; 8:15-17, 19-26; Daniel did not understand the vision [8:27]; 9:20-27; 10:10-14 [Daniel understood, 10:1]; the angel reveals the remainder of the book).

> Thus we are in a very different theological atmosphere from that of Old Testament prophecy. God no longer declares his ʿēṣā plainly through the dābār of his prophet, but his communications are hidden in the riddle-like contents of visions and dreams and are unintelligible except to those who have been initiated into their mysteries. The prophet has been replaced by the interpreter who, in virtue of his God-given bīnā, can crack the code in which God conceals his detailed plans for the future, and so has the same powers of exact prediction as the Babylonian specialists claimed to possess through their closely guarded techniques.[81]

Thus divination was no stranger to ancient Israel and to Judeans of the Hellenistic period. They clearly practiced various mantic techniques, forbade others, and placed all permissible ones within the framework of their monotheistic theology. Opposition to pagan divination centered on the fact that it was pagan, not that it was mantic. Dream interpretation (oneiromancy) continued from earlier times into the period when apocalyptic literature arose. As a result, to maintain that divination contributed to the rise of apocalypticism is not to assert an impossibility; this sort of wisdom was in many ways acceptable on Jewish soil.

Babylonian (Dan 1:20; 2:4-11, 27; 4:7, 18) dream interpreters. On these verses, see E. L. Ehrlich, *Der Traum im Alten Testament* (BZAW 73; Berlin: Töpelmann, 1953) 65-85; 90-122. Regarding Daniel's expertise in dream interpretation, see 1:17 (cf. McKane, *Prophets and Wise Men,* 98; Oppenheim, *The Interpretation of Dreams,* 210).

[80] McKane, *Prophets and Wise Men,* 98-99.

[81] Ibid., 100. See also D. S. Russell, *The Method and Message of Jewish Apocalyptic* (Old Testament Library; Philadelphia: Westminster, 1964) 161-63.

# IV

## ENOCH AND ASTRONOMICAL REVELATIONS

It was maintained above (chap. II) that Enoch's biblical life-span of 365 years indicated that already in the sixth or fifth century a priestly Jewish writer associated his name with astronomical phenomena and that this association appears to have derived ultimately from Enmeduranki's relationship with the solar deity Shamash. It may be that other writers in the Persian period (ca. 539–330) recorded or developed traditions about Enoch, but, if they did, their labors have vanished. In fact, the only other biblical reference to him is in the Chronicler's genealogy (1 Chr 1:3). Whatever may have been the fate of Enochic traditions—whether written or oral—in the centuries following the priestly redaction of the pentateuch, Enoch's association with astronomy was not forgotten but re-emerged with a vengeance in the Astronomical Book (= AB) of *1 Enoch* (chaps. 72–82). Since this is probably the oldest composition that circulated under his name, it is the natural place at which to begin a study of the evolution of Enochic traditions in ancient Judaism.

### A. Literary Issues

The contents of the AB distinguish it as a unit from its present literary environment.[1] Other sections of *1 Enoch* (e.g. the Book of Watchers, chaps. 1-36) deal with the sun, moon, and stars among other topics, but these 11 chapters are devoted almost exclusively to a highly schematic and decidedly primitive astronomy. For example, 72:2–37 detail the movement of the sun through six "gates" in a 12–month, 364–day year and give the varying ratios for hours of daylight and of night throughout the months. Chaps. 73 and 74 then add a somewhat contorted description of the laws by which the moon operates and contain a comparison of the lengths of lunar and solar years. It was not only in content, though, that early critics of *1 Enoch* separated the AB from the preceding Parables (37–71); they also viewed it as part of a

---

[1] It is also formally distinguished from chap. 71 by its opening words ("The book of the revolutions of the lights of heaven" [72:1]) and from chap. 83 by the introductory words of that new section ("And now, my son Methuselah, I will show you all the visions which I saw").

composition that was originally independent of the Parables. That is, for some time a prominent view about the structure of *1 Enoch* was that it consisted of three principal parts: 1) a "groundwork" which included 1–36 and 72–105; 2) the Parables (37–71); and 3) various Noachic additions (e.g., 6–11; 64–69; 106–7).[2] R. H. Charles, however, was able to demonstrate that *1 Enoch* consisted not of three but of five independent works—a position that remains standard today. These components are: 1) the Book of Watchers (1–36); 2) the Parables (37–71); 3) the AB (72–82); 4) the Book of Dreams (83–90); and 5) the Epistle of Enoch (91–107). Charles recognized that each of these parts combined elements from disparate sources, but in their present forms they have at least an editorial unity.[3]

The AB is, then, generally and properly regarded as an independent composition. In it, Enoch gives to his son Methuselah a detailed, first-person account of what the angel Uriel had revealed to him about the sun, moon, and stars. Students of these chapters have observed, however, that as it now stands in the Ethiopic version—the only complete text extant—the AB is neither completely unified nor in its pristine order.[4] As these matters are of importance for dating developments in the Enochic legends, they should be examined in this context.

Charles' argument that the AB was composite and re-arranged proceeded as follows.[5] 72:1, which is an introduction to the entire book, shows that the purpose of the AB was to describe the laws that govern the sun, moon, and stars.

> The book of the revolutions of the lights of heaven, each as it is, according to their classes, according to their (period of) rule and their times, according to their names and their places of origin, and according to their months, which Uriel, the holy angel who was with me and is their leader, showed to me; and he showed me all their regulations exactly as they are, for each year of the world and for ever, until the new creation shall be made which will last for ever.

---

[2] See the convenient survey of older theories in Charles, *The Book of Enoch or 1 Enoch* (Oxford: Clarendon, 1912) xxx–xlvi. Among the eminent scholars who defended a division of this sort were A. Dillmann and E. Schürer. H. Ewald saw essentially the same major units but divided the groundwork into two parts. F. Martin (*Le livre d'Hénoch* [Paris: Letouzey et Ané, 1906] lxii–lxxii) offers another survey of nineteenth–century views on these matters.

[3] He had argued for a pentateuchal division already in *The Book of Enoch* (Oxford: Clarendon, 1893; the 1912 volume is actually a second edition of this work, though Charles himself said that it was ". . . not so much a second edition as a new book"[v]). See *The Book of Enoch*, xlvi–lvi (this and all future references are to the 1912 edition).

[4] E.g., Beer, "Das Buch Henoch," 224–30; Martin, *Le livre d'Hénoch*, lxxxiii–lxxxiv; Charles, *The Book of Enoch*, xlix–l.

[5] *The Book of Enoch*, xlix–l; 147–49.

There is no hint in this verse that any but purely scientific interests motivate the author; the theological notice about the new creation serves merely to indicate that as long as the present creation endures the laws of the heavens will remain immutable. The writer relentlessly pursues his astronomical concerns (adding a few related geographical notes in 77) until 79:1 which, with the remainder of this summary chapter, appears to be a conclusion: "And now, my son Methuselah, I have shown you everything, and the whole law of the stars of heaven is complete." While reference is made to wrongdoing in 75:1–3, the evil in question consists only of failure to intercalate four days at the appropriate times in the year. Chap. 82 evidences a similar interest: its focus is astronomical, and transgressing is specified as not adding the four intercalary days (see vv 4–7).

The contents of chaps. 80–81 differ radically from those in 72–79, 82. The emphasis in 80, far from being scientific, is purely ethical. Furthermore, in this chapter it is said that the natural order will change in "the days of the sinners" (v 2) who are characterized as worshipers of the stars (v 7). The writer forecasts extraordinary celestial disruptions that will have severe repercussions on the earth: the year will grow shorter, crops will be tardy, the moon will appear at unusual times and with abnormal brightness, while the stars will alter their assigned courses and be visible at the wrong times (vv 2–7). Chap. 81, too, is hardly scientific. Here, at Uriel's bidding, Enoch reads from heavenly tablets the deeds of all humankind; righteous and sinner are distinguished but not by their calendrical preferences; and provision is made for Enoch to remain with his children for one year in order to teach them what he had learned. After one year, it is said, three angels[6] (who have not been mentioned before in the AB) would return to take Enoch from his family (v 6).

These data led Charles to the conclusion that the original components of the AB were 72–79, 82. Since, however, the latter part of 82 (vv 9–20), which narrates the "law of the stars" (v 9), seems to be the referent of 79:1 ("the whole law of the stars of heaven is complete"), he suggested that the original order was 72–78, 82, 79. It appears that Charles and others were correct in bracketing 80–81 as elements alien to the presumed original form of the AB, and one could add to the evidence that Enoch is mentioned by name only in 80–81 (80:1 and 81:1). Elsewhere, his identity can be deduced only from the speaker's words "my son Methuselah" (76:14; 79:1; 82:1; cf.

---

[6] One group of mss (Charles' β group, Knibb's Eth II) reads *three*, while mss from the other family (Charles' α, Knibb's Eth I) read *seven*. See Knibb, *The Ethiopic Book of Enoch*, 1.268; Charles, *The Ethiopic Version of the Book of Enoch* (Anecdota oxoniensia; Oxford: Clarendon, 1906) 154 n. 25.

81:5). Nevertheless, it is unnecessary to transfer all of chap. 82 to a position before 79. There is adequate reason for thinking that 82:9-20 belong there (although stars are mentioned in chap. 75), but 82:1-8 form a credible conclusion to the AB.[7] In this regard it is of some interest that 4QEnastr d, which probably preserves the end of 82 that is lacking in Ethiopic (on this see below), contains what appears to be a synchronization of the movements of the sun and stars. Thus it may be that in its original form chap. 82 was longer than in the Ethiopic version[8] and that it contained additional information about stars to which 79:1 refers.[9]

## B. The Date of the AB

Due to the results of the preceding literary analysis, one is faced in dating the AB with the complication that it now consists of an original treatise which has been subjected to at least one redaction and to some

---

[7] So Beer, "Das Buch Henoch," 228; Martin, Le livre d'Hénoch, lxxxiv. O. Neugebauer (The 'Astronomical' Chapters of the Ethiopic Book of Enoch [72-82]: Translation and Commentary, With Additional Notes on the Aramaic Fragments by Matthew Black [Det Kongelige Danske Videnskabernes Selskab Matematisk-fysiske Meddelelser, 40:10; Copenhagen: Munksgaard, 1981] 4-5) finds two versions: Chaps. 72-76 (74 is probably an intrusion) and 77-79:1, to which fragments have been added (the section 80:2-82:3 forms an apocalyptic intrusion). G. W. E. Nickelsburg (Jewish Literature Between the Bible and the Mishnah [Philadelphia: Fortress, 1981] 150-51) suggests that 72-80 belong together and that 81 and 82 are additions.

[8] There is general agreement that chap. 82 is incomplete in its Ethiopic form; see Martin, Le livre d'Hénoch, lxxxiv, 192; Charles, The Book of Enoch, 178; Milik, The Books of Enoch, 297. 4QEnastr[b] 26, which will be discussed in more detail below, gives some indication of a disturbance in order in the context of 79:1. Milik (ibid. 294) suggests that this Aramaic fragment reflects the order 79:3-5 + 78:17-79:2. The fragment is too damaged to be certain, but at least it shows that it is not implausible to propose that something other than the end of the present chap. 78 once stood in this vicinity.

[9] Some scholars have also raised questions about the authenticity of chap. 77, which deals with geographical matters (e.g., Martin, Le livre d'Hénoch, lxxxiv). Martin's difficulties with the chapter appear to be based on its contents alone: why should there be a geographical section in the middle of an astronomical work? However, 77 follows naturally on 76 which treats the 12 portals of heaven from which the winds emerge, three of which are located toward each of the four cardinal points of the compass (vv 2-3). These are detailed in the remainder of the chapter, and 77 develops the division further by describing the four quarters of the earth and their contents—three groups of seven prominent features: mountains, rivers, islands. In other words, chap. 77 is a natural development of 76 which in turn is at home in an astronomical work. Beer ("Das Buch Henoch," 228-29) objected that 72:1, which provides an overview of the book, does not prepare the reader for 76-77; but it is precarious to exclude parts from the book on this basis. Furthermore, there is no reason to believe that the author meant to list each of the following topics in this introductory verse; it functions as a summarizing, brief title of the composition. Also, see below for a suggestion regarding why geographical sections are in fact to be expected in an astronomical work such as the AB.

dislocation. Chaps. 80–81 can be set aside temporarily as later additions while attention should now be given to the evidence for dating the original work. It would be interesting and perhaps instructive to review what nine-teenth–and early–twentieth century scholars proposed on this issue,[10] but the evidence of the Qumrân manuscripts has rendered their efforts largely obsolete. These MSS have, nevertheless, introduced new sets of problems as they have assisted in solving old puzzles.

## 1. The Qumrân MSS of the AB

Milik, who labels his publication of the AB MSS "preliminary,"[11] has identified four copies of the book amid the mass of fragments from cave 4. On the basis of paleographic criteria he dates them as follows:

Enastr$^a$      end of the third/ beginning of the second century B.C.
Enastr$^b$      early years A.D.
Enastr$^c$      middle of the first century B.C.
Enastr$^d$      second half of the first century B.C.[12]

Enastr$^a$ is clearly of the greatest importance for dating the book, but, without explanation and to the dismay of his reviewers, Milik furnishes neither transcription, translation, nor photograph of it. Consequently at present one cannot check the basis of his verdict about its date, though his well known skill as an epigrapher inspires confidence in its accuracy.[13] The result is, if one accepts Milik's date for Enastr$^a$, that B.C. ± 200 becomes the *terminus ad quem* for the book.

Before one accepts this date, however, he should be aware that there are special problems related to the MSS that Milik has identified as belonging to the Aramaic version of the AB. His description of their contents highlights the issue pointedly:

> The majority of the fragments, those of Enastr$^a$ in their entirety and the great
> majority of those of Enastr$^b$, belong to an elaborately detailed and monotonous

---

[10] Many of the proposals are recorded in the surveys of Charles and Martin mentioned in n. 2. A date at some point in the second half of the second pre–Christian century was usually defended. For example, Martin and Charles correctly saw a reference to the AB in *Jub.* 4:17 (21) and used this allusion to fix a *terminus ad quem*—for Martin before 135 (*Le livre d'Hénoch*, xcviii) and for Charles before 110 (*The Book of Enoch*, liii). While their dating of *Jubilees* gave them a *terminus ad quem*, neither of these scholars was able to specify a *terminus a quo*.

[11] *The Books of Enoch*, 273.

[12] Ibid., 7, 273–74.

[13] Milik (ibid. 273) writes that the script is similar to an "archaic or early Hasmonaean semiformal script of *ca.* 175–125 B.C."—the label and date that F. M. Cross gives to the two scripts in Figure 1, 11. 6–7 of his "The Development of the Jewish Scripts" in *The Bible and the Ancient Near East* (ed. G. E. Wright; Garden City: Doubleday, 1965) 175. But Milik also thinks that the script of Enastr$^a$ resembles that in Figure 1, 11. 2–5 (Cross dates 11. 2–4 to the third century, 1. 5 to the early second).

calendar in which the phases of the moon, day by day, were synchronized with
the movements of the sun in the framework of a year of 364 days; the calendar
also described the movements of the two heavenly bodies from one "gate" of the
sky to another. *This part of the work no longer exists in the Ethiopic version.*
Enastr^b and Enastr^c contain passages which correspond to various paragraphs
of the third section of the Ethiopic, but in a much more developed form.
Enastr^d provides remains of the final part of the work, *a part which is also lost
in the Ethiopic tradition* (italics mine).[14]

Of the four MSS, only Enastr^b,c overlap with known parts of the AB; MSS a
and d have texts which correspond to nothing in the Ethiopic AB. Moreover,
a textual comparison of Enastr^b,c with the Ethiopic MSS shows that even
these two MSS offer in most cases a considerably different text than the
Ethiopic version. There are, to be sure, lines in which the Aramaic and
Ethiopic match closely (e.g., Enastr^c 1 ii 1 and 76:3; 1 ii 9 and 76:10; 1 ii 14
and 76:13–14), but in others there is little or no similarity (e.g., Enastr^c 1 ii 3
and 76:4; 1 ii 8 and 76:8–9; and 1 ii 17–18 which should correspond to
something in the context of 77:3).[15] Regarding these two Aramaic MSS, it is
safe to say that usually there is a similarity of content but not of text with the
Ethiopic version.[16] Therefore, since Enoch's name or an indication from
which one could infer that he was speaking is never found in published parts
of the four Aramaic MSS, and since other, apparently non-Enochic calendrical
texts have been found at Qumrân,[17] there is some reason to suspect that the
Aramaic texts belong to a work other than the AB.

Yet, while there is some room for scepticism, it still seems the most
reasonable conclusion that Milik has correctly identified these four MSS as
exemplars of the AB. A vital link in the argument is Enastr^b. There would be
little reason, judging from the published evidence, to connect the synchronic
calendar of Enastr^a with the AB, had not Enastr^b preserved both remains of
it and traces of other sections which almost certainly belong to the AB. Milik
has noted additionally that the Ethiopic version appears to have preserved a
garbled reflex of the synchronic calendar in 73:1–74:9. He suspects that this
long and repetitive section of the original AB was abbreviated by a justifiably weary scribe at some point in the textual adventures of the book.[18]

---

[14] *The Books of Enoch,* 7–8.

[15] See ibid. 284-88.

[16] Cf. Knibb, *The Ethiopic Book of Enoch,* 2.13. His analysis of the Aramaic fragments is
valuable and more cautious than is Milik's. He has also managed to give the correct text in
several places in which mistakes in transcription have crept into Milik's book. See also the
treatment of the fragments in Neugebauer/Black, *The 'Astronomical' Chapters,* 34–40.

[17] *The Books of Enoch,* 61–64, 68–69.

[18] Ibid., 273, 275.

Enastr[d], too, seems to belong to an earlier form of the AB though it likewise overlaps with nothing in the present Ethiopic text. Identifying it as part of the AB is plausible because chap. 82 is incomplete and Enastr[d] contains a section that supplies some of the missing material. 82:10–20 deal with the divisions of the year, particularly with the four seasons. Four angels are said to handle the assignment of dividing the year into quarters: Melkiel, Melemmelek, Meleyal, and Narel (v 13). Melkiel's season (spring) is described in vv 15–17, and vv 18–20 treat Helemmelek's time (summer). Here the book ends without mention of the other two seasons about which the reader has been led to expect some account. Enastr[d] 1 i fits at some remove from v 20 since it mentions the winter (*štw* i.4). The text breaks off soon after and resumes in a fragmentary way in cols. ii and iii which speak about the stars—a fact which is consistent with the critical view that the end of chap. 82 belongs before 79.[19]

There is no escaping the fact that noteworthy differences separate many lines of Enastr[b,c] from the readings of the Ethiopic texts, but these variations should be evaluated within the context of several other givens. First, the Ethiopic version is corrupt in places (the end of 82, for example); this means that where the Aramaic and Ethiopic differ, the Aramaic very likely preserves a superior text. Second, textual corruption seems to have overtaken the AB almost from the beginning. This can be shown from a comparison of Enastr[b] and Enastr[c] in the lines for which they overlap.[20] There are numerous variants between them, whether in spelling (e.g., Enastr[b] 23.5 *kwkbyn*; Enastr[c] 1 ii 16 *kwkby*), in vocabulary (in the same lines as in the preceding example Enastr[b] reads *wbdkn*, Enastr[c] *bdyl kn*), or in text (the end of Enastr[b] 23.7 seems to be at least eight words shorter than Enastr[c] 1 ii 18). Third, while it is true that no published Aramaic fragment connects any of the four manuscripts with Enoch explicitly, in several cases one can reasonably surmise that the Aramaic texts contained the same indications of the speaker's identity as the Ethiopic MSS. In Enastr[b] 23.2, which corresponds to 76:14 ("I have shown to you, my son Methuselah"), part of the verb is visible (*ʾḥ[zyt]*) and there is space in the following lacuna to reconstruct the entire expression (cf. also Enastr[c] 1 ii 14).[21] Enastr[b] 26.6, which seems to represent 79:1 ("And now, my son Methuselah, I have shown you everything"), comes within one word of a definite identification of the speaker: *wkʿn mḥwʾ ʾnh lk bry[*.[22] As a result, one should agree with Milik

---

[19] Ibid., 296–97.
[20] Ibid., 287–91.
[21] Ibid., 289, 288.
[22] Ibid., 294.

that his four MSS represent the Aramaic version (or, more precisely, versions) of the AB, but because of the significant differences between the Aramaic and Ethiopic, one should be cautious about relying too heavily on the wording of the later Ethiopic text.

## 2. Allusions in Other Texts

Once Milik's identification of the four Aramaic MSS with the AB is accepted, one must also admit B.C. ± 200 (the paleographically determined date of Enastr^a) as the *terminus ad quem* for the book. Some scholars who published their conclusions before discovery of the 4Q Enochic MSS in the early 1950's assigned the book a date toward the middle of the second century B.C. but no one dated it as early as Enastr^a appears to be.[23] In his attempt to specify a *terminus a quo* for the AB, Milik has gone so far as to speak of the late Persian or early Hellenistic period as the time of composition.[24] His case for this remarkably ancient dating is based on allusions to the AB in external, datable literature. The earliest reference to the AB, in his opinion, occurs in Gen 5:23, "where the writer, having fixed the age of the patriarch at 365 years, implies, in guarded terms, the existence of astronomical works circulating under the name of Enoch."[25] He follows the lead of A. Jaubert in believing that biblical chronology, especially in the pentateuch, presupposes the 364-day solar calendar that is found in the AB, but he proceeds beyond her hypothesis in claiming that at the time of the priestly editor this calendar was already associated with Enoch. He also postulates that the original form of Gen 5:23 read 364 years as Enoch's age and that only later was the number corrected to 365 in harmony with improved calendrical knowledge.[26] Enoch's peculiar age at his removal does, as argued above, hint at astronomical associations with the patriarch, but it is one thing to say that writers associated him with astronomy and quite another to claim that there were astronomical compositions that circulated under his name in the sixth century B.C. In the AB and in several later works Enoch is depicted as the first human recipient of revelation regarding the 364-day calendar, but this fact need not entail that the association had been made when P wrote. Moreover, Gen 5:23 says nothing about written works—even "in guarded terms." Finally, there is neither versional nor manuscript evidence that Gen 5:23 ever read 364 rather than 365.[27]

[23] See Charles, *The Book of Enoch*, xxxvi, xxxix–xlii for examples.
[24] *The Books of Enoch*, 8; cf. also his "Fragments grecs du livre d'Hénoch (P. Oxy. xvii 2069)," *Chronique d'Égypte* 46 (1971) 341. He does, however, except chap. 81 (though strangely not 80) which he believes was written after B.C. 164 (*The Books of Enoch*, 13–14).
[25] Ibid., 8.
[26] Ibid.
[27] Cf. the similar critical remarks in Jonas C. Greenfield and Michael E. Stone, "The

Without the prop of Gen 5:23, Milik's case for a date in the Persian period collapses. This is not to say that the AB was not written then; it means only that there is at present no evidence for such a date. There is more reason to believe, however, that the AB's existence in ca. B.C. 200 (as indicated by the script of 4QEnastrᵃ) is confirmed by Pseudo-Eupolemus' book about the Jews.[28] This author, whom authorities regard as a Samaritan,[29] holds a certain fascination for students of Jewish Enochic traditions because he, as did the authors of early Enochic books, fused biblical traditions with similar stories from ancient Near Eastern and Greek literature.[30] His book is no longer extant, but it, too, was cited by that avid collector Alexander Polyhistor in his work *On the Jews.* As was noted before, Polyhistor's book is also lost, but Eusebius quoted extensively from it in his *Praeparatio Evangelica.* The two fragments that are now identified as Pseudo–Eupolemus' writings were included in Eusebius' excerpts (IX.17, 2-9; 18,2). Polyhistor attributed (or Eusebius thought he did) the first of the two fragments to the Jewish historian Eupolemus who wrote a *History of the Jews* in ca. B.C. 158[31] and

Books of Enoch and the Traditions of Enoch," *Numen* 26 (1979) 92–93. These scholars also observe that even if Gen 5:23 did imply the existence of Enochic astronomical works, there would be no guarantee that the AB was one of them.

[28] For the text of the two preserved citations, see F. Jacoby, *Die Fragmenta der griechischen Historiker* (vol. III C part 2; Leiden: Brill, 1958) 678–79 (724 frgs. 1–2). Determining the ancient title of the book has proved difficult. The text suggests that Pseudo–Eupolemus called it *peri Ioudaiōn tēs Assyrias* ("On the Jews of Assyria"), but the awkward *tēs Assyrias* may modify the word *polin* which occurs two words later in the line (so. J. Freudenthal, *Hellenistische Studien* 1 & 2: *Alexander Polyhistor und die von ihm erhaltenen Reste judäischer und samaritanischer Geschichtswerke* [Breslau: H. Skutsch, 1875] 207). Even with this reading, however, the line remains strange because *polin* is further modified by *Babylōna*. B. Z. Wacholder ("Pseudo–Eupolemus' Two Greek Fragments on the Life of Abraham" in his *Essays on Jewish Chronology and Chronography* [New York: Ktav, 1976] 76–77) has raised a question about the other two words in the alleged title—*peri Ioudaiōn*: would a Samaritan author (see the next note) have entitled a book about Abraham "On the Jews"? He proposes that *peri Ioudaiōn* refers to the book's contents and is not its title; it was a descriptive tag that Alexander Polyhistor applied to it.

[29] Freudenthal (*Alexander Polyhistor*, 82–103) first advocated this thesis, and it has generally been accepted since then. The principal evidence for it is the way in which Pseudo–Eupolemus refers to Mt. Gerizim. He wrote that Abraham, after defeating the kings and rescuing his nephew, was entertained by the priest–king Melchizedek at the temple of *argarizin* which Pseudo–Eupolemus translates as "mount of the most high" (*oros hypsistou*).

[30] See Wacholder, "Pseudo–Eupolemus' Two Greek Fragments," 75–105, for extensive documentation.

[31] While the identification is not certain, the historian Eupolemus and the ambassador Eupolemus (cf. 1 Macc 8:17; 2 Macc 4:11; *Ant.* 12.10, 6 §415) are often regarded as the same man. If they are not identical, they lived at the same time, since the historian wrote at the time of Demetrius I (161–150). For a defense of this view and bibliography, see Wacholder, *Eupole-*

the second to an anonymous source (*en de adespotois*). Since the contents of the two citations are largely the same (the second summarizes the first) but clash with some material in Eupolemus' book,[32] they have been assigned to a single but different author conveniently dubbed Pseudo-Eupolemus. The nature and limited extent of the two citations make a precise dating of Pseudo-Eupolemus' book impossible now, but some threads of evidence suggest that he may have written in ca. B.C. 200 or shortly thereafter.[33]

The extant lines of Pseudo-Eupolemus' composition include an attempt to deflate the proud claims of Egyptians that they had "discovered" astrology and other sciences by exalting the role of Abraham in the origin and dissemination of such knowledge. Both fragments deal with Abraham as a student and teacher of astral sciences, but in the first and far longer citation Enoch figures in a way that renders the thesis that Pseudo-Eupolemus knew the AB highly probable. For him Abraham was an ancient worthy who "surpassed all men in nobility and wisdom, who also discovered astrology and Chaldaean [science (?)]."[34] After migrating to Phoenicia (Pseudo-Eupolemus' term for the area that includes ancient Canaan), he taught the citizens there about "the changes [*tropas*] of the sun and moon and all things of that kind." Similarly, while in Egypt during the famine, "Abraham lived with the Egyptian priests in Heliopolis [!], teaching them many things. And he intro-

---

*mus: A Study of Judaeo-Greek Literature* (Monographs of the Hebrew Union College 3; Cincinnati/New York/Los Angeles/Jerusalem: HUC, 1974) 1–7.

[32] Wacholder ("Pseudo-Eupolemus' Two Greek Fragments," 76) refers to a discrepancy between the role of Moses in Eupolemus and that of Abraham (and Enoch) in Pseudo-Eupolemus, as well as to stylistic differences.

[33] See the discussion in Wacholder, ibid. 77–79. As he recognizes, however, this dating is hardly conclusive. Milik (*The Books of Enoch*, 9) speaks of a date "from fairly far back in the third century, since one of its objectives was the exaltation of the temple of Gerizim, founded in the time of Alexander." This can hardly be a solid argument for placing Pseudo-Eupolemus in the third century for two reasons: since so little of the work has survived, it cannot be said with confidence that praise of this sanctuary was one of its objectives; and there is no compelling reason, if it was one of its objectives, why a Samaritan writer would not wish to exalt its reputation in, say, B.C. 150. Cf. the comments of Greenfield and Stone, "The Books of Enoch and the Traditions of Enoch," 94–95 (though they are too sceptical about Pseudo-Eupolemus' knowledge of the AB).

[34] Translation of Wacholder, "Pseudo-Eupolemus' Two Greek fragments," 93–94. All other English citations from Pseudo-Eupolemus are taken from Wacholder's convenient translation in *Eupolemus*, Appendix B, 313–14. In this particular passage, however, he (doubtless accidentally) omits the reference to astrology from his rendering (313). The motif of Abraham as an astrologer/astronomer derives from Gen 15:5, it seems. For later references, see J. Bowker, *The Targums and Rabbinic Literature* (Cambridge: Cambridge University, 1969) 201–02; and M. Hengel, *Judaism and Hellenism* (2 vols.; Philadelphia: Fortress, 1974) 2.62 n. 264. In *Jub.* 12:16–21 Abraham passes a negative verdict on his earlier astronomical concerns.

duced [*eisēgēsasthai*] astrology and other sciences to them, saying that the Babylonians and he himself discovered them, but he traced the discovery to Enoch. And he (Enoch) was the first to discover astrology, not the Egyptians." As it now reads at two removes from the original, the text seems somewhat disjointed; it leaves one with the impression that Abraham regarded himself and the Babylonians as the inventors of astrology but that at the same time he believed that Enoch had earlier made this discovery.[35] However the textual difficulties of this passage are resolved, it appears an unavoidable conclusion that Pseudo-Eupolemus identified Enoch as the first astrologer/astronomer.

Following a short genealogy which embodies a Babylonian claim that the Phoenicians and Egyptians were latter-day offshoots of the line of Babylonian Belus, Pseudo-Eupolemus is quoted as saying: "The Greeks say that Atlas discovered astrology, Atlas being the same as Enoch.[36] And Enoch had a son Methuselah, who learned all things through the angels of God, and thus we gained our knowledge." This remarkable passage, which illustrates so graphically the syncretistic tendencies in pre-Maccabean literary circles in Palestine,[37] is almost certainly corrupt at the end. There it appears that it was Methuselah, not Enoch, who learned a wide variety of subjects from the angels. Every other indication in the fragment opposes this inference, though, and favors the supposition that some words have disappeared from the text thus distorting its pristine meaning.[38] If the last line is brought into agreement with the contents of the remainder of the fragment and of all other sources about Enoch, then Pseudo-Eupolemus asserts that 1) Enoch introduced astral and other sciences (cf. *Jub.* 4:17); 2) which he had learned from the angels of God; 3) he transmitted all of this information to his son Methu-

---

[35] The relevant section reads: *phamenon babylōnious tauta kai hauton heurēkenai, tēn de heuresin autōn eis enōch anapempein.* It may be that Pseudo-Eupolemus wrote something of this sort: the Babylonians say that even they themselves (reading \**phamenous . . . hautous*) discovered these things, but he (i.e., Abraham) traced discovery of them back to Enoch. Cf. *Ant.* 1. 8, 2 §§ 166-68.

[36] *Einai de ton atlanta ton auton kai enōch.* Wacholder's rendering may leave the impression that the Greeks made this identification, but it seems clear enough that Pseudo-Eupolemus is articulating his view in this independent clause. It ought not, therefore, be left dangling from the sentence that precedes it. On Atlas and his connections with astronomy, see K. Wernicke, "Atlas," *PW* 2/2, 2119-33; Wacholder, "Pseudo-Eupolemus' Two Greek Fragments," 88.

[37] Cf. Hengel, *Judaism and Hellenism,* 1.88-92.

[38] See Wacholder, "Pseudo-Eupolemus' Two Greek Fragments," 90. The surviving text reads: *tou de enōch genesthai huion mathousalan, hon panta di² aggelōn theou gnōnai, kai hēmas houtōs epignōnai.* Presumably Pseudo-Eupolemus had written that Enoch had a son Methuselah whom he *taught* all that he (Enoch) had learned through God's angels and thus we have received our knowledge.

selah; 4) through whom posterity became acquainted with the same wisdom. Now, though it must be admitted that Pseudo–Eupolemus could have derived some of these data from Genesis 5 and the rest from oral sources or written ones which have perished, the facts that he seems generally to have relied on written sources and that his description so aptly characterizes the AB and no other known work lead inevitably to the conclusion that Pseudo–Eupolemus was referring to the AB.[39] In the AB the angel Uriel reveals astronomical information to Enoch (72:1; 74:2; 75:3–4; 78:10; 79:6 [cf. v 2]; 82:7), and the latter relates it to Methuselah his son (76:14; 79:1; 82:1) who is commissioned to pass this knowledge to his progeny forever (82:1–2). Enoch does, of course, receive astronomical revelations in other sections of *1 Enoch* (e.g., 33–36) and elsewhere he relates the contents of his visions to Methuselah (83:1; 85:1–2; 91:1–2); but only in the AB does he divulge revealed astronomical data to his son. Just one detail separates Pseudo–Eupolemus' description from the AB as it has been preserved in Ethiopic: he says that Enoch learned all things through the angels, whereas the AB has one angel—Uriel— reveal all to him. If the reading in Pseudo–Eupolemus is correct and the Ethiopic tradition intact, then the discrepancy may be explained in one (or more) of several ways. Pseudo–Eupolemus may have deduced Enoch's association with more than one angel from Gen 5:22, 24 or he was also familiar with the Book of Watchers (*1 Enoch* 1–36) which supplies Enoch with several angelic guides (e.g., 21:5; 22:3; 23:4; 24:6). Neither explanation excludes the other, of course.

The first fragment of Pseudo–Eupolemus' book is significant for the present study not only because it testifies to the existence of the AB in perhaps ca. B.C. 200 (the script of Enastr[a] does as much) but also because it sheds some welcome light on the contents of the AB at that time. Pseudo–Eupolemus was clearly acquainted with more than just the technical astronomical teachings of the book; he also knew the editorial framework into which the scientific material had been placed: Enoch learned his astronomy (and geography) from an angel, taught it to Methuselah, and Methuselah conveyed it to posterity. Moreover, there is no certain reference to the ethical concerns of chaps. 80–81, though one could argue that the author had no occasion to use them, since he was writing about the origin of scientific disciplines.

A *terminus ad quem* for the AB of ca. B.C. 200 is supported, then, from two sides: paleography and an allusion to it in another work of approxi-

---

[39] Cf. Wacholder, ibid. 89, though he says only that Pseudo–Eupolemus' statement that Enoch had discovered astrology "was taken from the Book of Enoch or a work dependent on it." See also Milik, *The Books of Enoch*, 9.

mately this time.[40] The issue of a *terminus a quo* is far more difficult and at present seems beyond definitive resolution. Though Milik's case for a date prior to Genesis 5 in its final form is thoroughly unconvincing, the AB may be considerably older than B.C. 200. There is reason to believe that it ante-dates the Book of Watchers (*1 Enoch* 1–36), the oldest preserved MS of which dates from the first half of the second century B.C. (see the following chapter). Thus, a third–century date for the AB is almost assured, while a more ancient one is not impossible.

### C. The Portrait of Enoch in the AB

The AB incorporates some elements from Gen 5:21–24 into its portrait of Enoch; there is no compelling reason for reversing the two as Milik proposes. One obvious borrowing is that Enoch is pictured as the father of Methuselah, a second that he enjoyed angelic company during some of his 365 years, and a third that he was associated with astronomical phenomena. However, in each case the author of the AB has not merely borrowed but has also elaborated these elements which were so cryptically expressed in Gen 5:21–24 and has added specificity to them.

### 1. Enoch the Father of Methuselah

The long–lived but faceless patriarch of Genesis 5 becomes in the AB the recipient of his father's revealed wisdom and the conduit through whom it was conveyed to posterity (as in the emended text of Pseudo–Eupolemus). The AB itself is cast as Enoch's first-person narrative to his son (76:14; 79:1; 82:1, etc.). The most detailed exposition of Methuselah's role is in 82:1–2.

> And now, my son Methuselah, all these things I recount to you and write down for you; *I have revealed everything to you*[41] and have given you books about all these things. Keep, my son Methuselah, the books from the hand of your father, that you may pass (them) on to the generations of eternity. I have given wisdom to you and to your children, and to those who will be your children, that they may give (it) to their children for all the generations for ever—this wisdom (which is) beyond their thoughts.

---

[40] Milik (ibid., 10–11) finds another early–second century allusion to the AB in Sir 44:16 (perhaps originally located at 49:14). He thinks that the phrase there *ʾwt dʿt* ("sign of knowledge") refers to astronomy, among other topics, and infers that the author intended both the AB and the Book of Watchers when he wrote this phrase. It does, however, seem more likely that the writer was referring to Enoch's role as witness against humankind (as in *Jub.* 4:24). On this, see D. Dimant, "The 'Fallen Angels,'" 120 n. 332.

[41] Knibb's policy in his translation of *1 Enoch* is to mark his emendations of his base text (Rylands Ethiopic MS. 23) by italics. At this passage the MS omits the italicized words which are found in several forms in many other MSS (for the readings, see Knibb, *The Ethiopic Book of Enoch*, 1.270; for the policy, ibid. 2.47).

A point of interest here is that at this early stage the revelation of scientific data given to Enoch is to be published; it is not to be hidden as is often the case in later Jewish apocalypses.

## 2. Enoch in Angelic Company

In a sense one can say that the entire AB is an elaboration of the theme of Enoch's 300-year sojourn in angelic company. If chaps. 80–81 are excluded from the original form of the AB as suggested above, then the only angel with whom Enoch associates directly is Uriel. In fact, no others are mentioned (other than the guides of the stars, etc.) in this form of the book. Uriel, whose name (God is my light) is well suited to his role and doubtless derived from it, is said to be the leader of the luminaries (72:1), the one whom God had placed in command over all celestial lights (75:3; cf. 79:8). The AB credits him alone with showing Enoch all of the astronomical laws and geographical data in the book (72:1; 74:2; 75:3–4; 78:10; 79:2, 6; 82:7). The close association between Uriel and Enoch, which is here attested for the first time, will continue for centuries in the traditions of Enochic lore.[42] The precise means through which Enoch received Uriel's revelations is never specified, but virtually the only expressions that are used in passages which describe the process are that Uriel *showed* the phenomena to Enoch (72:1 [twice]; 74:2 [twice]; 75:3, 4; 78:10; 79:2, 6; 82:7; in all of these passages the verb is *'ar'ayani* [= he showed me]; note that Enoch also *shows* the same material to Methuselah in 76:14; 79:1) and that Enoch *saw* (72:3; 73:1; 74:1, 9; 75:6, 8; 76:1; 77:4, 5, 8; the verb is always *re'iku* [= I saw]).[43] The book gives no indication that Enoch's experiences are visionary; rather, a journey seems to be presupposed and thus actual seeing of the phenomena that Uriel shows him (e.g., 76:1).[44]

## 3. Enoch and Astronomy

a. Principal Teachings: Gen 5:23 does appear to connect Enoch with the solar year by giving his final age as 365, but the AB is far more explicit about

---

[42] In *1 Enoch* Uriel appears by name also at 9:1; 10:1 (only in Syncellus' citation); 19:1; 20:2; 21:5, 9; 27:2; 33:4 (all in the Book of Watchers). In the list of the four presences in 40:9 he is not mentioned. See the discussion of this angel and other references in Y. Yadin, *The Scroll of the War of the Sons of Light Against the Sons of Darkness* (Oxford: Oxford University, 1962) 235–40. Cf. also Milik (*The Books of Enoch*, 172–73; 110–11) who properly identifies the Vreveil of *2 Enoch* 22–23 (B) with Uriel; and Eckhard Rau, "Kosmologie, Eschatologie und die Lehrautorität Henochs: Traditions- und formgeschichtliche Untersuchungen zum äth. Henochbuch und zu verwandten Schriften" (Unpublished Ph.D. dissertation, University of Hamburg, Hamburg, 1974) 140–50.

[43] In 82:7 Enoch says that Uriel "inspired me" (*nafḥa dibēya*).

[44] So also John J. Collins, "The Jewish Apocalypses," *Apocalypse: The Morphology of a Genre* (Semeia 14; Missoula: Scholars, 1979) 38.

this subject and about several other related ones as well. Indeed, one could almost say that the AB is an affirmative answer to the rhetorical question of Job 38:33: "Do you know the ordinances of the heavens?" (*hăyādaʿtā ḥuq-qôt šāmayim*).[45] Uriel's many revelations to Enoch regarding the sun, moon, and stars include calculations about the relative lengths of the solar and lunar years. Chap. 72 describes the annual movement of the sun through six "gates"[46] in each of which it spends 30 days twice a year. However, the third, sixth, ninth, and twelfth months last 31 days; thus, during them the sun stays in its gate an extra day "because of its sign" (72:13, 19; cf. vv 25, 31). As a result, the solar year lasts exactly 364 days (72:32; 74:10, 12; 82:4, 6). The author calculates the lunar year at 354 days: six months of 30 days each, and six months of 29 days each (78:15–16; but see also 78:9). In 74:10–17 one finds data about the discrepancies between solar and lunar years over periods of three, five, and eight years; in these statements the solar year continues to be reckoned at 364, the lunar at 354 days.[47]

The AB furnishes the earliest unequivocal reference in Jewish literature to a solar calendar of 364 days and attributes its promulgation to Enoch, the original astronomer. The early date of the AB proves that the Qumrân-based Essenes did not invent this intriguing system; it was known at least 50 and perhaps many more years before that community was formed. It may no longer be possible to ascertain whether it was employed in the temple cultus in ca. B.C. 200 and before, but the fact that the original AB defines error as failure to reckon the four intercalary days in a year does point toward use of it by some people in some context long before it was pressed into service by arch-conservatives on the shores of the Dead Sea.[48] It is also interesting to

---

[45] The AB assumes a positive stance toward the possibility of human knowledge of natural laws; in this respect it clashes with some biblical passages (e.g., Job 38–41; Eccl. 8:17; 11:5) and agrees with others (cf. 1 Kgs 4:29–34). On this issue see Stone, "Lists of Revealed Things," 414–52; and I. Gruenwald, *Apocalyptic and Merkavah Mysticism*, 3–28.

[46] For an analysis of what the writer means by these gates, through which the moon, too, rises and sets, see O. Neugebauer, "Notes on Ethiopic Astronomy," *Or* 33 (1964) 51–60 (cf. p. 50); and *Ethiopic Astronomy and Computus* (Österreiche Akademie der Wissenschaften, Philosophisch-Historische Klasse, Sitzungsberichte 347; Veröffentlichungen der Kommission für Geschichte der Mathematik, Naturwissenschaften und Medizin, Heft 22; Vienna: Akademie der Wissenschaften, 1979) 156–61. Neugebauer rejects the general assumption by interpreters of *1 Enoch* who are not astronomers that the gates are equivalent to the signs of the zodiac; in that case the sun would have to run backwards from six to one.

[47] 74:10a, 11 calculates the solar year at 360 days, thus omitting the four intercalary days. Naturally, these figures are puzzling because they contradict other calculations in the book. As Martin (*Le livre d'Hénoch*, 172) observed, the author protests against those who reckon the solar year at 360 days (75:2). For a suggestion regarding the origin of this discrepancy, see below.

[48] See VanderKam, "The Origin, Character, and Early History of the 364-Day Solar Calendar: A Reassessment of Jaubert's Hypotheses," *CBQ* 41 (1979) 390–411.

observe regarding the 364-day year that the AB preserves not the slightest trace of the sort of vigorous polemic found in *Jubilees* (6:32-38) against use of lunar phases as accurate gauges of time. In the AB the lengths of lunar months and years are revealed to Enoch in the same objective, detached manner in which the author describes solar periods. The writer gives no evidence that he or those in sympathy with him were engaged in a calendaric dispute with adherents of a lunar or luni-solar arrangement. Some radical changes must have occurred between the writing of the AB and the composition of *Jubilees* and the Qumrân texts whose authors defend the 364-day solar calendar against lunar rivals.

b. A Proposal regarding the Background of Enoch's Astronomy: As the Sumerian king Enmeduranki proved to be the model for much of the biblical portrait of Enoch and thus ultimately for the Enoch of the AB, it is methodologically advisable to investigate traditions that surrounded him for possible explanations of Enoch's association with astronomy in the AB. It is conceivable that the AB reflects a larger cycle of ancient traditions about Enmeduranki/Enoch than does the terse priestly notice in Genesis—whether that cycle consisted of traditions which had been transmitted for many years in Judaism (either orally or in literature that is no longer available) or even of lore that the author had learned through renewed contact with Mesopotamian sources (or both). Enmeduranki was, as explained in chap. II, an intimate of the solar deity Shamash—a motif that finds theologically modified expression in Enoch's biblical age of 365 years at his translation. It appears that this motif was further elaborated in the AB in which a relatively large amount of space is devoted to a 364-day solar calendar (72:2-37; 75:1-2; 82:4-6) and to the details of synchronizing it with a lunar year of 354 days (chaps. 73-74; 78-79). Yet, when due allowance has been made for the effect of this solar motif, one is still left with the strong impression that the solar associations of the seventh man fail to provide an adequate explanation for the rather elaborate astronomical contents of the AB in which the author deals with the moon at greater length than with any other celestial body and in which the stars and geographical topics also figure prominently.

It seems that a more satisfactory explanation for the connection of Enoch with astronomy can be reached if one broadens the inquiry by recalling that Enmeduranki was considered the founder of the *bārûtum*—the high-ranking guild of diviners which has been described above. In ancient Mesopotamia one of the most widely practiced mantic arts—perhaps the most frequently employed kind in the Neo-Assyrian period and later—was astrology. It appears that the *bārû*, though astrology was not regarded as his specialty, was expected to be familiar with the technical literature in this field as he was with the omen series in other categories.[49] This association suggests some interesting possibilities for the topic under discussion, and in the paragraphs that follow it will be proposed that the science of the AB reflects certain elements from a primitive level of Mesopotamian astronomy and that it shares several traits with astrological divination. It is quite possible that the author of the AB derived his schematic scientific data precisely from mantic contexts in which it would be likely that earlier levels of science survived. In other words, the tentative proposal will be advanced that the divinatory environment in which tradition lodged the seventh antediluvian king (his association with Shamash and Adad can be subsumed under this rubric as well) was a contributory factor in the process of making Enoch the primal Jewish recipient of astronomical information. The following sections offer evidence of similarities between the astronomy of the AB and some early Mesopotamian astronomical texts and will focus on some analogies between Enoch's science and divination.

Before turning to those topics, however, a few preliminary comments are in order. First, showing one or two isolated parallels between the contents of the AB and primitive scientific concepts (or mythological notions) in other systems (whether Babylonian, Egyptian, or Greek) offers little or no help in answering the question of historical derivation.[50] Doubtlessly people in different places and times could arrive at the same elementary conclusions about astronomical phenomena independently of one another. It would be far more useful if a series of parallels—a more systematic resemblance— could be demonstrated between the science of the AB and some other system. Second, the evidence regarding the origins of Enochic traditions points unmistakably to Mesopotamia, and this fact makes it the most plausible area in which to begin a search for the antecedents of Enoch's schematic astronomy. Naturally, evidence from other parts of the Ancient Near East and indeed of the Greek world ought not to be ignored, but Babylon is the logical starting point for the inquiry. Third, and this point is closely related to the

---

[49] Here it suffices to recall K 2486.18 where, in this constitution of the *bārûtum*, the astrological omen series *Enūma Anu Enlil* and possibly interpretations based upon it are mentioned. No other text shows that the *bārû* was involved with *Enūma Anu Enlil* but in the Late Babylonian period experts in astrological omens were called *tupšar Enūma Anu Enlil*—a cover term which may include *bārûs* or at least from which one cannot exclude them.

[50] It is fair criticism to charge that commentators on the AB have to date done little more than this. For instance, Beer ("Das Buch Henoch") adduces a number of parallels (see his notes to 72:2, 5, 6; 74:14 [where he sees possible Greek influence]; 77:1, 3, 4, 8; 78:2) but he gives no indication of his having searched for a pattern to them. The same can be said against Charles (*The Book of Enoch*) whose comments show no improvement in this regard (e.g., on 72:3; 74:13–16 [for Greek influence]; 77:8; 78:9 [another Greek borrowing]).

second, it is known that Jewish leaders borrowed heavily from Babylon in calendrical matters—an area which is intimately connected with astronomy and in which astronomical endeavors appear to have their roots[51] from ca. B.C. 600 onwards. All of the month names in the traditional Jewish calendar are derived from the Akkadian names for them, and the methods by which new moons were determined (after months of either 30 or 29 days as in the AB [78:15-16]) and intercalary months added also stem from Babylon.[52] It must be said that the solar calendrical system of *1 Enoch* is not the one which was or became orthodox in Judaism, but the salient point is that Babylonian influence in various areas affecting the Jewish calendar is documented. This fact too, supplies *a priori* warrant for looking to that source for antecedents to Enoch's celestial science.

One set of data that suggests a comparison between the AB and an early level of Mesopotamian astronomy is the table for the lengths of day and night during the 12 months of a year. These numbers, found throughout *1 Enoch* 72:8-34, also reveal something of the schematic and inaccurate character of Enoch's astronomy. The writer divides a full day into 18 parts and arrives at these results:

| month | day | night | | month | day | night |
|-------|-----|-------|--|-------|-----|-------|
| 1 | 9 | 9 | | 7 | 9 | 9 |
| 2 | 10 | 8 | | 8 | 8 | 10 |
| 3 | 11 | 7 | | 9 | 7 | 11 |
| 4 | 12 | 6 | | 10 | 6 | 12 |
| 5 | 11 | 7 | | 11 | 7 | 11 |
| 6 | 10 | 8 | | 12 | 8 | 10 |

In reality this is an impossible arrangement,[53] but the same ratios of day to night are attested in some astronomical texts from Mesopotamia. Long ago E. Weidner noted the resemblance between the Enochic system and an Akkadian one in which a full day consists of six parts, that is, one-third as many as in 1 Enoch. These numbers are given for the equinoxes and solstices of the year:

[51] Neugebauer, "The History of Ancient Astronomy," *JNES* 4 (1945) 14; B. L. van der Waerden, *Die Anfänge der Astronomie* (Erwachende Wissenschaft 2; Groningen: Noordhoff, 1965) 16-17.

[52] For the evidence, see Ben Zion Wacholder and David B. Weisberg, "Visibility of the New Moon in Cuneiform and Rabbinic Sources," in Wacholder, *Essays on Jewish Chronology and Chronography*, 59-74. Cf. also O. Neugebauer, *Ethiopic Astronomy and Computus*, 194-95. (In this volume Neugebauer has published the results of his studies in Ethiopic astronomical texts which include material from two types of sources: the astronomy of *1 Enoch* and the computus of the church calendar.)

[53] Neugebauer, "Notes on Ethiopic Astronomy," 60.

| date | day | night |
|------|-----|-------|
| 15 Nisannu (the vernal equinox) | 3 | 3 |
| 15 Dūzu (the summer solstice) | 4 | 2 |
| 15 Tašrītu (the autumnal equinox) | 3 | 3 |
| 15 Tebētu (the winter solstice) | 2 | 4 [54] |

The correspondences are exact for the same months (nos. 1, 4, 7, and 10 in the AB). In itself, this parallel may not be overly significant, since the two writers could have created the scheme independently; but the contexts in which the Mesopotamian arrangement is found are worth exploring in more detail because their similarities with the AB are not confined to the ratios of day to night.

The ratio of 2:1 for the longest day relative to the shortest night appears in several cuneiform documents, among which is a group that has been labelled *astrolabes*. These are early astronomical texts which supply the names of 36 stars and which arrange the stars either in a circular, graphic form or in lists of their names. Each of the astrolabes, whether circular or in list form, divides the 36 stars into three categories of 12 each. These groups of 12 correspond with the 12 months of the year, and the three stars which were thought to rise heliacally in a month are assigned to it. In this system each of the months has 30 days.[55] In the older astronomical system that finds expression in the astrolabes and several other texts, the vernal equinox is dated to the twelfth month (= XII), the fifteenth day, the summer solstice to III/15, etc.[56] However, according to a later system which is evidenced in,

---

[54] E. Weidner, "Babylonisches im Buche Henoch," *OLZ* 19 (1916) cols. 74–75. His summarizing comment should be quoted in full:

> Da das Schema bei dem Babylonier wie bei Henoch das gleiche ist und eine unabhängige doppelte Entstehung doch wohl nicht wahrscheinlich ist, das Buch Henoch auch sonst, zumal in seinem astronomischen Teile, ganz und gar die Vorstellungen der altorientalischen Weltanschauung wiedergibt, so kann kein Zweifel sein, dass auch hier bei Henoch altbabylonisches Kulturgut vorliegt (col. 75).

Neugebauer ("Notes on Ethiopic Astronomy," 60) observes correctly that the presence of this 2:1 ratio in cuneiform texts and in the AB does not prove mutual contacts, but, as the following paragraphs are intended to show, this precise agreement is part of a larger system of parallels, the combination of which provides the force of the argument for dependence of the AB on Babylonian models. See now his *The 'Astronomical' Chapters*, 4: "The linear pattern for the variation of the length of daylight as well as the ratio 2:1 at its extrema suggests an early Babylonian background" (cf. also pp. 11–12).

[55] For discussions of the four copies of astrolabes, see van der Waerden, *Die Anfänge der Astronomie*, 56–60, 62–64, 81–84. Van der Waerden groups the astrolabes with several other texts (including the fourteenth tablet of *Enūma Anu Enlil*) in which an older astronomical system comes to expression. He argues that the various texts of this group were composed in the second half of the second millennium B.C. (54; cf. also the chart on p. 70).

[56] Ibid., 81.

among other works, a compendium of astronomical information called
mulAPIN,[57] the vernal equinox is shifted to I/15, the summer solstice to
IV/15, etc. Nevertheless, even in this astronomical system, the ratio of the
longest day to the shortest night remains 2:1 (though in mulAPIN the more
accurate ratio of 3:2 is mentioned but not employed in calculations), and the
year consists of 12 30-day months which are arranged in four groups of
three months each.[58]

The astrolabes also provide names for their three lists of 12 stars: the
first group of 12 is called the stars of Ea, the second those of Anu, and the
third those of Enlil. As van der Waerden indicates, this distribution refers to
different zones in the sky: "Die Sterne des Anu waren in der Nähe des
Himmelsäquators angenommen, und die Sterne des Ea und des Enlil süd-
lich, bzw. nördlich davon."[59] There are two other texts which list 36 stars—
the same 36 as those in the astrolabes—but in them the three groups of 12
stars each are termed the stars of Elam, of Akkad, and of Amurru.[60] As there
appears to be no astronomical principle involved in naming the three groups
after these geographical areas, the explanation must lie elsewhere. After
considering other reasons for the selection of these three names, van der
Waerden remarks: "Möglich ist auch, dass die Liste angibt, auf welche Länder
sich die Bedeutung gewisser Omina erstrecken soll."[61] His reference to the
fact that astrological omens which were observed in specific parts of the sky
were believed to have import for particular areas on earth recalls a slightly
more complex division of the earth that is well attested in mantic literature.
C. J. Gadd summarized the facts about this other distribution thus:

> One of the most prominent features of this astrology is the constant use of a
> geographical scheme for the interpretation of heavenly signs; according to the
> direction in which a sign was observed, or the segment of the moon affected by a
> partial eclipse, the consequence was to concern Akkad, Subartu, Elam, or
> Amurru, roughly the south, north, east, or west.[62]

The sources indicate that there were actually three different arrangements of

---

[57] For mulAPIN see the convenient treatment in van der Waerden, ibid., 64–87. Though
the oldest exemplar of this two-tablet series comes from Aššur and dates itself to the equivalent
of B.C. 687, van der Waerden conjectures a Babylonian origin sometime before 700 (64). He
provides a summary of contents on p. 65.

[58] Ibid., 81; A. Sachs had also called attention to a point of similarity between mulAPIN
and *1 Enoch* regarding the 2:1 ratio of longest/shortest daylight; see Neugebauer, "Studies in
Ancient Astronomy. VIII. The Water Clock in Babylonian Astronomy," *Isis* 37 (1947) 40.

[59] Ibid. 60.

[60] Ibid., 61–62.

[61] Ibid. 62.

[62] *Ideas of Divine Rule in the Ancient East*, 53.

these four directions, but in each of them the names of the four lands (with Gutium at times combined with Subartu) remain constant.[63] Thus one reads in a letter from the scholar Mār–Ištar to the Assyrian king Esarhaddon: "'If Jupiter appears on the way of the Anu stars, a crown prince will rebel [against] his father (and) seize the throne.' The way of the Anu stars is (equal to) the Eastland; (i.e., in this case) the country of Elam has been intended."[64] Or, Akkullānu wrote: "[If] Mars approaches Perseus [which is in the way of the Anu stars], there will be a rebellion in the Westland [= KUR MAR.TU], (and) brother will slay his brother."[65] Given this geographical scheme in astrology and its close similarity with the division of the 36 stars into those of Ea, Anu, and Enlil, it is not unreasonable to suppose that the threefold division, too, had ominous significance and served as a means for determining which area of a tripartite earth was to be affected by an astrological sign. There would then be, should this prove correct, indications in astronomical/ astrological literature of both fourfold and threefold sectionings of the world. In passing it should also be noted how closely the concerns of what today would be distinguished rigidly as astronomy and astrology are intertwined in texts which date to the period of the astrolabes.

The extreme ratio of 2:1 for the longest day and shortest night thus appears alongside other kinds of information in early astronomical documents (only some of which have been mentioned), including the dates for equinoxes and solstices, 12 schematic months of 30 days, and the grouping of 36 stars into three zones which determine the segment of the earth for which an omen was intended. It can be shown that all of these elements are also present in the AB.

---

[63] A. Schott, "Vier Briefe Mâr-Ištars an Asarhaddon über Himmelserscheinungen der Jahre—670/668," *ZA* 47 (1942) 106–08; C. Bezold/F. Boll, *Sternglaube und Sterndeutung: Die Geschichte und das Wesen der Astrologie* (Aus Natur und Geisteswelt 638; Leipzig/Berlin: Teubner, 1918) 11–12. Constellations and in some cases individual stars were thought to be related to specific areas or cities on earth. For relevant texts, see Weidner, "Astrologische Geographie im Alten Orient," *AfO* 20 (1963) 117–21. Astrological geography is certainly attested elsewhere (e.g., in Greek and Latin texts), but, as Weidner noted: "Weder die Griechen noch die Römer haben die astrologische Geographie 'erfunden', ihre bescheidenen Anfänge gehen vielmehr auf die Babylonier und Assyrer zurück" (117). Cf. also F. Cumont, "La plus ancienne géographie astrologique," *Klio* 9 (1909) 263–73. It has often been said that another kind of astrological geography lies behind the references to the four beasts in Daniel 7 and the ram and he–goat in Daniel 8; see, for example, A. Caquot, "Sur les quatre bêtes de Daniel VII," *Sem* 5 (1955) 5–13.

[64] Translation of S. Parpola, *Letters from Assyrian Scholars to the Kings Esarhaddon and Assurbanipal, Part I: Texts* (AOAT 5/1; Kevelaer: Butzon & Bercker/Neukirchen-Vluyn: Neukirchener, 1970) 243 (no. 289). I have added the word *against* for the sake of the English. Note that in no. 290 (p. 245) Mār-Ištar revised his analysis.

[65] Ibid., 259 (no. 300).

The Enochic passages which express the 2:1 ratio of day to night and which therefore also date the equinoxes and solstices to the same months as in texts such as $^{mul}$APIN have been considered above. The remaining topics to be treated are the lengths of months and the geographical divisions in the AB.

First, regarding the number of days in a month, several passages in the AB are adamant that there are 12 months in a solar year, eight of which last 30 days (nos. 1, 2, 4, 5, 7, 8, 10 and 11; see 72:8, 11, 15, 17, 21, 23, 27, 29) and four 31 days (nos. 3, 6, 9, and 12; see 72:13, 19, 25, 31; 75:2; 82:4–6). For this arrangement the cuneiform sources which have been examined above offer no parallel, nor do any others. It has been observed that the Enochic scheme more nearly resembles the Egyptian solar calendar in which there were 12 months of 30 days each to which *five* days were added at the end of the year.[66] There certainly are analogies between these two calendars and it may be correct to see a historical connection between them, but, despite these similarities, the 364-day calendar of the AB differs in that it distributes the *four* surplus days throughout the year rather than bunching them together at the end in the Egyptian fashion. A close reading of the AB reveals in fact that the writer's scheme has more in common with the early Babylonian system than at first may appear to be the case. Several passages disclose that, though the author elsewhere speaks clearly and forcefully about 30- and 31-day months, he operates with a year which consists of 12 30-day months and that he assigns a special status to the four intercalary days outside the normal reckoning of the year. This becomes evident from the fact that some of his calculations presuppose a year of 360 days. For example, when he compares the lengths of lunar (=354 days; see, e.g., 74:14) and solar years, he writes: "*And (if) five years are added together, the sun has an excess of 30 days; . . .*" (74:10a) Simple multiplication and subtraction show that if he were computing with solar years of 364 days, the surplus would amount to 50 days (1820–1770 = 50); only a solar year of 360 days would permit the difference of 30 days (1800–1770 = 30). The author's total could be excused as a textual blunder, but it is not an isolated example (see 72:35; 74:11). Moreover, he expressly removes the extra four days from the year in unambiguous language: "And these [angelic leaders] serve on the four days which are not counted in the reckoning of the year [*wa-ʾellu yetqannayu 4-mawāʿela ʾella ʾi-yethassabu ba-hasaba ʿāmat*]" (75:1b; cf. 82:11). It is possible, on

---

[66] See, for example, Hengel, *Judaism and Hellenism*, 1.234–35 and the bibliography in n. 813 (2.158). Neugebauer (*Ethiopic Astronomy and Computus*, 109) writes: "This departure from the traditional Near Eastern lunar calendar towards a (only slightly modified) Egyptian-hellenistic pattern is perhaps the most remarkable feature of this heretical calendar." Also cf. p. 229.

the basis of such texts, to argue that the author of the AB began with a 12-month, 360-day scheme, which is familiar from cuneiform sources, and modified it (or his tradition did) to fit his sabbatarian, 364-day system. Traces of his polemic against advocates of the 360-day year are evident in the book (75:2; 82:4–6).[67]

Second, the fact that *1 Enoch* 76–77 depart from astronomy and turn to geography has puzzled commentators. As noted earlier in this chapter, both Beer and Martin questioned the authenticity of this section because the contents seemed out of place in a document which is otherwise devoted to the heavenly luminaries.[68] It must be granted that the brief characterization of the AB found in 72:1 does not prepare the reader for geographical discussions, though in itself this is hardly a weighty objection to their authenticity. Yet, if Enoch's astronomy is studied against the backdrop of an early stage of Babylonian astronomy in which scientific and superstitious interests were combined to some extent, geography proves to be a natural topic. Division of the sky into three zones and partition of the earth into four areas are solidly documented in cuneiform texts, and there is some reason to believe that at one time there may have been a tripartite arrangement of the world for divinatory purposes. In *1 Enoch* 76 one meets the same distribution of the earth into four *nafāsāt* (literally = winds); this term recurs, among other verses in this chapter, at v 14 where 4QEnastr[c] I ii 14 reads *rwḥy*, the construct plural form of *rwḥ* (= wind).[69] As a word for each of the quadrants of the earth or the four directions, *rwḥ* is used by biblical writers in several texts which date from the period of approximately the exile or later—i.e., the time when Babylonian influence was most direct or in subsequent times (Ezek 42:20; Zech 2:10; 6:5; Dan 7:2 [Aramaic: *ᵓrbᶜ rwḥy šmyᵓ*]; 8:8; 11:4; cf. also Jer 49:36; Ezek 37:9). The same usage is well attested in Akkadian documents, including letters from scholars who reported to Assyrian kings regarding the world region which an astrological sign was to affect and how (the term is *šāru* = wind).[70] *1 Enoch* 76 describes the four directions and locates three portals at the extremes of each. The simple fact that the AB divides the earth into four regions is hardly remarkable, but the fact that it is an astronomical treatise which denotes those regions with the very word

---

[67] Neugebauer (*Ethiopic Astronomy and Computus*, 231) sees here a reference to a sexagesimal division of the sidereal year in which the units are called *days* thus introducing confusion. "What is meant, however, is very simple: one lunar year amounts to 354 days, one sidereal year to 360 'days', hence the difference in 5 years is 5·6 = 30 'days', i.e., one 'month'" (231). That may be true, but there is, it seems, no indication of it in the text.

[68] See above, n. 9.

[69] Milik, *The Books of Enoch*, 288.

[70] Schott, "Vier Briefe Mâr-Ištars," 107.

which writers of Akkadian used in astronomical contexts is significant. With the other indicators which have been adduced it suggests influence from Mesopotamia upon the astronomy of Enoch.[71]

Some comments should also be added about lunar theory because it occupied a very prominent place in the thought of the author. The sections which deal with the moon, especially chaps. 73 and 78, are the most difficult in the AB. It may be that problems have been caused by textual errors in the Ethiopic version, but, as the Aramaic texts do not always coincide closely with the Ethiopic and as sizable portions of the Qumran fragments have not yet been published, one frequently has no alternative but to rely on the Ethiopic version. Despite difficulties, though, several points can be made about the author's lunar views. First, in all passages but one,[72] he operates with lunar months that last either 29 or 30 days (78:15-16). These durations were, of course, widely recognized in ancient calendrical systems, including

---

[71] Another geographical division is found at 77:3. The Ethiopic version states that one of the earth's quadrants—the northern—contains three parts and describes their contents. The Aramaic fragments which correspond to this verse, show, however, that originally 77:3 presented a tripartite division of the entire earth rather than just a quarter of it (4QEnastr b 23.8-9 [Milik, *The Books of Enoch*, 289]). Grelot ("La géographie mythique d'Hénoch et ses sources orientales," *RB* 65 [1958] 34–36, 67–68) and, following him, Milik (*The Books of Enoch*, 15–18, 288–89, 291; cf. already "Hénoch au pays des aromates [ch. XXVII à XXXII]: Fragments araméens de la grotte 4 de Qumran," *RB* 65 [1958] 76) have proposed that the scheme in the Aramaic version is modeled on a Babylonian *mappa mundi* in which the world is pictured as a circle surrounded by the Bitter River. Beyond the river are seven triangular areas, one of which is the abode of Utnapishtim, the survivor of the flood. Their argument does, however, greatly stretch the evidence of 77:3 which mentions no circle and no triangular regions beyond a watery section. It is tempting, given the presence of an astrologically conditioned geography in *1 Enoch* 76 and in the first verses of 77, to propose that the tripartite arrangement in 77:3 reflects the presumed three-part division of the world into areas corresponding to the stars of Ea, Anu, and Enlil. But this hypothesis, while not impossible perhaps, confronts a major difficulty in that the regions which are described in 77:3 do not seem to correspond with three areas of the earth in which people live as do the astrological regions.

[72] The exception is 78:9: "And in certain months the moon has twenty-nine days in each (month) and once twenty-eight." Mention of a 28-day month led Charles (*The Book of Enoch*, 168; he acknowledges that K. G. Wieseler first made this observation) to infer that the author knew the 76-year cycle of Callippus in which one 28-day month replaces one 29-day month every 76 years. It hardly needs saying that this is a large conclusion to base on such slender evidence; at the very least one must object that the author does not say when this 28-day month falls—whether once in a year or otherwise. No convincing explanation which incorporates the 28-day month into the system of the AB has yet been proposed, and no help is forthcoming from the Aramaic, since the only fragment which overlaps with 78:9—4QEnastr b 25—seems to preserve a word from v 9 in line 1 but not the one in question (see Milik, *The Books of Enoch*, 293, where he also says that if this verse reflects Callippus' cycle it is due to the Greek translator). Considering the reference to a 28-day month an addition at some later point in the book's textual history seems the simplest solution.

the traditional Jewish and Babylonian lunar calendars. The writer does show his characteristic penchant for symmetry by stating that each half year contained three 29-day and three 30-day months (78:15-16), but he makes no distinctive contributions regarding the lengths of the lunar months.

Second, in two passages (73:4-8; 78:6-14; cf. 74:2-3) the author details the varying amounts of the moon's surface which are illuminated during the nights of a lunar month. He prefaces both of these sections with the claim that the light of the full moon equals one-seventh that of the sun (73:3; 78:4). This fraction, which appears to be derived from Isa 30:26, is also used for divisions of the lunar surface and is at times halved into fourteenths. The clearest picture emerges from 78:6-8 which furnishes an arithmetic pattern for the lighted portions of the moon's surface in a 30-day month: during each of the 15 nights of its waxing (from new moon to full moon) the lighted part increases by one-fifteenth, and in each of the 15 nights of its waning the illumined section decreases by a fifteenth. There is an Aramaic fragment which corresponds to these verses in Ethiopic (4QEnastr$^c$ 1 iii 3-9), and it confirms the pattern of the Ethiopic text.[73] There appears to be no precise equivalent to this scheme in the cuneiform texts that have been discussed, but for comparative purposes another lunar pattern, which offers related information, should be adduced. In several of the older astronomical texts which van der Waerden treats one meets calculations which are geared to the 2:1 ratio for day to night and which give times for the rising and setting of the moon for the days of a month. Stated briefly, this system makes the

---

[73] Milik, *The Books of Enoch*, 292-93. The pattern or patterns in chap. 73 remain difficult; see the comments of Charles, *The Book of Enoch*, 157-58; Knibb, *The Ethiopic Book of Enoch*, 2.171-72. Milik (*The Books of Enoch*, 283) on the basis of some published and unpublished material, writes:

His plan . . . is as follows. During the first 14 days of each lunar month, the moon waxes from one half of the seventh part of its light up to the full moon, thus from 1/2 to 7 = 1/14 to 14/14. In the second half of each month, on the other hand, it wanes from 1/14 to 14/14 (= the astronomical new moon) between the 16th and the 29th of each month composed of 30 days, and between the 15th and the 28th day of each month composed of 29 days. Each new month . . . starts with 1/14 of the lunar light, borrowed, moreover, from the sun (Enoch 78:4).

The fractions should perhaps be expressed in fifteenths: one part (corresponding to the surface area added in each of the subsequent 14 days) is lighted on the first day and in the following 14 days equal parts are added until the fifteenth. If so, then the description in 78:6-8 would also fit chap. 73. Cf. Neugebauer (*Ethiopic Astronomy and Computus*, 195-96): "The two linear sequences of 14 days increasing and 14 days decreasing illumination vary between the extrema 0 and 1, which remain valid for one day each—a pattern well known from linear schemes in Babylonian, Greek, and Medieval astronomy" (196 [cf. n. 8: extrema actually cover 1 1/2 days—between the last morning visibility and first visibility the next evening—linear parts cover 13 1/2 days each]).

setting of the moon coincide with sunset on the day before the new moon
(thus making it invisible) and delays the moon's setting after sunset one–
fifteenth of the night for each of the first 15 nights of the month. On the
fifteenth night the moon rises at sunset and sets with sunrise so that it is
visible the entire night. For each of the remaining 15 nights the moon rises
one–fifteenth of the night later with the result that on the thirtieth day the
moon rises with the sun and is thus once again invisible.[74] Admittedly the
Enochic set of fractions and these do not refer to precisely the same entities,
but their close relationship is suggestive. The scheme in the AB may represent simply the transfer by the writer of this Babylonian arithmetic progres-
sion to the lighted portions of the lunar surface.

   The comparative material that has been assembled in the preceding
section gives, it can be said, warrant for the hypothesis that Enoch's science
is a Judaized refraction of an early stage in the development of Babylonian
astronomy—a stage that finds varied expression in texts such as the astrolabes, *Enūma Anu Enlil*, and mulAPIN. In it astronomical and astrological
concepts are intermingled and schematic arrangements at times predominate
over facts. There can be no question of comparing the science of the AB with
that of cuneiform astronomical texts from the Seleucid period or of Greek
documents from Ptolemaic Egypt for by that time scientists had advanced to
a far more sophisticated level.[75] No other source in relevant periods and
places presents so many similarities with the astronomy of the AB as does
the ancient stage of Babylonian astronomy that has been discussed;[76] in this
respect, too, the Enochic tradition appears to be firmly rooted in Mesopo-

---

[74] Van der Waerden, *Die Anfänge der Astronomie*, 82–88.

[75] Neugebauer, "Notes on Ethiopic Astronomy," 58: ". . . an extremely primitive level of
astronomy which shows no relation to the sophisticated Babylonian astronomy of the Seleucid
period nor to its Hellenistic Greek sequel." Cf. also *Ethiopic Astronomy and Computus*, 109;
and *The 'Astronomical' Chapters*, 4. The truth of his evaluation is readily apparent from
reading his *The Exact Sciences in Antiquity* (2nd ed.; Providence: Brown, 1957) or from perus-
ing his magisterial works *Astronomical Cuneiform Texts* (3 vols.; London: Lund Humphreys,
1955) and *A History of Ancient Mathematical Astronomy* (Studies in the History of Mathematical and Physical Sciences 1; 3 vols.; Berlin/Heidelberg/New York: Springer, 1975).

[76] Several of the parallels adduced are attested elsewhere, e.g., astrological geography in
Greece and Egypt (on the latter, see van der Waerden, *Die Anfänge der Astronomie*, 132–33; the
mantic geography of Greece and Egypt may be due to influences from Mesopotamia); 12
30–day months in the solar calendar of Egypt, etc. Nevertheless, there appears to be no source,
other than the early cuneiform astronomical texts, which provides all of the similarities that
have been presented above. Cf. Beer's statement ("Das Buch Henoch," 286) that "die letzte
Grundlage des Kalendersystems 'Henochs' ist die babyl. Astrologie und Mythologie" (comment
on 82:7); and also the general remark of Hengel, "Qumrān und der Hellenismus," *Qumran: Sa
piété, sa théologie et son milieu* (ed. M. Delcor; BETL 46; Paris-Gembloux: Editions Duculot/
Leuven: University Press, 1978) 369.

tamian soil.[77] Every indicator points to the conclusion that the author of the AB has fixed in writing a very old stage in the evolution of Enochic lore, a stage in which its eastern origins are clearly apparent and no admixture of Greek influences is yet demonstrable.[78]

By presenting the seventh biblical patriarch as the person to whom God chose to reveal astronomical information, the writer ranks Enoch alongside other culture heroes from the various peoples of the ancient world. There was a widespread belief in the ancient Near East and in the classical world that knowledge about the sun, moon, and stars had been divulged to special individuals at the dawn of history. One thinks, for instance, of Oannes in Berossus' *Babyloniaca*[79] or of Atlas and Prometheus in Greek mythology.[80]

---

[77] This is perhaps the place in which to mention some of the isolated parallels that commentators have proposed between motifs in the AB and in cuneiform literature. Beer ("Das Buch Henoch," 278), Zimmern (*Die Keilinschriften und das Alte Testament*, 619), and Charles (*The Book of Enoch*, 151) have all noted that the AB shares with *Enūma Elish* 5.9 and other texts the notion that there are heavenly portals through which the sun, moon, and stars rise and set (cf. A. Heidel, *The Babylonian Genesis* [2nd ed.; Chicago/London: University of Chicago, 1951] 44 n. 103). Beer (ibid.) also observed that reference to the sun's riding a chariot (e.g., 72:5) recalled the chariots of Shamash and of Greek Helios, while Re, the Egyptian sun god, was thought of as riding a bark. Although Beer (ibid., 283), Zimmern (ibid., 618), and Charles (ibid., 166) claimed that a sevenfold division of the earth in 77:4-8 reflected Babylonian sources, the text actually mentions no division of this sort. It merely lists groups of seven items (mountains, islands, etc.) which are located in various places in the world. It should be added that parallels such as the heavenly portals and solar chariots are hardly significant in themselves, but they, too, are consistent with a Mesopotamian background that is suggested by the more systematic parallels with early Babylonian astronomy.

[78] Especially Charles (*The Book of Enoch*, 150, 160; Beer ["Das Buch Henoch," 281] considers his view possible) has maintained that the comparative statistics for the number of days in three, five, and eight solar and lunar years (74:13-16) betray influence from the Greek eight-year cycle (as seen in n. 71 above, he also thought the 28-day month of 78:9 reflected Callippus' 76 year cycle). His point is simply that there is no reason for the author to bother with these particular calculations because in the Enochic system the difference between a lunar and solar year is always ten days, whereas in the eight-year cycle years three, five, and eight are lengthened by an intercalary month. However, there is now cuneiform evidence for use of eight-year cycles during the Persian period (see van der Waerden, *Die Anfänge der Astronomie*, 111-13) so that appeal to Greek influence, while possibly correct, is unnecessary. It is of some interest that nothing in the AB indicates the author's acquaintance with the later and more accurate 19-year cycle which was known in Greece (the Metonic cycle) and Babylon in the fifth century (cf. Neugebauer, *The Exact Sciences in Antiquity*, 7, 140; van der Waerden, ibid.; and Charles, ibid., 168).

[79] Schnabel, *Berossus*, 254 frgs. 9-10; cf. 253 frg. 8.

[80] For Atlas, see n. 36 above; and for Prometheus cf. Aeschylus, *Prometheus Bound*, 11. 454-59. It is interesting that Prometheus, who like the Mesopotamian Oannes and the *apkallūs* is said to have introduced all human culture, also first taught the arts of divination (*Prometheus Bound*, 11. 484-506). Josephus (*Ant.* 1.3, 9 §106), probably depending ultimately upon Berossus, also alludes to "discoveries in astronomy [variant: astrology]" by the long-lived patriarchs

It is noteworthy that, despite claims of this sort by his neighbors and contemporaries, the ancient scholar who penned the AB refrains from national-
istic or religious controversy, unlike Pseudo-Eupolemus for one.[81] He does
not dispute the claims of others but fashions his own candidate and borrows
freely from Mesopotamian sources to do so. He belonged to a scholarly
milieu which was, it seems, characterized by an openness to other cultures.[82]
Where that milieu was and when the writer was active can no longer be
specified, but there is an unconfirmed yet perhaps somewhat reliable tradition in the *de pietate* (ca. B.C. 315) of the Greek writer Theophrastus that
Jewish scholars were interested in astronomy: "During this whole time, being
philosophers by race, they [the Jews] converse with each other about the
deity, and at night-time they make observations of the stars, gazing at them
and calling on God by prayer."[83] There is no mistaking the idealizing twist to
his description of the Jews, but at least Theophrastus does mention Jewish
concern with astronomy at a time perhaps not too far removed from the
period when the AB was composed.

Whenever the AB was written and whatever may have been its sources,
it presents Enoch's astronomy as the record of angelic revelation about
unchanging natural phenomena. Since the sun, moon, and stars continue to
operate according to fixed laws and to pursue their unalterable courses, the
future cannot be read from them. A mantic background provides a satisfactory explanation for Enoch's concern with astronomy, but astrological motifs
have had to be modified in order to be incorporated into a monotheistic,
Jewish context. From beginning to end "scientific"[84] interests govern the

---

of the pre-deluge period (translation of H. St. J. Thackeray, *Josephus IV: Jewish Antiquities
Books I-IV* [LCL; Cambridge/London: Harvard University, 1930]). See also p. 51 n. a.

[81] See nn. 35-36 above.

[82] So Stone, "The Book of Enoch and Judaism in the Third Century B.C.E.," *CBQ* 40
(1978) 479-92.

[83] M. Stern, *Greek and Latin Authors on Jews and Judaism*, vol. 1: *From Herodotus to
Plutarch* (Jerusalem: Israel Academy of Sciences and Humanities, 1976) 10; for the date, see
pp. 8-9.

[84] Enoch's "astronomy" is, of course, clothed in mythological dress throughout. Uriel,
God's angelic deputy, reveals all astronomical information to him (72:1; 74:2; 75:3-4; 78:10;
79:2, 6; 82:7). Uriel is termed the *guide* (*marāxi*) of all celestial bodies (72:1) and is said to be the
one who is empowered to give light to mankind (82:8)—that is, light and darkness fall under
angelic control. Various stars are called *leaders* (*marāxeyān* [e.g., 72:3; 75:1; cf. 80:1; 82:18]) or
*heads over thousands* (*ʾarʾesta ʾaʾlāf*[75:1; 82:4, 12-14]), while, as noted before, the sun, moon,
and stars are pictured as riding chariots across the sky (sun, 72:5; 73:3; 82:8; moon, 73:2; 75:3;
82:8; stars, 75:3; 82:8). Other decidedly non-scientific expressions include the notion that various stars render special service on the four intercalary days (75:1) and that certain leaders watch
to insure that other celestial bodies appear at the correct times and places (82:10). It is not
surprising that modern estimates of the astronomy of the AB have been low; see Neugebauer,

original AB, and no eschatological or revelatory significance is attached to the motions of the heavenly bodies.

### 4. Enoch the Writer

The AB not only greatly expands several traits of Enoch that are mentioned briefly in Genesis 5 but also adds an entirely new role for him—writer of angelic disclosures. The motif of Enoch as writer or scribe, which is mentioned so frequently in later Jewish and Christian literature, figures in two passages in the AB. The first is in a context in which Uriel is revealing to Enoch details about the monthly journey or course of the moon. "And Uriel, the holy angel who is the leader of them all, showed me everything, and I wrote down their positions as he showed (them) to me; and I wrote down their months, as they are, and the appearance of their light until fifteen days have been completed" (74:2). The other instance is in 82:1 where the process by which the information in Enoch's books will be transmitted is under discussion:

> And now, my son Methuselah, all these things I recount to you and write down for you; *I have revealed everything to you* and have given you books about all these things. Keep, my son Methuselah, the books from the hand of your father that you may pass (them) on to the generations of eternity.

Precisely why more than one book is mentioned is not clear, but there is no mistaking the fact that Enoch relayed Uriel's revelations to Methuselah both orally and in writing. If chaps. 80–81 did not belong to the earliest form of the AB, then Enoch's books, which the context suggests refer only to the contents of the original AB, consisted of scientific information without ethical or theological elaboration (other than occasional references to the God who created the luminaries and appointed Uriel over them). It is noteworthy that the books are not to be hidden nor reserved for a later time; they are for all the generations of the world.

The assumption that the pre-deluge patriarch could and did write resembles claims made in other cultures in antiquity. According to Berossus, the art of writing was introduced in antediluvian times by Oannes and his followers.[85] Thus, as with astronomy, this late Babylonian source attributes

---

"Notes on Ethiopic Astronomy," 59–61, with 58. Charles (*The Book of Enoch*, 150) even wrote that the author espoused a 364–day solar calendar ". . . only through sheer incapacity for appreciating anything better" and suggested stupidity as a cause. Discovery of the Qumran literature has, though, cast a new light on some of the problems involved. Cf. also H. Bietenhard, *Die himmlische Welt im Urchristentum und Spätjudentum* (WUNT 2; Tübingen: Mohr, 1951) 21–25.

[85] Schnabel, *Berossos*, 253 frg. 8; 254 frg. 9.

discovery of the art to the period in which Jewish sources place Enoch. It should be noted, however, that the writer does not claim, as will the author of *Jubilees* (4:17), that Enoch was the first man who learned how to write. That issue is not addressed in the AB. It is simpy assumed that Enoch can write and that Methuselah and his offspring will be able to read what he has recorded. This device makes of Enoch the author of most of the AB and clothes the astronomical teachings in it with the authority of both Uriel and of this revered sage.

Summarizing the results of this chapter, one can say that the author of the original AB (72-78; 82:9-20; 79; 82:1-8), writing in ca. b.c. 200 or probably earlier, knew not only the terse biblical pericope about Enoch but also a far larger body of Enochic traditions, whether written or oral. It is reasonable to suppose that he borrowed the basic features of his Enochic portrait from Gen 5:21-24—his son was Methuselah, he was in angelic company, he was associated with astronomical phenomena—but in no case is the allusive account in Genesis adequate for explaining fully the contents of the AB. The writer has developed each of these biblical items considerably beyond the modest givens of Gen 5:21-24. Moreover, he has added to these elements a motif that is absent from Genesis—Enoch as a writer of books which contain angelic revelations about astronomy and geography. It is possible that in some cases the writer has refracted Mesopotamian traditions which were unknown to P and connected them with Enoch (e.g., the geography, some details of the astronomy, Enoch's scribal role); yet, one cannot exclude the possibility that he committed to writing a larger portion of Enochic traditions which had circulated for some time in post-exilic Judaism and of which P expressed only the proverbial tip of the iceberg. The works of authors such as Berossus (and of Greek scholars in Alexandria) show that ancient traditions were being collected and published in early Hellenistic times. Thus the author of the original AB may have had access to new sources about antediluvian times and heroes. Since, however, one cannot ascertain the extent of Enochic traditions that were available at the time of the priestly editor, one cannot rule out the possibility that the AB embodies native Palestinian Jewish development of Enochic lore. Perhaps the process which is now crystalized in the book involved a combination of new contact with foreign sources and native elaboration.

It is worth noting that in the AB (both in its original form and in the present one) there is no mention of the angels who sinned and consequently of Enoch's relationship with them. Furthermore, though Enoch is clearly regarded as the first astronomer, there is no overt polemic in the book against counter-claims by other nations that their ancestors had discovered this science. Finally, in its original form, the AB was almost completely devoid of eschatological references (72:1—the new creation—is the only

exception) and says nothing, for whatever reason, about Enoch's final removal from human society. Rather, in this composition Enoch assumes the
role of antediluvian sage who still experiences intimate contact with the
divine realm and who bridges the gap between human and divine by convey-
ing his special knowledge to humanity. In this way his function closely
resembles that of the Mesopotamian *apkallūs*.

### Appendix: Chaps. 80-81 and the AB as an Apocalypse

Chaps. 80-81 appear to be additions (not necessarily contemporaneous
ones) to the scientific core of the AB. The case for this conclusion was
presented above. The problems that remain are to locate the chapters in the
context of the evolving Enochic lore and to determine which nuances they
add to the original astronomical book.

Some features in chap. 81 suggest that they have been drawn from other
parts of *1 Enoch*, but the same does not appear to be the case for chap. 80,
aside from the editorial link in v 1. 80:2-8 give what could almost be called
an astrological twist to the AB in that, contrary to 72:1, this paragraph
predicts that the heavenly luminaries will reflect (or cause) the eschatological
chaos which will hasten upon the earth in the "days of the sinners." Prior to
the end, natural laws, which are considered unchanging elsewhere in the AB
and in *1 Enoch* as a whole (e.g., 2:1),[86] will no longer apply, just as humanity
will violate moral and religious laws. The heavily eschatological message of
80:2-8 is in starkest contrast to the scientific concerns of the original book.
Charles commented that 80:2-8, which he regarded as poetic, ". . . is mani-
festly an addition, made to give an ethical turn to a purely scientific treatise,
and so furnish it with some fitness for its present collocation."[87] But one
wonders why someone chose to add a poem that conflicts so strongly with
the remainder of the book. The poetic description of chaos in the celestial
sphere with its ominous implications for the terrestrial realm is an alien
element in *1 Enoch* and therefore difficult to ascribe to the editor of the
entire book. The views expressed in it have some similarity with *Jub.* 6:32-38;
there, however, no violation of natural law is anticipated, only human mis-
calculation of the year. Rau has argued at some length that 72:1 does indeed
prepare the reader for 80:2-8 and that it is not therefore foreign to the
material of the AB. For him, the first parts of 72:1 point forward to 72:2-79:6
while the latter section ("until the new creation shall be made which will last
for ever") limits the duration of natural laws—a situation reflected in the

---

[86] Cf. Charles, *The Book of Enoch*, 148.
[87] Ibid., 147.

eschatological 80:2-8.[88] Nevertheless, his analysis (the fullest one available regarding the antecedents and structure of the passage and parallels to it) involves a mis-reading of 72:1h-i. It claims that the laws of nature which Uriel is to show to Enoch will retain their validity as long as the present creation endures; but 80:2-8, which deal with a time when the old creation still survives, oppose that view. Before the old creation expires, the laws which had governed God's creation are repealed. As a result, despite Rau's efforts, these verses remain an incongruous section in the AB. When and why they were spliced into the AB remains an enigma.

More can be said about chap. 81. While it does contain some eschatological allusions (e.g., vv 2, 4), it is far more subdued in this respect than chap. 80. Charles wrote that "it is of the nature of a mosaic, and came probably from the editor of the complete Enoch."[89] An example that supports Charles' contention is the tablets of heaven on which someone other than Enoch had inscribed the deeds of the human race forever. Such tablets with similar contents are mentioned elsewhere in *1 Enoch* (93:2; 106:19). Another feature of chap. 81 not only resembles information found in another section but also indicates that it is derived from it—the sudden mention of three angels as though they had been part of the preceding narratives: "And these three holy ones brought me, and set me on the earth . . ." (v 5a). Since the remainder of the AB puts Uriel alone in contact with Enoch, these words are jarring. The writer of chap. 81 appears to have taken them from traditions such as those now embedded in *1 Enoch* 87:3-4; 90:31, where three angels conduct Enoch from place to place. Milik would, on this basis, date 81 after B.C. 164, which is his date for the Book of Dreams (*1 Enoch* 83-90).[90] One could object that the writer drew the detail about three angels from some other source, but the Book of Dreams certainly seems to be the most likely candidate. As a result, it appears that chap. 81 is later than the Book of Dreams, though it need not be placed much after it. In chap. 81 more attention is paid to the chronology of Enoch's life than elsewhere in the AB. According to vv 5-10, he is given one year after his return to earth to teach his children and write down what the angels had shown him. After one year he would be removed from them (regarding his testifying, see also *Jub.* 4:18-19).

Addition of chaps. 80-81 may change the genre of the AB. The original book belongs to the very general category of revelatory literature, and it shares with apocalypses several prominent features such as angelic revela-

---

[88] "Kosmologie," 279-305.
[89] *The Book of Enoch*, 148; cf. Milik, *The Books of Enoch*, 13-14.
[90] Ibid.

tions about the heavenly sphere, provision for publication (though Enoch
gave the order, not an angel), and a journey through the universe. Also, the
scientific interests of the AB are among those that Stone has isolated as a
constitutive element in apocalypses.[91] Since, therefore, the original AB had
many ingredients of an apocalypse, it would not have been difficult for an
editor to transform it into one. Yet, the older form of the book ought not to
be classed as an apocalypse—at least not in the sense in which Collins has
defined the genre. Even with the addition of chaps. 80–81 it qualifies only
with difficulty. Because this issue has some bearing on the understanding of
how Jewish apocalyptic literature developed, some space should be devoted
to it.

Collins writes:

> 'Apocalypse' is a genre of revelatory literature with a narrative framework, in
> which a revelation is mediated by an otherworldly being to a human recipient,
> disclosing a transcendent reality which is both temporal, insofar as it envis-
> ages eschatological salvation, and spatial insofar as it involves another, super-
> natural world.[92]

His definition fits the original AB until one reaches the words "disclosing a
transcendent reality." The AB, if it were an apocalypse, would have to be
classified under Collins' Type IIb: Otherworldly Journeys with Cosmic and/or
Political Eschatology";[93] but it seems unlikely that it qualifies. First, there is
just one possible allusion to a journey (76:1); otherwise one may well be
presupposed, but it is hardly a noticeable theme in the book. Second, the AB
does not disclose a "transcendent reality" in the sense that journey–centered
apocalypses do. Rather, it expresses a speculative set of theories about the
sun, moon, stars, winds, etc. It does not describe various heavens, nor does
Enoch enter the divine throne room. On the contrary, its concerns rarely
move beyond humanly observable phenomena; speculation is limited to subjects such as the gates from which the luminaries and winds are supposed to
emerge. Thus there is really no vision of a transcendent realm in the normal
sense of that term. And third, there is no explicit eschatology in the original
AB.

Collins is able to classify the AB as an apocalypse (Type IIb) because he
does not separate chaps. 80–81 from the scientific core. He speaks of it as a

---

[91] "Lists of Revealed Things," 414–52; see also his essay "The Book of Enoch and
Judaism in the Third Century B.C.E.," 479–92.

[92] "Introduction: Towards the Morphology of a Genre," *Apocalypse*, 9 (where it is italicized).

[93] Collins, "The Jewish Apocalypses," *Apocalypse*, 23, 38.

". . . rather peculiar adaptation of apocalyptic writing"[94] in that it focuses quite narrowly on the true calendar as the way in which astronomical bodies determine the lives of people; but he prefers to include it, nevertheless, among the Jewish apocalypses. It is of some interest that a substantial percentage of the characteristics that led him to this conclusion is found in chaps. 80–81: the eschatology of chap. 80 and the presupposition of some kind of afterlife in 81:4–10. To these he joins the reference to the new creation in 72:1.

Perhaps the present form of the AB is an apocalypse because of the narrative framework and the eschatological elements in chaps. 80–81, but it does not disclose a transcendent reality beyond the perceivable universe. It is advisable not to label the original AB an apocalypse, though its scientific, non–eschatological contents include several traits that would later be found in apocalypses. The sorts of scientific data found in it will, in other documents such as the Book of Watchers, be endowed with moral implications, but none of that is present in the original AB.

[94] Ibid., 38.

# V

## ENOCH IN THE BOOK OF WATCHERS (1 Enoch 1–36)

### A. Introduction

Parts of the Book of Watchers (= BW) are probably the most familiar sections of *1 Enoch*. In the booklet one reads the story of the angels who sinned (they are often called the Watchers),[1] and a verse from its majestic description of theophany (1:3b–9) is quoted in the NT (Jude 14b–15 = *1 Enoch* 1:9). Perhaps no other part of *1 Enoch* presents, however, such imposing literary problems as these chapters do. There is some reason for regarding the BW as a collection of several originally independent units which an editor has amalgamated into a passable literary unity.[2] Judging by content and to some extent by redactional transitions, the major divisions are:

| | |
|---|---|
| 1–5: | an eschatological admonition |
| 6–11: | stories about the angels' descent and sin |
| 12–16: | Enoch and the Watchers' petition |
| 17–19: | Enoch's first journey |
| 20–36: | Enoch's second journey. |

Enoch himself figures in each of these units except the crucial second one. His absence from this section demonstrates that there was once a form of the Watcher story in which he played no role (Noah is the only individual to whom it alludes).[3] Nevertheless, in chaps. 12–16 a writer brings Enoch into direct contact with the fallen angels. The figure of Enoch in the BW is a more complicated one than in the AB; as the analysis proceeds, it will become apparent that by the early Hellenistic period he had attracted to himself not only the traits that Gen 5:21–24 had ascribed to him but also mythological characteristics of disparate kinds and apparently from various sources.

---

[1] The term *Watchers* (Aramaic *ʿîrîn*) can refer to either good or bad angels. In Dan 4:13, 17, 23 it is used of angels who serve God; elsewhere, as in the BW, it is a title for the angels of Gen 6:1–4 who descended to earth and sinned with the daughters of men. For references, see Dimant, "The 'Fallen Angels,'" 32–33.

[2] Dimant (ibid., 22 n. 78) uses the term *catalog* to describe the composite nature of the BW.

[3] Even he is not mentioned by name but only as the son of Lamech (10:1).

The textual evidence for the BW is both more plentiful and less controversial than it was for the AB. The Ethiopic MSS again offer the only complete text, but for these chapters there are many Aramaic fragments and a nearly complete Greek translation.[4] Milik has published the remains of five MSS, all written in Aramaic; he has labeled them 4QEn[a-e]. According to his calculations, these MSS, with his restorations, preserve some 50% of the BW.[5] One should be aware, though, that his restorations constitute the greater part of that 50%.[6] More importantly, the preserved words and letters indicate that there is a much closer relationship between the Aramaic texts and the later versions (Greek and Ethiopic) than was the case for the AB.[7]

### B. The Date of the BW

While the dates that pre–Qumran scholars posited for the AB differed widely from the minimal dating that the Aramaic MSS require, there is a much smaller divergence for the BW. It is true that Beer favored, with due reservations, the end of the second century B.C.,[8] but both Martin and Charles opted for dates far earlier in that century: the former suggested ca. 166,[9] and the latter set ca. 170 as a *terminus ad quem.*[10]

One of the Qumran MSS—4QEn[a]—has proved that Martin and Charles, among others, were correct in assigning the BW to a period earlier than Beer

---

[4] The Greek texts have been edited most recently by M. Black, *Apocalypsis Henochi Graece* (PVTG 3; Leiden: Brill, 1970). Codex Panopolitanus (= Gr[Pan]) dates to the sixth century and offers a Greek version of chaps. 1–32, with a duplicate rendering of 19:3–21:9. The Byzantine chronographer George Syncellus quoted *1 Enoch* 6:1–9:4; 8:4–10:14; 15:8–16:1, though often in rather a different form than that found in Gr[Pan]. On the Greek material, see A. M. Denis, *Introduction aux pseudépigraphes grecs d'Ancien Testament* (SVTP 1; Leiden: Brill, 1970) 15–28; and Knibb, *The Ethiopic Book of Enoch,* 2.15–21.

[5] *The Books of Enoch,* 5, 22.

[6] See the review of Milik's book by Knibb and Ullendorff in *BSO(A)S* 40 (1977) 601–02. In fairness to Milik, however, it must be added that he himself is explicit about this (e.g., *The Books of Enoch,* 5).

[7] Knibb, *The Ethiopic Book of Enoch,* 2.12–13; cf. also Milik (*The Books of Enoch,* 143) who maintains that in general the Greek version more nearly resembles the Aramaic than does the Ethiopic. Recently S. Brock ("A Fragment of Enoch in Syriac," *JTS* 19 [1968] 626–31) has identified a Syriac citation of *1 Enoch* 6:1–7.

[8] "Das Buch Henoch," 230–32.

[9] *Le livre d'Hénoch,* xcv. He thought that it was later than the Apocalypse of Weeks (*1 Enoch* 93:1–10; 91:11–17), which was, in his opinion, written shortly before 170, and that passages such as 1:9 and 25:6 seemed to refer to the Antiochan persecution which began in 167. He did, however, exclude chaps. 1–5 from this dating and drew no conclusions regarding the time when they were composed.

[10] *The Book of Enoch,* lii. Charles saw no references to Antiochus' campaign against Judaism in the work.

allowed, but it also is consistent with a date even before 170. On paleographical grounds Milik has dated 4QEn[a], which preserves parts of *1 Enoch* 1–12,
to the first half of the second century B.C.[11] Moreover, there is some reason to
think that it was copied from a model dating from the third century.[12] 4QEn[b]
appears to be a copy from the mid–second century, while the other three
copies were made in the last century B.C. and the first century A.D.[13] The
antiquity of En[a,b] implies that the BW, including chaps. 1–5 which had often
been considered a late introduction to the entire *1 Enoch*,[14] was written
before the Maccabean period and well before the priestly schism that gave
birth to the Qumran community in the mid–second century. Milik believes
that both En[a] and En[b] contained only the BW, while it seems clear that En[c]
included with it the newly identified Book of Giants, the Book of Dreams
(*1 Enoch* 83–90), and the Epistle of Enoch (*1 Enoch* 91–107).[15] At least
by the time of En[c], then, Enochic compositions were being gathered into
larger collections.

Paleographical considerations require a date no later than the first half
of the second century for the BW, but, while they establish this lower limit,
they leave unanswered the question of when the unit was edited and certainly
when its parts were written. Milik himself assigns the book to the mid–third
century[16] and maintains that one of its principal sources—chaps. 6–19—is

---

[11] *The Books of Enoch*, 140. He notes that the script is related to semicursive hands of the
third–second centuries B.C. but that "it does not fit very well into the scribal traditions of the
Jewish copyists of Judaea or even Egypt; the scribe would perhaps be dependent upon the
Aramaic scripts and the scribal customs of Northern Syria or Mesopotamia."

[12] Ibid., 141. He claims that the old copy was ". . . from the third century at the very
least." This he infers from examples of purely consonantal orthography and confusion of
certain letters which would be more likely to occur in scripts of the third century (e.g., *y* and *p*)
than in later ones.

[13] For 4QEn[b] see ibid., 164; for En[c] pp. 178 and 23; for En[d] pp. 217 and 22; and for En[e]
p. 225.

[14] That chaps. 1–5 had been written as a general introduction to the entire book of
*1 Enoch* was a common view among specialists. See, for example, Beer, "Das Buch Henoch,"
224; Martin, *Le livre d'Hénoch*, lxxviii; and Charles, *The Book of Enoch*, 2–3. This position has
now been excluded because these chapters are represented on MSS which antedate other parts of
*1 Enoch*. Cf. Dimant, "The 'Fallen Angels,'" 22 n. 78; Rau, "Kosmologie," 34–35.

[15] *The Books of Enoch*, 22, 178, 182–84. Nickelsburg (*Jewish Literature*, 48–55) includes
*1 Enoch* 1–36 among the Jewish writings which pre-date B.C. 175.

[16] *The Books of Enoch*, 28. "We may conclude that it was in Palestine under Lagid
hegemony, towards the middle of the third century B.C., at the height of the intensive commer-
cial and cultural exchanges between East and West, that the Judaean author of the Enochic
Book of Watchers lived and prospered, as a merchant and a writer." Milik derives his notion
that the writer was a merchant from his analysis of Enoch's travels at the end of the BW; the
narratives of those journeys will be examined below.

more ancient still. He detects the earliest allusion to this source, which he names the Visions of Enoch, in an unpublished fragment of the Aramaic Testament of Levi (4QTestLevi[a] 8 iii 6-7), where, in a context in which priests are being admonished, the following words appear:

]ᵓ hlᵓ qbl ẖn̂ŵk [
]nᵓ wᶜl mn thwᵓ ḥwbtᵓ
] Did not Enoch accuse [. . .]?
] And with whom will the blame lie, . . .?[17]

He comments that in these lines ". . . there was certainly an allusion to the accusations made by the patriarch against the Watchers (En. 13-16), who were responsible for the evil which had spread among men (En. 13:2 and 16:3)."[18] He hopes, when he publishes the evidence, to show that the Testament of Levi was composed in the third or perhaps the fourth century B.C. If he proves correct about this, then the reference that he finds in it to chaps. 6–19 of the BW would date the Visions of Enoch to a time no later than the third century and the composition itself would probably have to be placed even earlier.

Milik is probably correct in assigning the BW to the third century, but he has almost certainly overstepped the evidence in his inference from 4QTestLevi[a]. In the first place, even the reading of the name *Enoch* is most uncertain as the circles above three of the four consonants indicate. Second, the verb *qbl* would more likely mean "received" or something of the sort than Milik's "accused." And third, even if Milik were correct about the preceding two dubious points, it would not necessarily follow that the reference was to Enoch's accusations against the angels (though he may have more unpublished evidence that would clarify the context). Moreover, if the words *ḥnwk qbl* did reflect precisely these accusations, it would not be certain that they alluded to the version of this story that is found in the BW.

A more controversial point that Milik has raised is his contention that the Visions of Enoch (i.e., *1 Enoch* 6-19) antedates the version of the story about the angels that appears in Gen 6:1-4.[19] Strangely, he offers no detailed case for his remarkable proposition—one which reverses the order that is otherwise accepted in scholarly literature. Apparently the "abridged and allusive formulation"[20] of Gen 6:1-4 brands it as a summary of the longer account in *1 Enoch*. Yet there is no readily discernible reason why one should not see in *1 Enoch's* version a development of the terse biblical peri-

[17] Ibid., 23–24.
[18] Ibid., 24.
[19] Ibid., 30-32.
[20] Ibid., 31.

cope and of other traditions in a manner analogous to that found in other demonstrably later works such as *Jubilees* and the Genesis Apocryphon.[21]

As a result, it must be said that both attempts by Milik to find allusions to the BW, or more precisely to the Visions of Enoch, in very old literature fail for lack of evidence. His approach to the problem of establishing a date is an appropriate one, but it founders on the paucity of Jewish texts that can be assigned to the fourth and third centuries. The fact that so little is known about Palestinian Judaism in this period makes it unlikely that at present the BW or its parts can be dated more precisely than paleographical data permit. Thus, for dating, the situation is the same as that for the AB: a paleographically determined *terminus ad quem* of ca. 200 or slightly later is reasonably certain, but there is no firm evidence that would allow one to specify a *terminus a quo*. It is possible and indeed likely that the BW is a third–century composition; it is almost certain that it is pre–Maccabean and that it had assumed its present form by the time of 4QEn[a]. It is probably later than the AB, since chaps. 33–36 seem to summarize information from it (see below).

### C. Enoch in the BW

Because their contents differ considerably, it will be convenient to study separately the portraits of Enoch that emerge from the various sections of the BW. In general one can say, though, that the descriptions of Enoch in each of the parts of the BW are elaborations of the biblical theme that he "walked with the *ʾĕlōhîm*" and that the *ʾĕlōhîm* are always understood to be angels.

### 1. Enoch in *1 Enoch* 1–5

The opening lines of the BW present the patriarch in a rather different light than did the original AB:

> 1. The words of the blessing of Enoch according to which he blessed the chosen[22] and righteous who must be present on the day of distress (which is appointed) for the removal of all the wicked and impious.[23] 2. And Enoch answered and

[21] See Nickelsburg's review of *The Books of Enoch* in *CBQ* 40 (1978) 416.

[22] At this point 4QEn[a] 1 i 1 reads: ]ñ ḥn[w]k lbḥ[yryn (Milik, *The Books of Enoch*, 141).

[23] Gr[Pan] has *kai sōthēsontai dikaioi* (and [the] just will be saved) rather than a second term for the wicked. Milik (*The Books of Enoch*, 142) restores the Aramaic equivalent of the Greek ([wqšyṭyn yplṭwn]).

said:[24] (there was)[25] a righteous man whose eyes were opened by the Lord, and he saw a holy vision[26] in the heavens which the angels[27] showed to me. And I heard everything from them, and I understood what I saw, but not for this generation, but for a distant generation[28] which will come. 3. Concerning the chosen I spoke, and I uttered a parable concerning them . . . (1:1–3a).

a. Enoch and Balaam (1:2–3a): Commentators regularly note that the introductory paragraph, which tells the reader very little about the identity of Enoch,[29] begins with words modeled on Deut 33:1 and then continues with several phrases borrowed from the Balaam stories in Numbers 22–24.[30]

---

[24] Gr$^{Pan}$ reads in place of the bland "answered and said" the words *kai analabōn tēn parabolēn autou eipen* (he took up his parable and said). 4QEn$^a$ 1 i 2 confirms the Greek in that the expression *mtlwh[y w$^{>}$]mř* appears here, though the plural form (*mtlwhy*) is different. This expression derives, as indicated below, from the Balaam stories in Numbers 22–24 where his oracles are introduced by the words *wayyiśśā$^{>}$ mašlô wayyō$^{>}$mar* (23:7, 18; 24:3, 15, 20, 21, 23). In Numbers the singular *mašlô* is always used. In the Aramaic form of *1 Enoch* 93:1, 3a (4QEn$^g$ 1 iii 18, 23), one finds *nsb ḥnwk mtlh* (Enoch took up his parable). See Milik, *The Books of Enoch*, 142, 263–64.

[25] Though there is an awkward change from third to first person in v 2 (for a similar interchange see 93:1–3a), it seems preferable to regard the words "a righteous man whose eyes were opened by the Lord, and he saw a holy vision in the heavens" as standing in apposition to the word *Enoch* and not as the first, peculiar words of his speech, as Knibb punctuates it.

[26] The Ethiopic MSS read either *rā$^c$ya qeddus* (a vision of the Holy One) or *rā$^c$ya qeddusa* (a holy vision). The Greek text agrees with the former (*tēn horasin tou hagiou*).

[27] There are several textual problems at this juncture. Gr$^{Pan}$ reads: *edeixen moi kai hagiologōn hagiōn ēkousa egō* (he showed to me, and I heard holy words of holy ones [?]). The word *hagiologōn* is strange and may be the product of a confusion, perhaps conditioned by the word *hagiōn* which follows. The Aramaic (En$^a$ 1 i 3), which Milik reads as *wmn ml$^{>}$ [$^c$yryn]* *wqdyšyn* (*The Books of Enoch*, 142) and Knibb as *wmn ml̊$^{>}$kyn] wqdyšyn* (*The Ethiopic Book of Enoch*, 2.57), suggests that the Greek is a corruption of *apo logōn hagiōn* (so Milik, ibid., 143). The singular *edeixen* remains a problem It may be that originally a plural *edeixan* appeared, followed by *aggeloi* or *egrēgoroi* and that *aggeloi* was omitted by homoioteleuton with *moi*. Once the plural subject had disappeared and it was noticed that only singular subjects had been mentioned before (God and the Holy One), the plural was emended to a singular.

[28] All texts agree that Enoch speaks for a distant generation, not for his contemporaries, but the wording varies somewhat. The Aramaic reads: *lhd]n drh lhn ld[r r]ḥyq $^{>}$nh $^{>}$m̊[ll* (for) this generation, but for a faroff generation I shall speak [Milik, *The Books of Enoch*, 142]).

[29] Beer ("Das Buch Henoch," 224) argued from the fact that these verses say so little about who Enoch is that they drew upon a more extensive Enochic tradition in which there was a report about him and how he had attained the eminent position that he occupies in chaps. 1–5.

[30] See, for example, Charles, *The Book of Enoch*, 4–5, though his notes do not indicate the full extent of the borrowing. More complete are the studies of L. Hartman: *Prophecy Interpreted: The Formation of Some Jewish Apocalyptic Texts and of the Eschatological Discourse Mark 13 Par.* (ConB 1; Lund: Gleerup, 1966) 112–14; and *Asking for a Meaning: A Study of 1 Enoch 1–5* (ConB 12; Lund: Gleerup, 1979) 22–23. Even Hartman, however, does not deal adequately with the problem of why the writer should describe Enoch as another Balaam in effect. See also Rau, "Kosmologie," 34–41. Rau (38) also observes that 1:2a, 3a,b

The extent of the borrowing from Numbers can be seen from the following comparison.

| Expression | 1 Enoch | Numbers |
|---|---|---|
| took up his parable and said | 1:2 (Aramaic, GrPan), 3 | 23:7, 18; 24:3, 15, 20, 21, 23 |
| whose eyes were opened by the Lord | 1:2 | 22:31; 24:3–4, 15–16 |
| he saw a vision of the holy one | 1:2 (GrPan, some Ethiopic MSS) | 24:4, 16 (*šadday* is used) |
| heard everything from them[31] | 1:2 | cf. 24:4, 16 (one who hears the words of *ʾēl*) |
| not for this generation, but for a distant generation which will come | 1:2 | cf. 24:14, 17. |

It may seem puzzling at first glance that the author of the BW would portray Enoch in language that draws so heavily on the stories about Balaam, a foreign diviner who, though summoned to curse the Israelites, was eventually compelled to bless them. Why would a Jewish writer turn to this pericope for phrases with which to introduce his visionary hero Enoch?

Several features of Balaam's character in Numbers 22–24 may have suggested to the author that Balaam and Enoch were not as different as one might suppose. Enoch was, according to the argument of the preceding chapters, a Jewish version of the Mesopotamian diviner–king Enmeduranki. Most of the traits ascribed to Enoch in Gen 5:21–24 and in the AB are explicable on the basis of that traditional model. The point of connection between Enoch and Balaam seems to be the fact that both have strong associations with the world of divination and more specifically with the *bārûtum*.[32] Balaam is unmistakably depicted as a diviner who hails from the

---

correspond to an introduction to a wisdom speech (comparing Job 27:1; 29:1). Enoch's blessing is thus presented as a wisdom address.

[31] If with Milik (*The Books of Enoch*, 142) one reads *wmn mly* rather than *wmn ml[ʾkyn]* as Knibb (*The Ethiopic Book of Enoch*, 2.57) proposes, the parallel with Num 24:4, 16 would be closer, since there the *words* of God are mentioned. There seems to be a trace of a letter at the edge of the fragment, but it is most difficult to decipher it.

[32] Similarities between Balaam and the *bārûs* have been detailed, more or less convincingly, by several scholars. S. Daiches ("Balaam—a Babylonian *bārū*: The episode of Num 22, 2–24, 24 and some Babylonian parallels" in *Hilprecht Anniversary Volume: Studies in Assyriology and Archaeology* [Leipzig: Hinrichs, 1909] 60–70) discussed several features of the Numbers texts that are paralleled in ritual texts for the *bārûs*: divining in the morning, accompanying

northern Euphrates region (22:5; cf. 23:6),[33] and in the narratives and poems of these chapters standard mantic terms are employed. One learns that messengers from Balak, king of Moab, gave him fees for his divinatory services (qĕsāmîm; 22:7); that he received revelations from God at night (22:8, 19–20); that he followed the well attested mantic practice of performing sacrificial rituals prior to receiving communications from the deity (23:1–6, 14-17, 29–30); and that he regularly sought oracles (nĕḥāšîm; 24:1). It happens, however, that though Balak had summoned Balaam to curse Israel the diviner is eventually forced to the conclusion that "there is no enchantment [naḥaš] against Jacob, no divination [qesem] against Israel" (23:23).[34] Moreover, the fact that Balaam, under divine illumination (24:4, 16 [maḥăzēh šadday]), sees a vision in which the star/sceptre will come to judge Israel's foes, naturally enhanced the relevance of these chapters for the writer of 1 Enoch 1:1–9, since, according to him, angels revealed (at God's command) to Enoch information about the great day of judgment when God will destroy the evil and bless the righteous (cf. 1:3b–9). It is particularly important for the connection with Enoch that Balaam informs Balak that his words concerned what Israel would succeed in doing to his people "in the latter days" (24:14 [bĕʾaḥărît hayyāmîm]). This phrase may well have had a rather limited historical scope in the mind of the author of Numbers 24,[35] but for a Jewish

---

sacrifices by both diviner and the one for whom he divines; the term šepî (23:3) meaning "quietly, with hindered step"; Balaam's titles, etc. R. Largement ("Les oracles de Bileᶜam et la mantique suméro-akkadienne," École des langues orientales anciennes de l'Institut Catholique de Paris: Mémorial du cinquantenaire 1914-1964 [Travaux de l'Institut Catholique de Paris 10; Paris: Bloud et Gay, 1964] 37–50) compared many aspects of the Balaam chapters with Mesopotamian omens and practices. He even considered seriously the implausible and philologically erroneous suggestion that bĕᶜôr—the name of Balaam's father—represents a scribal misunderstanding of the word bārû. However, the name of the diviner's father (spelled bᶜr) is now attested in the recently published text from Deir ᶜAlla (e.g., 1, 5, 13) so that the bārû-suggestion becomes even more unlikely. Balaam also appears as a diviner in the Deir ᶜAlla text: he is called ʾš ḥzh ʾlhn (I, 2 [a man who sees gods]) and from the gods he receives a night vision that deals with the future (I, 3–7). For the text see J. Hoftijzer and G. van der Kooij, Aramaic Texts from Deir ᶜAllā (Documenta et Monumenta Orientis Antiqui 19; Leiden: Brill, 1976); and the review essay of B. Levine, "The Deir ᶜAlla Plaster Inscriptions," JAOS 101 (1981) 195-205 (his line numbering is used above). Albright ("Balaam: Critical View," Encyclopaedia Judaica 4.122) pointed to the similarities between Balaam and the bārûs of Mari who accompanied armies into battle.

[33] Regarding the identity of Balaam's homeland, see M. Noth, Numbers (Old Testament Library; Philadelphia: Westminster, 1968) 173–74; Albright, "Balaam: Critical View," 122; and Largement, "Les oracles," 38.

[34] G. Gray (Numbers [ICC; Edinburgh: Clark, 1903] 355) translates: "There is no observation of omens in Jacob, Nor divining by lots in Israel." His literal rendering of the two instances of the preposition bĕ- is unnecessary and does not suit the context.

[35] So Noth, Numbers, 192.

writer of the Hellenistic age it would naturally have aroused eschatological thoughts. If this is correct, then it is perhaps noteworthy, in light of the discussion regarding divination and eschatology in chap. I (above), that for the writer of *1 Enoch* 1 a diviner (Balaam) could be speaking about the *eschaton*.

*1 Enoch* 1:1–3a serves, then, to authenticate the following words of Enoch, not by appeal to Gen 5:21–24 or to the AB, but by introducing him as a diviner-seer in the mold of Balaam. Both of these figures belong in mantic contexts, both speak under divine inspiration in such circumstances, and both pronounce future blessings upon the people of God and curses on their enemies. The author of this chapter seems, therefore, to have viewed Balaam in a favorable light; otherwise it is difficult to understand why he would describe Enoch and his visionary experience in terms that are borrowed from the Balaam stories.[36]

*1 Enoch* 1:3a, which also draws upon the Balaam chapters, labels the speech of Enoch that follows a *parable*. Since the word is taken from Num 23:7, 18; 24:3, 15, 20, 21, and 23, where it categorizes Balaam's various addresses, one could perhaps glean something of the sense in which the author of *1 Enoch* 1 used this flexible term from its meaning(s) in Numbers 23–24. Regarding the meaning of *māšāl* in the Balaam pericope A. R. Johnson has written:

> . . . it denotes, not a parallel which already exists and thus serves as an example whereby its like may be avoided or brought into being, but one which is first pictured in the mind, possibly under so-called 'ecstatic' conditions, and then given colourful expression in words with a view to its corresponding appearance in actual life, i.e., the pattern or shape of things to come as envisaged by the speaker in terms of Yahweh's purposeful action. In the passages in question it clearly forms the pattern of a blessing or curse, expressed here and there in somewhat allegorical language, and, as such, it serves as an instrument of magical or, better perhaps, magico–religious action—in short a spell which can be effective in and of itself.[37]

The "parable" of Enoch in chaps. 1–5 involves blessings for the righteous

---

[36] In this assessment he was not alone, as Balaam occupied a lofty position according to some rabbinic authorities. He was considered one of the seven prophets to the nations (*b. B. Bat.* 15b), and in some respects he was held to be greater than Moses (*Num. Rab.* 20.1). See Y. M. Grintz, "Balaam: In the Aggadah," *Encyclopaedia Judaica* 4.123.

[37] "*Māšāl*" in *Wisdom in Israel and in the Ancient Near East* (VTSup 3; ed. M. Noth and D. Winton Thomas; Leiden: Brill, 1960) 167–68. See also D. W. Suter, "*MĀŠĀL* in the Similitudes of Enoch," *JBL* 100 (1981) 193–212. He notes that in *1 Enoch* 37–71 the term applies to comparisons between the fate of the righteous and wicked and between cosmology and eschatology.

and curses for the sinners, and it rivets the reader's attention on the *eschaton*, particularly the final judgment.

   b. *1 Enoch* 1–5 as an Eschatological Text: Because of its strong interest in the final judgment and the contrasting fates of the righteous and wicked during it *1 Enoch* 1–5 can be characterized as an eschatological work. In 1:3b–9 one reads a magnificent description of theophany in which the Lord, as he did in Israel's ancient wars, comes to destroy his wicked foes and to save his righteous people. But here theophany is future and functions as a prelude to the ultimate judgment. *1 Enoch* 2:1–5:3 describe the unwavering and eternal obedience of nature to the laws which God had designed for its many parts, while 5:4–9 sharply contrast this praise–inspiring regularity with the perpetual disobedience of sinners to the divine ordinances. These last verses also depict the differing rewards of the sinners and the righteous.

   Recent studies have disclosed how completely the theophany in 1:3b–9[38] and the eschatological curses and blessings of 5:4–9[39] rest upon biblical foundations. In fact, it is safe to say that there is no clear evidence that the author has advanced beyond his biblical models in expressing his eschatological convictions. Obviously biblical writers, too, awaited a future divine judgment of some sort upon the evil and a reward for the obedient. Hence, in *1 Enoch* 1–5 one moves in an eschatological world and indeed Enoch is, for the first time in surviving literature, brought into relation with the *eschaton*; but the eschatology expressed here remains archaic and somewhat restrained in comparison with some of the more elaborate treatments of the end in later works (the same can be said of *1 Enoch* 10:16–11:2). In addition, one should note that there is no survey of world history, no effort to organize it into epochs, and no detailing of final woes. The only eschatological event of importance is the judgment. As a result, though Enoch learns of the future through a vision, it seems inappropriate to label *1 Enoch* 1–5 an apocalypse or its contents apocalyptic eschatology. These chapters stand in the tradition of Israel's prophets and wise men.

   c. Enoch and the Creator's Laws: As he was in the AB (but certainly not in 80:2–8), Enoch continues in the BW to be associated with the unalterable laws which regulate natural phenomena. In fact, 2:1 may have been

---

[38] Hartman, *Prophecy Interpreted*, 71–73, 112–18; *Asking for a Meaning*, 22–26; Vander-Kam, "The Theophany of Enoch i 3b–7, 9," *VT* 23 (1973) 129–50; Rau, "Kosmologie," 42–66.

[39] Hartman (*Asking for a Meaning*, especially 18–21 [literary observations] and 30–38 [use of OT passages]) has discussed this pericope in great detail and concludes that to a large extent it is an interpretative re–presentation of elements drawn from Moses' farewell speech in Deuteronomy 27–32 and from the priestly benediction of Num 6:24–26. "Beyond any doubt the text as a whole [i.e., *1 Enoch* 1–5]—except for the details of 2:1–5:3 (on the order of nature)—grows out of a soil consisting of an interpreted OT" (37–38).

inspired by the AB: "*Contemplate* all the events in heaven, how the lights in heaven do not change their courses, how each rises and sets in order, each at its proper time, and they do not transgress their law."[40] There follow very brief sections which illustrate the obedience of different parts of nature to the laws which the Creator had designed for them: the earth and what is done on it (2:2); the two seasons summer and winter (2:3); the trees (chap. 3); the days and heat of summer (chap. 4); trees again (5:1);[41] and seas and rivers (5:3). Immediately before this last section the writer inserts the general comment: "And understand in respect of everything and perceive how He who lives for ever made all these things for you; and (how) his works (are) before him in each succeeding year, and all his works serve him and do not change, but as God has decreed, so everything is done" (5:1b–2).[42] While the sapiential principle of unchanging natural order is the same as in the AB and astronomy and calendrical matters figure prominently,[43] the range of subjects is expanded. The most important innovation *vis-à-vis* the AB is that in *1 Enoch* 2–5 the orderliness of nature—its subjection to divine law—becomes the basis of Enoch's exhortation. It and the penchant of the righteous for noticing it serve as a contrast to the behavior of the sinners, who, though they will be judged by God (unlike nature), consistently violate the statutes which he had ordained for them and fail to take note of natural laws. As a result, they are to be condemned and to suffer the curses of the covenant after the judgment that is pictured so graphically in 1:3b–9.

Appeal to natural order as a foundation for parenesis is unprecedented in the OT, but Hartman has made a major contribution to understanding

---

[40] 4QEn^c 1 i 17–19 preserves a few words of this verse, and, though the meaning is largely the same as in the Ethiopic, the wording is somewhat different. Also, there is an additional clause at the beginning. Milik (*The Books of Enoch*, 185) translates thus: "[Consider] all (His) work, and observe ye the work(s) of the heavens, [and the luminaries which do not change their courses] in the stations of their lights, that all arise [and set, each one of them in its order]." En^a 1 ii 1 preserves a few letters from the end of the verse, including the word *srkn* (their order; ibid., 145).

[41] Knibb (*The Ethiopic Book of Enoch*, 2.62) draws attention to the fact that 2:3 with chap. 3 parallels chap. 4 with 5:1. Hartman (*Asking for a Meaning*, 17–18) offers a detailed study of the carefully designed structure of 2:1–5:3.

[42] There are textual problems here, too, but the meaning in the versions does not differ in ways that are important for the present purposes. For the Aramaic evidence from En^a,c, see Milik, *The Books of Enoch*, 146–48, 185; and Knibb, *The Ethiopic Book of Enoch*, 2.64–65. Rau ("Kosmologie," 66–92) argues at length that the major purpose of 2:1–5:3 is not to celebrate nature's predictability but to elicit praise for the creator. Failure by the wicked to observe nature properly leads to their apostasy from God. He explores parallels in various late sapiential texts (see below for examples) and in biblical passages that belong to the wisdom traditions of Israel (e.g., Psalm 148).

[43] Milik (*The Books of Enoch*, 148) thinks that chap. 3 is dependent on the AB.

this Enochic theme by demonstrating that natural entities here occupy the place filled by the sun, moon, and other natural phenomena in OT treaty contexts. There they are summoned as witnesses to the proceedings, but in *1 Enoch* 2-5 that ancient and originally mythological usage is modified so that the many parts of God's creation become examples which are to elicit praise and obedience.[44] Nature's orderliness, interpreted as obedience to the Creator's laws, surfaces in other Jewish works, especially in wisdom texts, yet chaps. 2-5 appear to be the earliest instance of the particular use to which the author puts it. In his search for parallels, Charles drew attention to Sir 16:26-28:[45]

> When the Lord created his works in the beginning,
> and after making them defined their boundaries,
> he disposed them in an eternal order
> and fixed their influences for all time.
> They do not grow hungry or weary,
> or abandon their tasks;
> one does not jostle another;
> they never disobey his word (*NEB*).

*BS "hymn to creation?" [handwritten] En ch. 43 [handwritten]*

Parenetic use of natural order is not as immediately apparent here as in *1 Enoch* 2-5, but the context in Ben Sira includes this element as well (note the treatment of humankind as God's creation in chap. 17). A closer parallel to *1 Enoch* 2-5 is found in *T. Naph.* 3:2-5 (e.g., v 2: "Sun and moon and stars change not their order; so do ye also change not the law of God in the disorderliness of your doings").[46] But it is clear that these verses are dependent on the BW. In these and other passages like them, as in the AB, it is assumed that humankind can and does have a grasp of the fundamental

---

[44] There is no biblical precedent for a hortatory appeal to nature's laws. Hartman (*Asking for a Meaning*, 29-30) shows that *Sifre* Deut 32:1 (the biblical passage calls on heaven and earth as witnesses) interprets the verse much as *1 Enoch* 2:1-5:3 does: "In both cases we encounter admonitions to observe how creation does not change its orders, and in both nature's order is contrasted to man's disobedience. In both texts, also, the text may be connected with the covenantal context of Dt, . . ." (29). On pp. 65-71 he adduces other relevant texts and locates most of them in the context of covenant and *rib* (e.g., Jer 5:22-23; Job 12:7-8). One does, of course, find biblical references to nature and concern by Israel's sages with observation and classification of it (e.g., 1 Kgs 4:29-34 [Hebrew 5:9-14]; cf. also Prov 30:4, 18-19, 24-28, 29-31; and the long list of rhetorical questions and observations in Job 38-41). For analyses of this *Listenwissenschaft* and parallels to it in Egyptian and Mesopotamian literature, see A. Alt, "Die Weisheit Salomos," *TLZ* 76 (1951) cols. 139-44; and von Rad, "Hiob xxxviii und die altägyptische Weisheit" in *Wisdom in Israel and in the Ancient Near East*, 293-301. But parenesis is never appended to these passages.

[45] *The Book of Enoch*, 8-9; Hartman, *Asking for a Meaning*, 65-71.

[46] Translation of Charles in *APOT* 2.

principles by which nature operates. Only in this way would it be possible to appeal to natural laws as examples of obedience to the creator and as a spur to ethical conduct.[47]

In summary, *1 Enoch* 1–5 re-uses and significantly develops older themes that had clustered about the person of Enoch. The introduction shows that these chapters and indeed the entire BW are a further elaboration of the biblical theme that Enoch sojourned with the *ʾĕlōhîm* (i.e., angels). His associations with the mantic world are reaffirmed in that he is presented in language that is unmistakably drawn from the Balaam stories and poems of Numbers 22–24. Divining necessarily entails prediction, and here Enoch does predict; but in these chapters a new and momentous step is taken in that Enoch becomes a herald of the *eschaton*. As noted above, the reference in Num 24:14 to the *ʾaḥărît hayyāmîm* (understood in an eschatological sense) probably facilitated in part the process of assimilating Enoch to Balaam. Henceforth Enoch will never be dissociated from eschatological prediction, though his efforts at this early point are limited almost exclusively to the day of judgment and are thus on a relatively restricted scale. His scientific interests, which were so important in the AB, re-appear in 2:1–5:3, but they serve new ends: they are not presented simply as information but as the platform from which the patriarch exhorts his readers to praise and morality in obedience to the creator and from which he castigates the wicked for their failure to observe, praise, and obey.

### 2. Enoch in *1 Enoch* 12–16

These chapters, which critics have usually regarded as a distinct unit within the BW,[48] serve in their present environment to develop and elaborate chaps. 6–11 and to introduce or prepare for the accounts of Enoch's journeys in chaps. 17–19 and 21–36.

---

[47] Opposed to this position is another, found already in the OT (e.g., Eccl 8:17; 11:5; Job 38–41), that stresses humanity's inability to comprehend the ways of God and his creation. For the texts and analyses of them see Stone, "Lists of Revealed Things," 414–52; and Gruenwald, *Apocalyptic and Merkavah Mysticism*, 3–28.

[48] See, e.g., Beer, "Das Buch Henoch," 225; Charles, *The Book of Enoch*, xlvii, 27–28; C. Newsom, "The Development of *1 Enoch* 6–19: Cosmology and Judgment," *CBQ* 42 (1980) 315–23. Milik (*The Books of Enoch*, 25) speaks of chaps. 6–19 as ". . . an early written source which he [the author of the BW] incorporated without any great changes in his own work. . . ." His discussion, which concludes with the observation that "all the laborious critical 'vivisection' of our document by 'many hands' (Charles, p. 1) accomplished during the last century and a half is shown to be useless and mistaken," (25) really does not touch on the issues raised by the "vivisectionists" and certainly does not refute their arguments. It seems likely that a single editor has imposed a loose unity on chaps. 6–19, but much of the material now contained in this section probably once existed in several independent parts.

a. Chaps. 12–16 in Relation to 6–11: Since chaps. 12–16 build on 6–11, it will be useful to add a few comments regarding the latter section's versions of the story about the angels who sinned, though Enoch himself does not appear in these chapters.

1) Notes on *1 Enoch* 6–11: Beginning already with Dillmann, commentators had noticed that *1 Enoch* 6–11 offer two different stories about the angels who were held responsible for the hideous evil and violence in the immediate antediluvian period.[49] The longer narrative centers about a 200–member angelic company at whose head stands a Watcher named Shemihazah (*šĕmîḥāzâ*), and it includes several major elements.

1. From heaven the Watchers saw and desired the daughters of men; they swore an oath that they would act according to their desires (6:1–8).
2. They descended, married, and defiled themselves with women (7:1abc).[50]
[3. They taught women about charms, spells, root–cutting, and plants (7:1de)].[51]

---

[49] Dillmann, "Pseudepigraphen des Alten Testaments," *RE*[2] 12.352; Beer ("Das Buch Henoch," 225) found version a in 6:2b–8; 7:3–6; 8:4; 9:1–5, 9–11; 10:4–11:2; and version b in 7:1b; 8:1–3; 9:6–8; and 10:1–3. He thought that 6:1–2 and 7:1a, 2 were common to the two narratives. Charles (*The Book of Enoch*, 13–14) with Dillmann assigns 6:3–8; 8:1–3; 9:7; and 10:11 to a Shemihazah cycle. He attributed 10:1–3 to a Noah Apocalypse. More recently, Paul Hanson ("Rebellion in Heaven, Azazel, and Euhemeristic Heroes in 1 Enoch 6–11," *JBL* 96 [1977] 197–233) has assigned all of the section to the Shemihazah story except 7:1de; 8:1–3; 9:6; 8c; and 10:4–10; and Nickelsburg ("Apocalyptic and Myth in 1 Enoch 6–11," *JBL* 96 [1977] 383–405) has distinguished as Asael material 8:1–2; 9:6; and 10:4–8. He also claims that 7:1de; 8:3; 9:8c; and 10:7 are a "secondary contamination" in the Shemihazah cycle from the Asael version (386). Dimant ("The 'Fallen Angels,'" 23–72), whose analysis of the haggadic sources in chaps. 6–11 is the most thorough one available, finds three versions of a story in the section: 1. the angels defile themselves with women and from them engender giants who are the source of evil and violence (this version, which is related to Gen 6:1–4, was not originally connected with the flood); 2. the angels sin through teaching forbidden secrets to humankind and thus lead them to sin (this version, which is also related to Gen 6:1–4, seems to present the flood as a punishment on sinful humanity); and 3. Asael corrupts people by his teachings (this version, which relates more closely to Gen 6:11–12, explains the corruption on the earth before the flood and thus supplies a reason why the punishment was sent).

[50] At 7:1c the Ethiopic reads *wa-taddammaru meslēhomu* ("and were promiscuous with them"), but both Gr[Pan] and Syncellus have *kai miainesthai in autais* (and to defile themselves with them). Knibb (*The Ethiopic Book of Enoch*, 2.77) proposes that confusion of the Aramaic verbs *ṭmʾ* (to be unclean, defiled) and *ṭmᶜ* (to be mixed up) underlies the variants. The meaning "defiled" better suits the interpretation of the Shemihazah story found in 15:3–7.

[51] Nickelsburg ("Apocalyptic and Myth," 384–86), Hanson ("Rebellion in Heaven," 226–32), and R. Bartelmus (*Heroentum in Israel und seiner Umwelt* [ATANT 65; Zurich: Theologischer, 1979] 160–66) have maintained that the teaching passages are an intrusion from the Asael story. It must be admitted that this motif plays a more meaningful role in the Asael

4. The women gave birth to giants who, after exhausting human food supplies, turned to cannibalism and drinking blood (7:2–5).
[5. Different angels are said to have taught various arts including those mentioned in 3. above and astrology (8:3)].
6. Oppressed human survivors of the giants' attacks cried to heaven for help (8:4; cf. 7:6 where the earth is said to have accused the lawless).
7. Angels who had not sinned brought humanity's suit before God (9:1–5, 7–11).
8. God consequently ordered punishment in several stages: slaying of the mortal giants before their fathers' eyes (10:9–10);[52] binding of the immortal Watchers themselves beneath the hills for 70 generations until the day of judgment (10:11–12); and, after the final judgment, imprisoning them forever in a fiery abyss (10:13).

This Shemihazah version, in which the Watchers and their gigantic offspring cause the ensuing difficulties and not angelic teachings, differs markedly with the seemingly abbreviated[53] Asael (*ʿăśāʾēl*) cycle in several ways. According to the parts of this latter story that have been spliced into the first (8:1–2; 9:6; 10:4–6, 8), the angel Asael, who bears the same name as the tenth leader in Shemihazah's group (6:7),[54] becomes a teacher of heav-

---

narrative than in the Shemihazah story where it has no function. Dimant ("The 'Fallen Angels,'" 52–65), however, makes a strong case that the teaching angels other than Asael are traces of another version of the story about the angels and that these passages do not derive from the Asael version. She thinks that the story in which angels teach (no. 2 in n. 49 above) was fused with the Shemihazah material before the Asael passages were added. The presence of the teaching elements in the Shemihazah version led to the addition of the Asael verses in which teaching also has an important part.

[52] It is not at all clear how the flood is supposed to be connected with the story. In 10:1–3, which critics have often identified as part of a book of Noah, the writer may have felt compelled to reproduce the biblical juxtaposition of human–angel marriages and the announcement of the flood, but the deluge affects neither the Watchers nor the giants—only supposedly innocent people. As noted above, Dimant argues that the Shemihazah version originally had no connection with the flood. The issue of a book of Noah, potentially a most significant subject, is complicated by the fact that the various sections of *1 Enoch* that have been assigned to it are far from unified. See the discussion in Dimant, "The 'Fallen Angels,'" 122–27.

[53] In *1 Enoch* 86:1–2 the Asael story begins with his descent from heaven; later, other angels join him. For later versions of the Shemihazah and Asael accounts, see Milik, *The Books of Enoch*, 321–39.

[54] The two narratives may have been combined not only because of their related content but also because of this overlap of names. Syncellus already considered them the same, as his version of 8:1 indicates (*azaēl ho dekatos tōn archontōn* [Asael the tenth of the rulers]); but he does not spell the two in the same way (in 6:7 the form is *azalzēl*). Gr[Pan], too, spells the names differently: in 6:7 it is *aseal* but in 8:1 *azaēl*. In Ethiopic there is also a difference: *ʾasāʾēl* (6:7) and *ʾazāzeʾēl* (8:1). These variations in spelling could lead one to conclude that the two names

enly secrets. It is these teachings that lead humankind to sin. He instructs people in two subjects: making weapons of war[55] and preparing cosmetics by which women seduced the holy angels.[56] Heavenly angels then charge Asael before the Lord with the crimes of teaching impiety and revealing heavenly secrets. In other words, the arts which he taught were previously unknown to humankind and were not meant to be communicated to them by Asael. Only a revolt against heavenly authority led to his revelation of them. The angel Gabriel was assigned the task of punishing the convicted rebel by binding him hand and foot and throwing him into the darkness amid sharp, jagged rocks. Asael's punishment, like that of Shemihazah and his associates, was to unfold in two stages: after his rocky confinement he would be hurled into fire on the day of judgment. *1 Enoch* 10:6, in which the Lord speaks, seems to allude to a fuller version of the Asael myth: "And the whole earth has been ruined by the teaching of the works of Azazel, and against him write down all sin."

Although *1 Enoch* 6–11 is a composite narrative in which at least two strands have been imperfectly interwoven, it is unmistakably based on Gen 6:1–2, 4—the terse paragraph about the sons of God and the daughters of men. It is, however, no less apparent that the writers have made extensive changes in and additions to the biblical model. Taken in itself, the Genesis

---

entail there were two different angels behind them (so Dimant, "The 'Fallen Angels'" 55 n. 205). However, the Aramaic evidence now shows that on the original level of the text there was no distinction: ʿsʾl (4QEnᵃ 1 iii 9 = 6:7); ʿš[ʾl] (Enᶜ ii 26 = 6:7); and ˚ˢ˚[l] (Enᵇ 1 ii 26 = 8:1). A complicating factor at some point in the tradition may have been influence from stories about the ʿăzāʾzēl of Leviticus 16. Hanson ("Rebellion in Heaven," 220–26) ascribes a very important role to Leviticus 16 in the development of the Asael materials, but his explanation is not as convincing as the Prometheus parallel mentioned below (so Nickelsburg, "Apocalyptic and Myth, 403–05). See also Delcor, "La mythe de la chute," 35–37.

[55] In 8:1b the Ethiopic MSS read *za-ʾem dexrēhomu* ("the things after these"); Grᴾᵃⁿⁿⁿⁿⁿⁿⁿ has *ta megala* (the large/great things); and Syncellus *ta metalla* (the metals). Grᴾᵃⁿⁿⁿ can be explained as a corruption of the superior reading attested in Syncellus, while the Ethiopic represents a mis-division of *ta metalla* as *ta metʾ alla* (see Knibb, *The Ethiopic Book of Enoch*, 2.80, though *ta metʾ alla* is to be preferred to his *ta metʾ auta*; cf. Milik, *The Books of Enoch*, 169). Knibb's suggestion that the Ethiopic and Greek variants could have arisen from ". . . Aramaic *mṭwl*— understood by Eth to mean 'after', and by Gr to mean 'metal'" is not convincing, since *mṭwl* means "on account of," not "after," in Aramaic, and *mṭwl* meaning "metal" is not attested, however similar the sounds may be.

[56] The reading in Syncellus, which Nickelsburg ("Apocalyptic and Myth," 398) is inclined to accept as original at the end of 8:2, is *kai parebēsan kai eplanēsan tous hagious* (and they transgressed and led astray the holy ones). Ethiopic reads: "and they went astray, and all their ways became corrupt." The difference could be explained by appeal to a confusion between Greek *hagious* (holy ones) and *hodous* (ways). Though 4QEnᵇ 1 iii 1 supplies part of 8:2, this section of the verse is lost (Milik, *The Books of Enoch*, 170). See also Dimant, "The 'Fallen Angels,'" 56–57.

pericope is neutral about the commingling of angels and women and about the character of their children.[57] In fact, it is possible to argue that the extraordinary offspring of these marriages were meant to be humankind's protectors against the giants who lived at that time.[58] But in *1 Enoch* 6-11, from beginning to end, these unions of divine and human individuals are condemned with no mincing of words as the root of evil and violence (note, for example, the oath in 6:3-5; the description of the giants in 7:2-5; and the punishments meted out to fathers and sons in 10:4-15).[59] Editorial interference that alters the *Tendenz* of a section so decisively raises questions about purpose and sources. One major effect of these editorial labors is to cast a negative light on the crafts and arts—the secrets—which the angels revealed. It is significant that among these are included not only manufacture of weapons and cosmetics but also several mantic arts (such as astrology) or information essential to practice of them.

> Šemî-ḥazah taught spell-binding [and cutting of roots. Ḥermonî taught the loosing of spells,] magic, sorcery, and skill. [Baraqʾel taught the signs of thunders. Kôkabʾel taught] the signs of the stars. Zêqʾel [taught the signs of lightning-flashes. Arʿtaqoph taught the signs of the earth]. Šamšîʾel taught the signs of the sun. [Šahrîʾel taught the signs of the] moon. [And they all began to reveal] secrets to their wives (8:3, Aramaic).[60]

The context shows that the author considers this particular revelation of such knowledge to be sin; these arts lead to untold wickedness and misery. This appraoch to the secrets stands in a certain tension, it appears, with the AB in which astronomical information was revealed to Enoch with no effort to suppress it (cf. also 2:1-5:3),[61] but it also acts as a foil for Enoch's reception and transmission of revealed knowledge in the remainder of the AB.

Issues of sources, purpose, and date are difficult to separate for these chapters. Scholars both ancient and modern have noticed similarities between features of the Shemihazah–Asael stories and some tales from Greek mythology. Josephus wrote about Gen 6:1-4: "For many angels of God now consorted with women and begat sons who were overbearing and disdainful of

---

[57] See the extended analysis in Bartelmus, *Heroentum in Israel*, 15-30; cf. also Delcor, "La mythe de la chute," 4-17. Both of these scholars, with many others, consider Gen 6:3 an addition to the text. It is not cited in the angel story of *1 Enoch* 6-11; however, the concern about length of life in 10:9-10 may be a reflection of it.

[58] So Bartelmus, *Heroentum in Israel*, 152, 156-60.

[59] Ibid., 156-68.

[60] Milik, *The Books of Enoch*, 158.

[61] Bartelmus (*Heroentum in Israel*, 154-55) sees in this tension a reason for regarding 6-11 as originally non-Enochic. With others, he prefers to view it as Noachic.

every virtue, such confidence had they in their strength; in fact the deeds that tradition ascribes to them resemble the audacious exploits told by the Greeks of the giants" (*Ant.* 1.3, 1 §73).[62] It may be, too, that the LXX already reflects awareness of the parallel, since it renders the terms *hannĕpilîm* and *haggibbōrîm* (nephilim and mighty men) of Gen 6:4 with *hoi gigantes*—a term that has a more negative connotation.[63] The Shemihazah cycle does bear some resemblance to Hesiod's *titanomachia* and *gigantomachia* or to the account preserved in his *Catalogues of Women and Eoiae*, though other revolts by lower-ranking deities against the reigning god are widely attested in the ancient Near East;[64] but the Asael story exhibits remarkable affinities with the Prometheus myth (Prometheus was a titan), especially as Aeschylus gave shape to it. Bartelmus summarizes the systematic parallels thus:

> . . . in beiden Traditionen handelt ein göttliches Wesen, das in der Vergangenheit einmal mehr Macht hatte, das aber nichtsdestoweniger nach wie vor göttlich bleibt; beide Male wird das Geschehen als eine Durchbrechung des göttlichen Rechts gewertet, der Vorgang selbst ist Verrat. Zwischen dem Hauptgott und dem Täter besteht aufgrund dessen eine Feindschaft, die eine möglichst vollkommene Ausschaltung des Rechtsbrechers nach sich zieht. Was verraten wird, sind handwerkliche Fähigkeiten, die Kenntnis von Heilmitteln, die Entdeckung von Bodenschätzen, Methoden der Zeichendeutung, Astronomie und Kunde der Erdzeichen, also ein ganzer Katalog von wesentlichen Kulturellen Errungenschaften der Menschen.[65]

It would be inappropriate to dismiss the contributions which native Jewish traditions have made to the re-interpretation of Gen 6:1–2, 4 in *1 Enoch*

---

[62] Translation of H. St. J. Thackeray, *Josephus* IV: *Jewish Antiquities* (LCL; Cambridge: Harvard University, 1930).

[63] See Bartelmus, *Heroentum in Israel*, 158–59; and Delcor, "La mythe de la chute," 14–15 (who refers to other passages in the LXX where titans, giants, etc. are mentioned).

[64] Nickelsburg, "Apocalyptic and Myth," 395–96 (but with hesitation); Bartelmus, *Heroentum in Israel*, 171–73 (Hesiod's *Catalogue of Women*, especially for the punishment of Shemihazah and his colleagues; he also thinks that the description of Asael's place of punishment is borrowed from the titan myth of Hesiod [166]); and T. Francis Glasson, *Greek Influence in Jewish Eschatology* (London: SPCK, 1961), 59–61 (*Catalogue of Women*; for influence of the titan myth on the account of the Watchers' punishment, see pp. 62–64). Cf. also Beer, "Das Buch Henoch," 242; and Charles' note to the term *valley* in 10:12 (*The Book of Enoch*, 24).

[65] *Heroentum in Israel*, 164–65 (and all of 161–66). See also Nickelsburg, "Apocalyptic and Myth," 399–404; and Glasson, *Greek Influence in Jewish Eschatology*, 64–67. Hengel (*Judaism and Hellenism*, 1.190), too, accepts influence from the Greek accounts about the titans, especially Aeschylus' *Prometheus Bound*, but adds: "It should, of course, be noted that the doctrine of the fall of the Titans, based on Hesiod's theogony, is probably of ancient oriental origin . . ." (2.127 n. 540). While this may well be true, no oriental parallels are as close, nor would there be any need to posit an eastern inspiration for this motif, if the BW dates from the Hellenistic period.

6-11,[66] but the argument for borrowing from Greek sources is rather compelling, especially the claim that the Asael version reflects elements of the Prometheus story. *1 Enoch* 6-11, then, offers the first reasonably certain instance in Enochic literature of Greek influence, since none was discernible in the AB and surely not in Gen 5:21-24 (in Hebrew, that is).

Nickelsburg and Bartelmus have recently moved beyond this observation of Greek influence to the related issue of purpose. They have maintained that the motif of divine-human marriages which produced gigantic, violent, and rapacious offspring is a veiled literary attack on the *diadochoi*, the successors of Alexander the Great as rulers of his empire. Since they were supposed to be descendants of divine-human unions, they claimed divinity for themselves. They were notorious for maintaining and attempting to improve their positions through an endless string of wars and constant rapine.[67] Bartelmus has also tried to use this approach as a means for dating *1 Enoch* 6-11, and he concludes that composition in the time of Antiochus IV Epiphanes, who made divine claims for himself and whose military adventures directly affected Judea, is most likely.[68] However, even if one admits that the Enochic giants are a literary representation of the *diadochoi* (a plausible suggestion), the facts that Ptolemaic and Seleucid rulers inaugurated royal cults in the early third century[69] and that throughout the same century their destructive campaigns crisscrossed the Syro-Palestinian region many times entail that an earlier date is possible. There is no statement, either in *1 Enoch* 6-11 or in the remainder of the BW, which clearly refers to Antiochus IV. And, since 4QEn^a, which preserves sections of chaps. 1-5, 6-11, and 12, is to be dated to the first half of the second century,[70] an earlier date than the beginning of Antiochus' reign (175) seems much more likely for chaps. 6-11. Conversely, if the giants are camouflaged literary representations of Alexander's successors, then a *terminus a quo* for 6-11 (and therefore also for the complete BW) would be fixed in the first half of the third century B.C. That issue should remain open, but Greek influence on these chapters is clear, and its presence in them makes similar claims for other parts of the BW more plausible.

---

[66] Dimant ("The 'Fallen Angels,'" 45-48) prefers a biblical derivation for the story of the giants and points to possible influence from the fact that some versions use the term *giants* for various Canaanite peoples. The Prometheus-Asael parallel, though, is the strongest argument for Greek influence.

[67] Nickelsburg, "Apocalyptic and Myth," 396-97 (tentatively); Bartelmus, *Heroentum in Israel*, 175-79.

[68] Ibid., 179-83.

[69] For a short summary of the evidence, see VanderKam, "2 Maccabees 6,7a and Calendrical Change in Jerusalem," *JSJ* 12 (1981) 63-67.

[70] Milik, *The Books of Enoch*, 5, 139-40.

It should be added that the eschatological section that concludes *1 Enoch* 6-11 (10:16-11:2) remains within the relatively narrow limits of biblical eschatology. The final judgment is mentioned several times just before this section in connection with the punishment of the angels (10:6, 12-14), and 10:16-11:2 describe the future paradisaical conditions of the righteous in some detail. There is, nevertheless, no extended picture of the judgment, no historical survey of any sort, and no tour of the heavenly realm. Eschatology is decidedly in evidence, but the literary form through which it comes to expression ought not to be termed an apocalypse.[71]

2) Chaps. 12-16 as an Elaboration of 6-11: When one turns from chaps. 6-11 to their continuation in 12-16, it soon becomes obvious that the two main stories that have been blended in 6-11 are both presupposed, but the writer of the new section makes significant additions to and alterations of these accounts as he brings the Watchers into direct contact with Enoch for the first time. Actually, though the finished text indicates the author's knowledge of both stories (or, rather, an editor's awareness of them), aside from 13:1-2 which is most awkward in its present context, chaps. 12-16 recapitulate and expand only the version associated with Shemihazah (without ever mentioning his name).[72] Several paraphrases of events in 6-11 (e.g., 12:4-6; 14:4-7) serve to cement the later chapters to the earlier ones. It is apparent, despite the fact that the unit 12-16 now follows 6-11, that the author conceived of the events in 12-16 as happening at some point during, not after, the episodes of 6-11. The angels have already descended and engendered

---

[71] Biblical interpretation is one of the most important elements in the text but there is naturally much more. Hanson ("Rebellion in Heaven," 232) terms chaps. 6-11 an "expository narrative" (see pp. 195-97 for his review of other proposals). Nickelsburg (*Jewish Literature*, 51) writes: "In addition to being biblical interpretation this story is myth. Conditions in the author's world are the result of events in the unseen heavenly realm. Moreover, the end-time will be characterized by a quality that is beyond human ken and experience."

[72] For an analysis of these chapters in relation to 6-11, see Dimant, "The 'Fallen Angels,'" 72-79; and Newsom, "The Development of *1 Enoch* 6-19," 316-19. Cf. also Nickelsburg, *Jewish Literature*, 52-54. Charles (*The Book of Enoch*, xlvii, 1-2, 27) argued for a major rearrangement of the material in chaps. 12-16: "The original order, therefore of this section was, so far as the present fragmentary text goes: $14^1$ . . . $13^{1-2}$ $13^3$ $12^3$ $13^{4-10}$ $14^{2-16}$ $12^{4-6}$ ‖ $16^{3-4}$ . $12^{1-2}$ is an editorial introduction" (27). Such radical surgery is unnecessary, if 13:1-2 are recognized as an addition from the Asael cycle (possibly with 16:3; 10:7 says that secrets were revealed by the Watchers, but 9:6 ascribes them to Asael). Without these supplementary verses the text proceeds smoothly, and the repetition of 12:4-6 in 16:3-4 can be regarded as an editorial *inclusio* (so Newsom). Newsom's further conclusion that 12-16 were written when 6-11 related only the story about the Watchers' sin with women (319), while possible, is hardly required by the evidence. The writer could have selected only those parts of 6-11 that served his purposes.

giants through their marriages, but, as in chap. 10, the punishments for the angels have been determined in heaven and have yet to be announced to the Watchers and giants. Enoch himself is commissioned to inform them of their sentences (12:4–6; 13:1–3). Thus the situation in 12–16 is in some respects that of chap. 10, but with some noteworthy differences. First, whereas in chap. 10 four angels were commanded to punish Asael, the Watchers, and the giants (and one to announce the coming of the flood), in 12–16 Enoch apprises the guilty parties of what is to befall them. He does so at the behest of one or more Watchers who had remained faithful (12:3–6).[73] So, Enoch assumes the role of a mediator between heaven and the angels who had left their celestial home: in 13:1–2 he executes part of the order that was given to Raphael in 10:4–6 (punishment of Asael), and in 12:3–6; 14:4–7; 15:2–16:4 he performs a task that had been assigned to Michael in 10:11–13 (punishment for Shemihazah and his colleagues). It is of interest, however, that he is not commissioned to announce the impending deluge to the son of Lamech (that is, Noah) as the angel Sariel[74] had been in 10:1–3. The omission may be significant for locating the events of 12–16 in Enoch's career.

b. The Eminence of Enoch in 12–16: It may appear that the author of 12–16 records scenes from Enoch's life after his ultimate assumption by God (Gen 5:24), since the editorial introduction in 12:1–2 takes up several phrases from Gen 5:24. "And before everything[75] Enoch had been hidden [GrPan: *elēmphthē* (was taken)], and none of the sons of men knew where he was hidden [GrPan: *elēmphthē*], or where he was, or what had happened. And all his doings [GrPan: *ta erga* (the works, deeds)] (were) with the Holy Ones and with the Watchers in his days [GrPan: *hai hēmerai* (the days)]."[76] The verbs

---

[73] If Milik (*The Books of Enoch*, 190, 192) has placed frg. i correctly, then 4QEn<sup>c</sup> 1 v 19 reads at 12:3: *w]ʾrw ᵉ[y]rʾ* ("behold, the . . . Watcher")—that is, just one Watcher would be addressing Enoch. The Greek and Ethiopic texts read a plural.

[74] At 10:1 Syncellus gives as the angel's name *ouriēl*, GrPan *istraēl*, and the Ethiopic mss a variety of unlikely forms (e.g., *āresyalāleyur* in Knibb's ms). 4QEn<sup>b</sup> 1 iii 7 (= 9:1) has *śryʾ[l* = Sariel. This may well have been the original form in 10:1 too. See Milik, *The Books of Enoch*, 172–74.

[75] Knibb's ms reads *wa-ʾem–qedma kʷellu nagar* (and before everything), but this seems to be a corruption of *wa-ʾem-qedma ʾellu nagar* (and before these things; so, e.g. Tana 9). The latter is supported by GrPan (*pro toutōn tōn logōn*). Thus the text says only that the events of chap. 12 happened before those of the preceding section. See also Beer, "Das Buch Henoch," 243.

[76] Charles (*The Book of Enoch*, 27) notes that Ethiopic *takabta* (was hidden) is a rendering of the LXX's *metethēken* (was removed) in Gen 5:24. See also Dillmann, *Das Buch Henoch Uebersetzt und erklärt* (Leipzig: Vogel, 1853) 104. The Greek verb offers a passive translation of Hebrew *lqḥ* (to take). As Nickelsburg ("Apocalyptic and Myth," 401) observes, the words *erga* and *hēmerai* remind one of the title of Hesiod's *Works and Days*.

used here come from Gen 5:24, while the clauses "none of the sons of men knew where he was hidden, or where he was, or what had happened" seem to be attempts at explicating the cryptic *ʾênenni* ("and he was not") of the same biblical verse. It should be recalled, though, that in Gen 5:22 and 24 there are two references to Enoch's "walk" with the *ʾĕlōhîm*—one during and one after his 365 years. There is reason to believe, despite the wording of 12:1-2, that for the writer Enoch's embassy to God occurred during, not after, his 365 years. *1 Enoch* 13:7 pictures him as still on the inhabited earth (in Dan) and in special contact with the angels (12:3-6). *Jub.* 4:21-22 supplies later support for this reading of the evidence.[77] If this is correct, then there is a natural explanation why Enoch does not announce the coming of the flood to Noah (as he does in *1 Enoch* 65-66, after his final assumption): Noah has perhaps not yet been born and the flood is, at any rate, many years in the future.[78]

In *1 Enoch* 12-16 the patriarch assumes a status far higher than he had enjoyed in earlier descriptions of him. In the AB he relayed to his son and posterity the scientific information that Uriel had divulged to him, but here he becomes a mediating agent between the Lord and the angels on whose behalf he intercedes. He now, during his 365 years, attains at least the status of an angel (though he is not called one), and, as a comparison of 14:21 with 14:24-15:1 shows, he was even granted the privilege of entering the luminous divine presence—a privilege denied to some angels though apparently not the Holy Ones (cf. 14:23). Consequently, in these chapters one sees him not only associating with angels (whether good or bad) but outranking at least some of them. Enoch's entry into God's throne room is reminiscent of Enme-duranki's admission to the presence of Shamash and Adad, but, while the ancient king there learned divinatory techniques, Enoch is told in a forth-right way (though in a dream—a common mantic medium) what will befall the angels who had sinned. He discovers, moreover, greater detail about the future in that he hears of the fact that evil will continue to exist in the world until the final judgment. A new motif provides the explanation: spirits which

---

[77] Cf. Charles, *The Book of Enoch*, 27-28; Beer, "Das Buch Henoch," 243. Dillmann (*Das Buch Henoch*, 104, vi-viii) favored the view that the setting of 12:1 is after Enoch's 365 years, though he was, of course, aware of the other possibility.

[78] This conclusion follows from the chronologies in the MT and LXX for the ages of the antediluvian patriarchs. In the MT Enoch's years are 622-987 (from creation), but the flood does not come until 1656. In the LXX his dates are 1122-1487, with the deluge coming in 2242. However, in the Samaritan Pentateuch and in *Jubilees* he lives from 522-887, and the flood begins in 1307. Thus, in this system, Noah, who was 600 years of age when the flood began, was born during Enoch's 365 years. Nevertheless, in each chronology the flood lies far in the future in Enoch's time, and for this reason it was inappropriate or at least less pressing for him to announce the flood to Noah. A similar chronology may underlie *1 Enoch* 106-107 (see chap. VI).

apparently emerge from the bodies of the fallen giants will insure that violence and evil remain.[79] Once again, though, the conditions that will prevail
from the present until the judgment are simply outlined; no detailed survey
of history or description of the assize is offered. Something of Enoch's status
in these chapters can be gleaned from 13:3: 'Then I [Enoch] went and spoke
to them all [the Watchers] together, and they were all afraid; fear and trembling seized them." These are virtually the same words as those which describe the reaction of the Watchers to *God's* advent in 1:5: "And all will be
afraid, and the Watchers will shake, and fear and great trembling will seize
them unto the ends of the earth" (cf. 65:1–5).

Several other characteristics of the exalted Enoch of 12–16 should be
noted. First, he is called the scribe (12:3) or the scribe of righteousness (12:4;
15:1). Enoch recorded Uriel's revelations in the AB (82:1), but here his
scribal role is official and one that suits perfectly the principal function that
he performs, viz., composing a proper copy of the angels' petition and of the
indictment which replies to it (13:4–6; 14:1–16:4).[80] Enoch becomes an official
mediator for the angels because their crimes had made them too ashamed to
approach their former heavenly home again (13:5). They assume rightly that
Enoch will have access to God himself. It is not claimed here that Enoch was
the first man who learned how to write (as *Jub.* 4:17 asserts); his ability with
the pen is simply presupposed. Gunkel, Zimmern, and Charles maintained
that Enoch's role as scribe was another borrowing from Mesopotamia, since
in this respect he resembles the god Nabu.[81] The parallels are that both
function as heavenly scribes who are brought into connection with heavenly
tablets on which are recorded the fates of humankind. But a number of
objections make their derivation of Enoch's writing rather unlikely. At least
in the ways in which they are presented in the AB and BW, Enoch's scribal

---

[79] *1 Enoch* 15:8 calls the giants evil spirits, but 15:9 and 16:1 claim that evil spirits emerge
from their flesh. There may be, as Dimant ("The 'Fallen Angels,'" 61–62 [with regard to 10:15],
76–78) proposes, a blending here of two originally independent traditions: one in which the
giants were the offspring of the union between angels and women, and one in which evil spirits
resulted from their co-habitation. On the term *nplym* in the sense of untimely born offspring
(miscarriages; deriving the word from *nēpel*) who become evil spirits, see Dimant, ibid., 49.

[80] Cf. Milik, *The Books of Enoch*, 237, 262, 305 for the Aramaic terms and 103–07 for
references to later literature. See also F. Dexinger, *Henochs Zehnwochenapokalypse und offene
Probleme der Apokalyptikforschung* (SPB 29; Leiden: Brill, 1977) 146–50. In the *Frg. Tg.* Gen
5:24 he is called the great scribe.

[81] H. Gunkel, "Der Schreiberengel Nabû im A. T. und in Judentum," *ARW* 1 (1898)
294–300; Zimmern, *Die Keilinschriften und das Alte Testament*, 400–06; Charles, *The Book
of Enoch*, 28. Zimmern added in a footnote (405 n. 1) that the scribal character of Enoch could
have been derived from the Enmeduranki traditions in that he had received divine tablets
from Shamash.

labors are suited to their specific contexts and have nothing to do with the tablets of destiny (in a later addition to the AB [81:1-2 (cf. 93:2; 106:19)] he *reads* what is written on the heavenly tablets). Nothing that is said in either of the compositions about his writing corresponds in distinctive ways with traditions about Nabu, the scribe of the gods. The fact that Enoch is a scribe of *righteousness* also reflects the context of chaps. 12–16: he is a righteous man (15:1), and he records the legitimate sentence that awaits the sinful angels and giants.[82]

A second feature that highlights Enoch's lofty position in 12–16 is a series of contrasts between him and the sinful Watchers. Several are made explicit in the divine indictment of 15:2–16:4, while others can be inferred.

1. The angels descended from heaven to earth (6:6; 12:4; 14:5; 15:3; 16:2–3), but Enoch ascended from earth to heaven (13:4; 14:8–16:4).

2. The angels, who were spiritual beings, contaminated themselves with humans (12:4; 15:3–10), but Enoch, who was human, associated with spiritual beings (12:2–3; 14:8–16:4).[83]

3. The angels, whose duty it was to intercede for humankind (15:2), misled them into corruption (15:2–16:4), but Enoch, who should have enjoyed the benefits of angelic assistance, interceded for them and reproved them (13:4, 6–10; 14:1, 3–7; 15:2; 16:2–4).[84]

4. Though little is made of this point in 12–16, the angels are accused of revealing improper knowledge—secrets not meant for people (13:2; 16:3), but Enoch, especially in the AB and in the succeeding chapters in the BW (17–36), receives and imparts revealed knowledge (cf. 14:2–3). Both Enoch and the angels function as sorts of culture-bringers, but what they bring and how they do so are evaluated very differently.

c. The Throne Vision in *1 Enoch* 14:8–25: The unit *1 Enoch* 12–16 is highly significant not only for evolution of the Enochic portrait but also for the development of the genre apocalypse because of the throne vision or

[82] See Charles, *The Book of Enoch*, 28.

[83] Cf. Nickelsburg, *Jewish Literature*, 53; Newsom ("The Development of *1 Enoch* 6–19," 316): "The real difference between chaps. 6–11 and 12–16 is that for the latter the problem of evil is perceived as a rupture in the order of the universe, . . ." Dimant ("The 'Fallen Angels," 74–77) speaks of a dualism of pure and impure, of flesh and spirit. The sin under consideration in 12–16 consists of a violation of these limits that the creator had established. Emphasis is not placed on violation of Noachic laws as had been the case in 6–11. Elsewhere (pp. 43, 73) she has drawn attention to the possibility that 15:4 means that the angels had mated with women during their menstrual impurity.

[84] Note the contrast with the situation in 9–10 (Charles, *The Book of Enoch*, 27). Another contrast worthy of attention is that the phrase "the Watchers and the impious ones" (16:1) is a negative form of the words "Watchers" and "holy ones" in Dan 4:17 (cf. 4:13, 23 for the same terms in the singular).

dream which the patriarch describes in 14:8–25. The throne theophany serves
as the awesome setting for the indictment of the angels that is revealed to
Enoch and as a confirmation of what is said. Such visions or dreams are an important ingredient in apocalypses, and, though they are crafted from biblical
materials, they tend to aim at different ends. In many ways *1 Enoch* 14:8–25
is a pastiche of biblical phrases and motifs that have been drawn primarily
from 1 Kgs 22:19–22, Isaiah 6, and Ezekiel 1 (also 8 and 10); later examples
can be found in Daniel 7 and Revelation 4, and some of the vocabulary also
appears in 4Q*Serek Šîrôt ʿÔlat Haššabbāt*.[85] There are strong ties, too, with
the later *merkavah* literature. As Gruenwald has written: "Indeed, one can
consider this particular vision a model-vision of Merkavah mysticism."[86]
Enoch begins to describe his experience in 13:7–9a:

> And I went and sat down by the waters of Dan in Dan which is south-west of
> Hermon [Hermon is the mountain to which the rebellious angels descended
> according to the word-play in 6:6]; and I read out the record of their petition
> until I fell asleep. And behold a dream came to me, and visions fell upon me,
> and I saw a vision of wrath, (namely) that I should speak to the sons of heaven
> and reprove them. And I woke up and went to them, . . .

He then says that he related his vision to them (13:10), and 14:1–16:4 provide
a detailed account of it. It appears that the terms *dream* (13:8; 4QEnᶜ 1 vi 10
reads *ḥlmʾ* in 14:1)[87] and *vision* are used interchangeably for Enoch's experience, but it is stressed that it came during his sleep (see also 13:10; 14:2).
That is, Enoch, whom tradition associated with mantic traits, here obtains
knowledge about the future through one of the most popular of divinatory
media. The author does not say that Enoch went to a temple, but it is evident
that he chose a particular site for reading out the angels' petition.[88] In this

---

[85] Many of the biblical passages that underlie the description are mentioned by Charles,
*The Book of Enoch*, 33–35; Beer, "Das Buch Henoch," 244–46; Black, "The Throne-Theophany Prophetic Commission and the 'Son of Man': A Study in Tradition-History," *Jews, Greeks
and Christians: Religious Cultures in Late Antiquity* (W. D. Davies Festschrift; ed. R. Hammer-
ton-Kelly and R. Scroggs; SJLA 21; Leiden: Brill, 1976) 57–73; and Gruenwald, *Apocalyptic
and Merkavah Mysticism*, 32–37. For the Qumran text, see J. Strugnell, "The Angelic Liturgy
at Qumran, 4QSerek Šîrôt ʿÔlat Haššabbāt," *Congress Volume, Oxford 1959* (VTSup 7; Leiden:
Brill, 1960) 318–45, especially 335–45. Note that *1 Enoch* 14:8 echoes the language of Elijah's
removal to heaven (2 Kgs 2:11).

[86] Gruenwald, *Apocalyptic and Merkavah Mysticism*, 36.

[87] Milik, *The Books of Enoch*, 193.

[88] Richard J. Clifford (*The Cosmic Mountain in Canaan and the Old Testament* [HSM 4;
Cambridge: Harvard University, 1972] 187) observes about the location:
> It is likely that the site was chosen with a view to the symbolism of the place. The waters of
> Dan are at the source of the Jordan, the river of Palestine, and the waters are the base of
> Hermon, a sacred mountain. These characteristics seem to make it a cosmic site, in the

respect his dream resembles incubation dreams that are widely attested in the ancient world. Enoch's dream vision (of the scriptural throne visions, only Daniel's is said to have come in a dream [e.g., 7:1]) clearly stands in a literary tradition, but it introduces some new elements which will recur in later examples of the type. First, in his dream vision, rather than simply seeing a celestial scene, Enoch ascends to heaven (14:8) and is brought near the door of the divine throne room itself (14:25). Second, not only does he ascend to heaven but he does so without angelic accompaniment.[89] He does not go on an extensive journey through the heavens; he merely describes the two splendid houses that he sees as the setting for the indictment of the angels that is entrusted to him. His vertical ascent in chap. 14 marks Enoch's first approach to the divine throne; later, angels who lead him on a horizontal journey will show him a mountain that resembles the throne of the Lord (18:8; 25:3) and that is located in the northwest. That throne is, however, the place from which the deity will pronounce judgment and is not identical to the one in chap. 14.[90]

These five short chapters have proven to be of great interest for the two principal subjects of the present investigation: the growth of traditions about Enoch himself and of apocalyptic literature. The AB showed how natural, scientific concerns, which remain important later in apocalyptic literature, were at home in Enochic lore; in the BW a mystical, visionary element becomes prominent. At this early point in the tradition the man Enoch has already assumed astonishing, superhuman traits. Eschatology, too, plays a role, but as with the other Enochic compositions to this date the eschatological theme does not predominate.[91]

### 3. Enoch in *1 Enoch* 17–36

The final 20 chapters of the BW include three units: Enoch's westward journey (17–19), a list of six or seven[92] angels (20), and his second journey

---

tradition of El's mountain, the source of the Two Rivers, of the Double-Deep, and an appropriate locale for divine–human encounter.

[89] Gruenwald, *Apocalyptic and Merkavah Mysticism*, 36.

[90] See Milik, *The Books of Enoch*, 35.

[91] Cf. Newsom, "The Development of *1 Enoch* 6–19," 316.

[92] The Ethiopic MSS list six but Gr[Pan] has a seventh. The first four of the angels—Uriel (21:9; 33:3), Raphael (22:3, 6; 27:2; 32:6), Raguel (23:4), and Michael (24:6)—are mentioned in the account of the second journey. The puzzling Zotiel (32:2) is most easily explained as a Greek corruption of *zophos* or *zophōdēs*, either of which would be a correct translation of Aramaic *ḥšwkʾ* (darkness; 4QEn[e] 1 xxvi 21). See Milik, "Hénoch au pays des aromates," 71, 76; *The Books of Enoch*, 232, 234; Knibb, *The Ethiopic Book of Enoch*, 2.122.

which eventually takes him around the world (21-36).[93] The account of the second trip pictures travels to the west (21-25), to the vicinity of Jerusalem (26-27), and to the east (28-32); and it culminates in a voyage around the world (33-36). The westward journey of 21-25 has obvious points of contact with 17-19,[94] while 33-36 excerpt information from the AB.[95] Despite these numerous divisions and the likelihood that some parts differ from others in authorship and date, *1 Enoch* 17-36 can, for the purposes of the present investigation, be treated as a unit. The portrait of Enoch that emerges from the various sections is largely the same.

*1 Enoch* 17-36 may appear at first glance to have very little in common with the first 16 chapters of the BW. In 1-16 there are no cosmic journeys but they dominate 17-36. A closer look reveals, nonetheless, that several familiar Enochic themes re-surface in the cosmological section of the book. For example, the angels who sinned are mentioned in both itineraries (19:1-2; 21:10), and in both Enoch travels about in angelic company (18:14; 19:1; 21:9; 22:3; 23:4; 24:6; 27:2; 32:6; 33:3). Moreover, the patriarch, who had approached God's throne in a vertical direction in 14-16, now travels on a horizontal plane to a throne where God will sit when he executes judgment at the end (18:8; 25:3).[96] The final judgment, which is a prominent theme

---

[93] Charles (*The Book of Enoch*, xlviii, 2) takes chap. 20 with 21-36 on the grounds that several of the angels in chap. 20 figure in the chapters that follow (see also pp. 38, 43, 44). Beer ("Das Buch Henoch," 222, 226-27) argued that the list in 20 was distilled from 21-36 and later expanded to include a more respectable total of seven angels. Martin (*Le livre d'Hénoch*, lxxx-lxxxi), too, joined 20 to 21-36 and believed that 20-36 belonged to the same source as 6-11.

[94] E.g. Charles, *The Book of Enoch*, xlviii, 38. Milik (*The Books of Enoch*, 25) calls 21-25 a re-working of 17-19 ". . . mainly from the eschatological point of view." He has advocated the novel hypothesis that 17-19 form the conclusion of the "venerable model" (chaps. 6-19) which the author of the BW included in his larger work (ibid., 25-41). That "venerable model," seems to have, though, a number of divisions within it and hardly constitutes an original unity. Newsom ("The Development of *1 Enoch* 6-19," 324-28) sees in the positioning of 17-19 after 12-16 a reflection of a Near Eastern diplomatic practice in which a monarch would exhibit his wealth and power to visitors to demonstrate his worth as an ally, etc. (as Hezekiah did for the emissaries from Merodach-baladan [2 Kgs 20:12-13]). The parallel is not particularly close with *1 Enoch* 17-19 (perhaps chap. 14 would be better) and the concerns are different. The emphasis in *1 Enoch* is on punishment for sin more than on the wonders of God's creation. Moreover, a more precise literary or traditional model is the Greek *nekyia* (see below and n. 100 below). For a critique of Newsom's proposal, cf. Collins, "The Apocalyptic Technique: Setting and Function in the Book of Watchers," *CBQ* 44 (1982) 104.

[95] Milik, *The Books of Enoch*, 38.

[96] Ibid., 35.

in all parts of the BW, continues to be a concern in 17–36, particularly in 21–36.[97]

There is no explicit indication in 17–36 regarding the stage in Enoch's career at which his travels are supposed to have taken place, but the editorial location of the cosmological section favors the view that the writer/editor thought they belonged in the 300-year period during which Enoch was with the angels before his return to human society and his final translation. The vague opening words of 17:1 ("And they [the angels] took me to a place ...") connect the events that follow with the time of 12–16, which was, as noted above, the time of his 300-year "walk" with the angels.

In the course of his two journeys Enoch learns about the structure of the world and especially about places located at the ends of the earth. In the AB the angel Uriel had disclosed astronomical information to the patriarch, though the subject of geography did arise (76–77); in 17–36 the same angel (with assistance from three others in 21–36) shows and explains all sorts of geographical features, though astronomical topics are not ignored (e.g., 33–36). Enoch's already impressive knowledge is expanded to truly encyclopedic dimensions so that, with the range of information at his disposal as a result of Uriel's revelations, his wisdom outranks that of any other mythological culture-bringer. Indeed, he himself claims, much like Gilgamesh, that his experience was unique: "And I, Enoch, alone saw the sight, the ends[98] of everything; and no man has seen what I have seen" (19:3).

Though in some instances one can recognize descriptions of actual places (Jerusalem and environs in 26–27),[99] the geography of the travelogues is transparently mythical. It has been observed that Enoch's travels are charted according to a fanciful scheme which resembles fictitious geographical plans in myths of the ancient Near East and of Greece. The accounts of travels which show the nearest parallels are the Epic of Gilgamesh (especially tablets IX and X) and the Odyssey (particularly Book XI).[100] Milik and Grelot have

---

[97] Regarding the common themes that sound throughout the BW, see Hartman, *Asking for a Meaning*, 138–45.

[98] Milik (*The Books of Enoch*, 35) thinks that the *perata* of the Greek text reflects the translator's mis-reading of *swp* as *syp*. *Extremities* would, however, be natural in this context.

[99] Milik ("Hénoch au pays des aromates," 70–77; cf. also *The Books of Enoch*, 36–37) has attempted to locate various areas in chaps. 28–32 by means of the spices, etc. which are said to be found in them. M. Gil ("ḥnwk b'rṣ hḥyym [Enoch in the Land of Life]," *Tarbiz* 38 [1968–69] 322–37) has effectively shown how precarious the argument is. He notes that the spices, etc. in question grow in more places than the ones Milik names and that this fact prevents one from making definite identifications of areas.

[100] Charles, *The Book of Enoch*, 38–42, 49; Beer, "Das Buch Henoch," especially 248; Bousset-Gressmann, *Die Religion des Judentums*, 498; Jansen, *Die Henochgestalt*, 69–74 (he thought that the Chaldeans attached their cosmological teachings to works such as the Epic of

maintained that a Late Babylonian *mappa mundi* also reflects a very similar geographical arrangement.[101] The geography of *1 Enoch* 17-36 differs from all of these "maps" or schemes in a number of features and displays its own interests (e.g., incorporating biblical notions about the location of paradise), but it is true that several phenomena which are placed at the ends of the earth are similar in all of these "maps." For example, 17:5 mentions a "river of fire whose fire flows like water and pours out into the great sea which (is) towards the west." This fiery river has understandably been compared with the *pyriphlegethon* of Greek mythology. The next verse refers to "the great rivers" beyond which lies a region of darkness.[102] These rivers remind one of the streams of Hades: Styx, Acheron, and Cocytus. Furthermore, the large body of water located at the ends of the earth is reminiscent of the Greek *Okeanos* and the Bitter River of the Late Babylonian map to which Milik and Grelot have referred (see 17:7-8; 18:10). Grelot, besides pointing to these ancient parallels, has also isolated the biblical background of some features of the Enochic geography and has argued that scriptural information dictated that the author impose a scheme of two paradises on a mythological arrangement.

Gilgamesh); Grelot, "La géographie mythique d'Hénoch," 33-69 (he fashions an impressive argument that even some motifs which more nearly resemble Greek themes are of Babylonian origin; he also points to the biblical bases for some geographical features); Glasson, *Greek Influence in Jewish Eschatology*, especially 8-11 (his claim that "*Enoch 1-36* is a Jewish *Nekyia*" [8] is extreme. If correct at all, it would be true only of 17-19, 21-36; but even 17-19 and large parts of 21-36 do not deal with the realm of the dead). For an overview of other Hellenistic material, see Hengel, *Judaism and Hellenism*, 1.210-18. Nickelsburg (*Jewish Literature*, 54) also finds that the Greek *nekyia* is the model behind the Enochic material. It should be added that both Milik and Grelot see Phoenician or Ugaritic motifs in the geography of Enoch. Collins ("The Apocalyptic Technique." 105-07) rapidly surveys the various proposals and concludes: "In short, there is a wealth of suggestive possibilities and an acute lack of decisive evidence" (107).

    [101] Grelot, "La géographie mythique d'Hénoch," 38-44 (for chaps. 17-36); Milik, *The Books of Enoch*, 34-41.

    [102] Albrecht Dieterich (*Nekyia: Beiträge zur Erklärung der neuentdeckten Petrusapokalypse* [2nd ed.; Leipzig/Berlin: Teubner, 1913] 218-19) noted similarities between the realm of the dead in Enoch and in Greek literature (in the west; a dark land through which great rivers flow) and commented: "Ich weiss nicht, warum man einer gewissen Modeneigung für die Babylonier folgend die längst erkannte klare Anlehnung an das griechische Totenreich im Westen mit seinen bekannten Strömen abweist" (219). Milik (*The Books of Enoch*, 38) apparently believes that the region of darkness corresponds to the area which a Babylonian *mappa mundi* labels *ašar* ᵈ*šamši la innamar(u)* ("a place where Shamash is not seen"). There are, nevertheless, too few points of contact between the geographical notices in *1 Enoch* and the Babylonian map to justify the consequences that Milik draws. See VanderKam, "1 Enoch 77, 3 and a Babylonian Map of the World" *RevQ* 11(1983) 271-78.

L'élément caractéristique de ce voyage est le dédoublement du paradis. On se l'explique comme une tentative pour harmoniser entre elles des donnés divergentes également traditionelles: celle de *Gen.*, II, qui place le jardin d'Éden 'du côté de l'Orient'; celle d'*Is.*, XIV, qui place le séjour divin sur la montagne du Nord; celle d'*Ez.*, XXVIII, qui identifie l'Éden et la montagne divine. Le résultat est une synthèse qu'on pourrait résumer comme suit. Dieu réside au paradis sur la montagne du N.-O. Avant de créer l'homme, il a planté un 'jardin de justice' au N.-E.; c'était une réplique du 'jardin de justice' du paradis. Il y a temporairement transporté l'arbre de vie; mais après la chute il l'a ramené au paradis du N.-O. C'est dans ce paradis qu'il a transféré Hénoch, pour l'y mettre en réserve en attendant le jour du jugement.[103]

There may be a kind of doubling present in the geography of the BW (see 18:6-8/24:2-3 compared with 32:1, although the Aramaic at this point—4QEn^e 1 xxvi 16-17—lacks the number *seven* for the mountains),[104] but there is no clear indication, either in the AB or in the BW, that a *paradise* is located in the northwest. The mountain of God is situated there as is a special tree which is described as though it were the tree of life (24:4-25:7); yet, unlike the eastern group of mountains, this region is not termed the/a garden of righteousness (32:3).

No complete map could be drawn on the basis of the information in 17-19 and 21-36, but the features which are present strongly suggest that the writers have borrowed mythological geographical motifs from the literature and/or traditions of their international environment. It is not impossible that they drew them from Mesopotamian, Phoenician, Classical, and biblical sources or from sources in which these traditions were somehow combined. The authors of the BW, like the writer of the AB, were open to foreign influences, borrowed from them, and refashioned them to attain their particular ends. Moreover, their interests tended toward pseudoscientific subjects such as cosmology. In these chapters Enoch continues to figure as the unique Jewish hero who has experiences that resemble to some extent those of mythological characters in the ancient world; but he receives absolutely trustworthy information through divine revelation. His knowledge extends to the limits of heaven and earth. From this substantial base it would be just one step—and an easily understandable one—to expand his revealed knowledge to encompass past, present, and future as well. His grasp of the universe and its ways was complete; extension along the time line was all that remained.

103 "La géographie mythique d'Hénoch," 43.
104 Milik, *The Books of Enoch*, 232, 234.

The writers of *1 Enoch* 17–36 do not, however, take the decisive step that would make Enoch a seer of apocalyptic surveys of history and the *eschaton*. Yet the role of eschatology in these chapters shows that the way was already paved for a new emphasis. Eschatology is particularly prominent in the account of the second journey and actually proves to be something built into the cosmos itself. That is, insofar as the places of punishment and bliss are already prepared and used and the throne from which God will preside over the final assize is already available, eschatology becomes an unavoidable corollary to learning about the created order.[105]

Among the eschatological sections there is one which betrays a significant development in the Enochic literature: in 22:1–13 sheol, the realm of the dead, is divided into three or four sections, each of which is reserved for a different sort of resident (this is another aspect of these chapters for which Greek parallels have been adduced).[106] Apart from the new disclosures about sheol, however, the eschatology of the cosmological sections of the BW remains within the relatively narrow and ancient confines that have been met before. The fact remains that at this very early stage in the development of Enochic lore a "scientific" interest still dominates traditions associated with the man. One still finds no apocalyptic surveys of history, though in later Enochic literature they become popular. His "science" is, of course, lodged within a theological framework: his cosmological travels are not simply pedagogical exercises but serve to assure the faithful that the justice of God is constructed into the creation. Sinners will indeed be punished, and the righteous rewarded; their respective places are already prepared. Enoch punctuates his travels at several places in the second journey with praise for the creator; these expressions of wonder function as a structuring device around his tour of the earth (22:14; 25:7; 27:5; 36:4). Throughout the BW the creation evokes wonder and awe at God's power and wisdom.

In the BW Enoch plays the part of a magnet that attracts heterogeneous mythological materials apparently from a variety of sources including the Bible. It is highly likely that here, for the first time in Enochic literature, the influence of Greek ideas and traditions makes itself felt. In the last 20 chapters of the BW the divinatory associations of the patriarch are not as clear as, say, in chaps. 1–5, but his "science" reflects or resembles the diviner's concern with nature as a medium for divine communication.

---

[105] See Collins, "Cosmos and Salvation," 128–40; "The Apocalyptic Technique," 107–09.
[106] On 22:1–13 see Charles, *Eschatology*, 215–20; Dieterich, *Nekyia*, 218; and Glasson, *Greek Influence in Jewish Eschatology*, 12–19.

# VI

## THE FIRST ENOCHIC APOCALYPSES
## WITH HISTORICAL SURVEYS

The preceding chapters have traced the growth of Enochic traditions in Jewish literature from Genesis through the Book of Watchers (= BW). It has been argued that the Jewish Enoch embodies the major traits of Enmeduranki who was the seventh antediluvian king and aboriginal diviner in Mesopotamian lore. The principal features of Enoch's biography reflect, often in modified shape, those of Enmeduranki, and the media through which Enoch receives revelations and to some extent their contents as well echo those of the diviner. In the Astronomical Book (= AB) and BW Enoch learns sundry data about the structure and functioning of the universe. The final judgment against the evil and the vindication of the righteous certainly come into consideration in the latter, but this happens largely through Enoch's early association with the myth of the angels who sinned or as a corollary to his cosmological explorations. That is, both the AB and the BW, the only extant Enochic compositions that date from before B.C. 200, have an emphatic scientific interest. They demonstrate that through inspired guidance into the mysteries of the cosmos one can arrive at theological truth.

The next booklets in chronological order are the Epistle of Enoch (*1 Enoch* 91–105; 106–107 may be an addition; 108 certainly is) and the Book of Dreams (= BD; *1 Enoch* 83–90). Both the Epistle and the BD contain, with other material, units which can be called apocalypses with historical surveys in the form of *vaticinia ex eventu*. As the first Enochic compositions to incorporate such surveys they occupy a special place both in the development of lore about Enoch and in the evolution of apocalyptic literature. In them the authors move one momentous step beyond the earlier, more cosmologically oriented books: they extend Enoch's already encyclopedic knowledge along the time–line and make his understanding of the course of history as comprehensive and insightful as his grasp of the universe. His traditional associations with divination made Enoch a natural candidate for the role of seer; in fact, the first two Jewish heroes to whom apocalyptic surveys of history were disclosed—Enoch and Daniel—both have unmistakable mantic qualities.[1] The method employed in the historical apocalypses is essentially the same as the interpretative one that underlies the AB and the BW: as one can learn about God and divine his plan by studying nature with the requisite insight, so one can discern the pattern and goal of the divine governance of history through inspired scrutiny of the Scriptures.

The Epistle and the BD also furnish an opportunity for identifying with a fair degree of precision the historical circumstances within which savants made this innovative advance in Enochic literature. The major apocalypses in each of the booklets—the Apocalypse of Weeks (= ApW; 93:1–10; 91:11–17) and the Animal Apocalypse (= AA; 85–90)—can be dated relatively precisely because the writers used the device of *vaticinia ex eventu* and thus betray their historical position at that point at which their predictions change from disguised accounts of the past to actual forecasts. In standard apocalyptic fashion they understood their age as the pivotal one in the history of God's dealings with his people—as standing immediately adjacent to that line which separates history from the *eschaton*. It will be argued below that both apocalypses were written in those critical years when adherents of traditional forms of Judaism suffered under the staggering consequences of Antiochus IV's energetic campaign of hellenizing. The seers viewed these events not simply as part of another significant moment in history but as the ultimately decisive acts whose gravity would trigger divine intervention and eschatological judgment.

## A. The Epistle of Enoch and the Apocalypse of Weeks

It will be shown below that the ApW is the earlier of the two historical apocalypses. It will, therefore, be considered first and the AA after it. The chapter will conclude with shorter sections that are devoted to the remaining parts of the Epistle.

### 1. The Date of the Apocalypse of Weeks and of the Epistle of Enoch

There is widespread agreement today that the Epistle dates from the end of the second or beginning of the first century B.C. but that the ApW is an earlier and independent composition that the writer of the Epistle incorporated into his larger work.[2] This claim about the ApW will have to be

---

[1] For Daniel as a mantic sage, see H. P. Müller, "Magisch–mantische Weisheit und die Gestalt Daniels," *UF* 1 (1969) 79–94.

[2] Charles (*The Book of Enoch*, li, liii, 218, 221–27) said that the ApW may be pre–Maccabean but that the Epistle (defined as chaps. 91–104) is from the first third of the first century B.C. Beer ("Das Buch Henoch," 230–31) affirmed that the ApW was pre–167 B.C. but that the remainder of the Epistle (91:1–11; 94–105) probably belonged to the period from B.C. 104–78. Similarly Martin (*Le Livre d'Hénoch*, xciv, xcvi–xcvii) placed the apocalypse before 170 and chaps. 91–105 in the time from 95–78. See also Eissfeldt, *The Old Testament*, 619. Milik (*The*

examined, but the related issue of when the Epistle itself was composed should be addressed first. Charles, whose views about these matters are generally accepted, supported his dating of the Epistle in large part by identifying two groups who are mentioned often in the text—the righteous and the sinners—as Pharisees and Sadducees respectively.

> Here they [the Maccabees] are leagued with the Sadducees and are the foes of the Pharisaic party. This section [chaps. 91–104] was written, therefore, after 109 B.C., when (?) the breach between John Hyrcanus and the Pharisees took place. But a later date must be assumed according to the literal interpretation of 103$^{14,15}$, where the rulers are said to uphold the Sadducean oppressors and share in the murder of the righteous. This charge is not justified before 95 B.C. As for the later limit, the Herodian princes cannot be the rulers here mentioned; for the Sadducees were irrevocably opposed to these as aliens and usurpers. The date, therefore, may be either 95–79 B.C. or 70–64 B.C., during which periods the Pharisees were oppressed by both rulers and Sadducees.[3]

He also held that the Epistle was dependent on the Book of *Jubilees* which he dated toward the end of the second century B.C.[4]

Charles' identification of the righteous and sinners as Pharisees and Sadducees can hardly be correct. The writer of the Epistle does distinguish the righteous from the sinners who distort the law (99:2) and he attributes to the righteous an expectation that the virtuous dead will in some sense rise (see 91:10; 92:3),[5] but these and other characteristics are too imprecise to support Charles' hypothesis. Such points of view would have been acceptable to the author of Daniel 10–12—chapters that were written in ca. 165 B.C. Moreover, the sinners are described in terms that even an ardent opponent would have recognized as inappropriate or false for the Sadducees. They were a wealthy faction in Jewish society, as the sinners appear to have been, and were probably more willing to accommodate change than were conservative groups; but the charge of idolatry simply does not tally with fact (e.g., 99:7).[6] It is difficult to recognize in the righteous and sinners of the Epistle any traits that are specific enough to justify party labels. They are pictured in

---

*Books of Enoch*, 255–56) agrees that the Epistle was written at the end of the second or beginning of the first century B.C. but also assigns the ApW to that period.

[3] *The Book of Enoch*, liii–liv. Beer ("Das Buch Henoch," 230–31) and Martin (*Le Livre d'Hénoch*, xcvi–xcvii) also thought the righteous were Pharisees and the sinners Sadducees.

[4] Ibid., liv, where he refers to his *The Book of Jubilees*, lxix–lxxi.

[5] On the type of rising here envisaged, see Nickelsburg, *Resurrection, Immortality, and Eternal Life in Intertestamental Judaism* (HTS 26; Cambridge: Harvard University, 1972) 123–24 (for chaps. 102–04). He shows that no resurrection of the body is intended, only of spirits— hardly a pharisaic doctrine.

[6] So Milik, *The Books of Enoch*, 49; cf. Eissfeldt, *The Old Testament*, 619.

general terms which could fit a variety of opposing groups throughout the second pre–Christian century (and other periods) including the hellenizing factions of pre– and early Maccabean days and their more orthodox opponents. Actually the descriptions of the righteous and sinners are more suitable for these groups than for the Pharisees and Sadducees (1 Macc 1:43 specifically charges the Jewish Hellenizers with idolatry). It is, in addition, only an assumption that the rulers who figure in the Epistle are Hasmoneans, and there is no compelling reason for thinking that the text mirrors Alexander Jannaeus' slaughter of his pharisaic opponents.

Charles' argument from an alleged dependence of the Epistle on *Jubilees* is now misleading and certainly not convincing. There is a growing body of evidence, derived especially from the Qumran texts (which were, of course, unknown to Charles), that *Jubilees* dates from a time no later than the mid–second century.[7] Thus, if another work borrowed from it, it would not imply, as it did for Charles, that the former was written no earlier than the last years of the second or the first years of the first century B.C. Moreover, the passages which suggested to Charles that the writer of the Epistle used *Jubilees* consist in most cases only of similar phrases from which the issue of dependence cannot be settled. In other instances the passages in question are biblical citations or are too general to demonstrate either dependence or the direction in which it went.[8] Also, there is a group of passages in *Jubilees* which may reflect its author's use of the Epistle (*Jub.* 4:17, 18, 19; 7:29; 10:17).[9] These verses, too, are inconclusive, but they do show that dependence may lie on the side of the writer of *Jubilees*.

Paleographical data from the two Aramaic MSS that preserve parts of the Epistle are consistent with but do not prove an earlier date for the book. Milik assigns 4QEn$^g$ to the mid–first century B.C. and 4QEn$^c$ to the last third of the same century.[10] He suspects, though, that since both MSS contain archaisms (e.g., an instance of *zy* rather than *dy* in 4QEn$^g$ 1 iii 25) they were copied from models that were written in ca. 100 B.C.[11] If one allows this highly tenuous extension of the paleographical argument, then it is likely that the Epistle was written before 100 B.C.

The parenetic and therefore rather timeless character of much of the Epistle frustrates any attempt to date it precisely. The only more securely

---

[7] See VanderKam, *Textual and Historical Studies in the Book of Jubilees*, 214–85.

[8] For the passages and arguments, see Charles, *The Book of Jubilees*, lxix–lxxi.

[9] See VanderKam, "Enoch Traditions in Jubilees and Other Second–Century Sources," SBLASP (1978) 1.231–41; Nickelsburg, *Jewish Literature*, 149–50.

[10] *The Books of Enoch*, 48, 178.

[11] Ibid., 48–49, 264–65.

datable segment of it is the ApW, but most scholars consider it an earlier composition that the compiler of the Epistle included in his book. Their conclusion may be correct, but it rests on weak arguments. There is no doubt that the ApW is a self-contained, discrete unit (though not all have agreed on which verses to assign to it),[12] but that is not to say that it once existed independently. It is worth noting that the ApW shares a number of traits with the remainder of the Epistle. The most obvious one—the distinction between righteous and sinner and the concern with righteousness or uprightness—is prominent in it too: sinners (93:4; cf. 93:9; 91:11, 12; 91:14); sin (91:17); righteous (93:10; 91:2; cf. 93:6); righteousness/uprightness (93:2, 3, 5, 10; 91:12, 13, 14, 17). Also, heavenly tablets appear in the ApW (93:2) and elsewhere in the Epistle (103:2; 106:19). These observations support Milik's contention that "no serious evidence exists to disprove that the author of this apocalypse of weeks is the same author as composed the rest of the Epistle, . . ."[13] If so, the date of the ApW would be that of the Epistle as well (or at least the two would probably be virtually contemporaneous).

Scholarly estimates about the date of the ApW range narrowly between a time just before the Antiochan decrees against Judaism (B.C. 167 and therefore just prior to the outbreak of the Maccabean revolt) and a point early in the period of resistance, shortly after the decrees were promulgated.[14] A decision between the two options hinges on the way in which one interprets the words that are used to describe the seventh (93:9-10; 91:11) and eighth weeks (91:12-13), but it should be interjected that whichever choice one makes (and these two possibilities seem the only plausible candidates)

---

[12] For different proposals, see F. Dexinger, *Henochs Zehnwochenapokalypse und offene Probleme der Apokalyptikforschung* (SPB 29; Leiden: Brill, 1977) 106.

[13] *The Books of Enoch*, 255-56. Matthew Black ("The Apocalypse of Weeks in the Light of 4Q En^G," *VT* 28 [1978] 464-69) finds evidence of redactional developments in the vicinity of the ApW and takes this as an indication that the apocalypse was an older source which the writer of the Epistle worked in his composition. There is a problem, however, in identifying at which stage the editorial labors occurred; there is no indisputable evidence for it on the Aramaic level. Dexinger (*Henochs Zehnwochenapokalypse*, 106-09) has proposed and very briefly defended an elaborate three-stage process from which the present arrangement of 91:1-93:14 is supposed to have resulted. His thesis certainly would require more backing than he gives it to be convincing.

[14] Pre-Maccabean dating: Charles (*The Book of Enoch*, liii): ". . . may have been written before the Maccabean revolt. There is no reference in it to the persecution of Antiochus. But the date is wholly doubtful." Beer ("Das Buch Henoch," 230): ". . . dürfte ihre Ausprägung in der mündlichen oder schriftlichen Überlieferung noch vor 167 v. Chr. erfolgt sein." Martin (*Le Livre d'Hénoch*, xciv-xcv): ". . . un peu avant 170." Others who have held similar views are mentioned by Dexinger (*Henochs Zehnwochenapokalypse*, 136-40), but he himself defends a Maccabean dating (see 138-40 where he refers to other advocates of this position).

the difference will be slight—perhaps just a year or two, possibly five or ten. Those who advocate a pre-Maccabean date maintain that the description of the seventh week, which according to them brings the account to the author's time, fails to mention the extraordinarily significant events of B.C. 167 and the following years. As the lines that portray the eighth week are authentic prediction, the author must have composed the ApW before 167. Those who prefer a later date at the very beginning of Maccabean times claim that the *sword* which in 91:12 is given to the righteous in the eighth week represents the Maccabean uprising. F. Dexinger, who has recently defended the latter position, argues that since the account which follows does not harmonize with the subsequent course of the revolt, the ApW must have been written early in the Maccabean period, possibly in 166.[15]

The ApW divides biblical history into six "weeks" of years and alludes in cryptic fashion to major events and/or characters in each. The writer groups in the sixth week (93:8) the apostasy of the divided monarchy period, the ascension of Elijah, the destruction of Jerusalem or the davidic kingdom, and the exile of the chosen people. Then for the seventh week he writes:

*Ethiopic*

93:9 And after this in the seventh week an apostate generation will arise, and many (will be) its deeds, but all its deeds (will be) apostasy.

93:10 And at its end the chosen righteous from the eternal plant of righteousness will be chosen to whom will be given sevenfold teaching concerning his whole creation.

91:11 And after this the roots of iniquity will be cut off, and the sinners will be destroyed by the sword; from the blasphemers they will be cut off in every place, and those who plan wrongdoing and those who commit blasphemy will be destroyed by the sword.

*Aramaic*

[. . . and all] its [deeds shall be (done)] in a[postasy. And with its end] there shall be chosen the elect, for witnesses to righteousness, from the eternal plant of righteousness, [to whom] shall be given sevenfold wisdom and knowledge. And they will have rooted out the foundations of violence and the structure of falsehood therein, to execute [judgement].[16]

---

[15] Ibid., 139.

[16] Translation and reconstruction of Milik, *The Books of Enoch*, 266. See also M. Black, "The Fragments of the Aramaic Enoch from Qumran," *La littérature juive entre Tenach et Mischna. Quelques problèmes* (ed. W. C. van Unnik; RechBib 9; Leiden: Brill, 1974) 24–25. As is well known, the Ethiopic version breaks up the ApW, placing the description of weeks one through seven in 93:3–10 and of weeks eight through ten in 91:12–17. Regarding the proper location of 91:11, see below.

The fact that 91:11 must be read, in a shorter form, as part of the section devoted to the seventh week[17] casts a new light on what is said about both weeks seven and eight. It is quite possible that what is in the future for the author is under consideration already at 91:11 (note that though the word *sword* is used twice in Ethiopic 91:11, it is absent from the Aramaic). The obvious implication would then be that 91:12 does not refer to the dawn of the Maccabean revolt. A natural explanation for the "apostate generation" of 93:9 is to understand it as a reference to the rise of a strong hellenizing party in Jewish society at the beginning of Antiochus IV's reign. The attraction of Hellenistic ways had made itself felt long before 175, but the sources trace a new turn in the hellenizing of Jerusalem and Judaism to the first years of this monarch's rule. As 1 Macc 1:10–13 pictures it:

> A wicked shoot sprouted from this stock, Antiochus Epiphanes, son of King Antiochus. This Antiochus Epiphanes, after having been a hostage in Rome, became king in the year 137 [= B.C. 175] of the Hellenistic dynasty. At that time, lawless men arose in Israel and seduced many with their plea, 'Come, let us make a covenant with the gentiles around us, because ever since we have kept ourselves separated from them we have suffered many evils.' The plea got so favorable a reception that some of the people took it upon themselves to apply to the king, who granted them liberty to follow the practices of the gentiles.[18]

It seems likely that these ardent Hellenizers among the Judean population are the "apostate generation" of the ApW and that the community of the writer constitutes the elect of the last time (they are part of the "eternal plant of righteousness"—the designation for the offspring of Abraham according to 93:5). These elect now have access through Enoch to special knowledge

---

[17] As 4QEn⁸ shows, 91:11 follows immediately on the material that corresponds with 93:10; it is, consequently, part of the paragraph devoted to the seventh week. See Dexinger, *Henochs Zehnwochenapokalypse*, 103–04; Knibb, *The Ethiopic Book of Enoch*, 2.218; and Black, "The Apocalypse of Weeks," 464–65. The older commentators had regarded 91:11 as redactional (e.g., Charles, *The Book of Enoch*, 227–28; Beer, "Das Buch Henoch," 299 n. k).

[18] Translation of J. Goldstein, *1 Maccabees* (AB 41; Garden City: Doubleday, 1976). 2 Macc 1:7 also traces the beginning of greater troubles to the high priesthood of Jason—i.e., early in Antiochus' reign. It should be recalled that the sinners of the Epistle are probably these same Hellenizing Jews. Günter Reese ("Die Geschichte Israels in der Auffassung des frühen Judentums: Eine Untersuchung der Tiervision und der Zehnwochenapokalypse des äthiopischen Henochbuches, der Geschichtsdarstellung der Assumptio Mosis und der des 4 Esrabuches" [Unpublished Ph.D. dissertation, Ruprecht-Karl-Universität, Heidelberg, 1967] 77–78) understands the opposing groups in 93:9–10 against the same historical foil since he regards the "chosen righteous from the eternal plant of righteousness" (93:10) as the *Hasidim*. Since he thinks, however, that the ApW is dependent on the Animal Apocalypse (*1 Enoch* 85–90), he is forced to move the ApW to a date some years after the beginning of the Maccabean revolt (85–88).

and wisdom (93:10 Aramaic). Their ultimate triumph is predicted in 91:11. There is no reference here, whether clear or veiled, to the decrees of Antiochus nor to the Maccabean response. Since those events had such enormous theological significance for the ones who later wrote about them, it is unlikely that the ApW was written after 167 (contrast Dan 11:30–31).

The wording and location of 91:12–13 indicate that the final and still future process of judgment begins at this point:

*Ethiopic*
91:12 And after this there will be another week, the eighth, that of righteousness, and a sword will be given to it that the *righteous judgement* may be executed on those who do wrong, and the sinners will be handed over into the hands of the righteous. 91:13 And at its end they will acquire houses because of their righteousness, and a house will be built for the great king *in glory* for ever.

*Aramaic*
And thereafter shall arise the eighth Week, that of righteousness, in which [a sword] shall be given to the righteous, to exact a righteous judgement from all the wicked, and they shall be delivered into their hands. And with its end they shall acquire riches in righteousness, and there shall be built the royal Temple of the Great One in His glorious splendour, for all generations forever. [19]

As noted earlier, advocates of a Maccabean dating see in the *sword* of 91:12 an allusion to Judas and his first troops. A thorny problem, assuming the Maccabean hypothesis, is to explain why the Antiochan decrees and desecration of the temple find no place in the ApW. Dexinger has attempted to cope with the difficulty in several ways (e.g., Jewish promotion of Hellenism [93:9] was, on the author's view, a more heinous crime than defiling the sanctuary and thus more worthy of mention;[20] or possibly the persecution and Jewish deviation from the covenant are included in the cover-term "an apostate generation"). He also observes that 91:12 (part of the paragraph about the eighth week) speaks of judgment against *oppressors*; these could be the enemies of the Maccabees.[21] However, the Aramaic reading at this point—

[19] Milik, *The Books of Enoch*, 266–67.

[20] The whole issue is complicated by the fact that the ApW also omits any reference to the first temple and to the post–exilic reconstruction of it. The *house* of 93:7 can hardly be the Solomonic temple as vv 7–8 demonstrate (note especially the phrase "all those who live in it"); it is more likely the davidic kingdom. Since neither temple figures in the ApW, it is difficult to decide whether the author belongs to that group of post–exilic writers who opposed the second temple. Regarding the various negative estimates of the post–exilic period and of the second temple, see Knibb, "The Exile in the Literature of the Intertestamental Period," *HeyJ* 17 (1976) 253–72.

[21] *Henochs Zehnwochenapokalypse*, 137–38. He adds that the same language is used in 1 Macc 3:3 (cf. 3:12) where the unremarkable fact that Judas Maccabeus bore the sword is recorded. Knibb's translation of 91:12 lacks the term *oppressors*; he renders ʾella yegaffeʿu too weakly as "those who do wrong." Charles translated these words more forcefully and correctly as "the oppressors."

*the wicked*—is far less specific and so weakens his case.[22] Thus it is apparent that none of his arguments removes the obstacles in the way of a Maccabean dating. The sword that the righteous receive is rather to be interpreted with most commentators as an allusion to an eschatological battle between the righteous and sinners. The words that summarize key events of the seventh week cannot very well be made to include the momentous happenings of 167, but the sword of the eighth week (the events of which are otherwise purely eschatological) can be explained plausibly as a reference to the sort of eschatological war that is depicted in other Jewish sources.

The seventh week, then, brings the historical drama to the author's time. 91:11, from the section that treats the seventh week, may even refer to events which the writer thought lay in the very near future. The "apostate generation" is probably that avidly hellenizing segment of Jewish society—the group whose enthusiastic sponsorship of hellenizing measures the authors of 1 and 2 Maccabees place early in the reign of Antiochus IV. One may, therefore, conclude that the ApW was written between 175 (his first regnal year) and 167 (the year of the decrees and of the desecration of the temple). This dating implies that the ApW is the oldest surviving Jewish apocalypse that includes a historical survey, although it antedates several others (Daniel 7; 8; 9; 10–12; the Animal Apocalypse) by just a few years. The acute crisis that gave rise to this historical apocalypse was the muscular challenge that the transformation of Jerusalem into a Hellenistic city posed for traditional forms of Judaism. A dating between 175 and 167 also entails that the Epistle, if—as argued above—its author and the writer of the ApW were the same person, was composed at some point early in the reign of Antiochus.

## 2. Features of the Apocalypse of Weeks

Dating the ApW specifies some of the immediate circumstances amid which it was penned, but it says little about the literary and intellectual soil in which the new apocalyptic form grew and flowered. A study of the introduction to and two leading characteristics of the ApW—dividing history into periods and "predicting" the past—should help to clarify these matters.

a. The Introduction (*1 Enoch* 93:1–3a):[23] In the introduction to the

---

[22] 4QEn^g 1 iv 16: *mn kwl ršy'yn* (Milik, *The Books of Enoch*, 266).

[23] These verses introduce only the ApW, but the Epistle itself begins with a preface that opens into an apocalypse (91:1–10). 92:1 also appears to be the introduction to a composition—perhaps to the remainder of the Epistle (see Charles, *The Book of Enoch*, 224). The present form of 93:1–3a may be the result of editorial expansion (v 2) and repetition (see Dexinger, *Henochs Zehnwochenapokalypse*, 106–09; Rau, "Kosmologie," 350–51), but the concern here is more with the extant shape of the ApW. As a result the very hypothetical pre–history of the text will not be discussed further.

apocalypse one meets a variety of features, some familiar and some new in the Enochic traditions. Verses 1–3a mention both the sources of Enoch's information and the group to which he disclosed it. *1 Enoch* 93:2, like 92:1 and 94:1, says that the patriarch spoke to his sons.[24] Gen 5:23 indicates that he had other sons besides Methuselah, but the fact that Methuselah is frequently the only named recipient of his father's teachings (79:1; 82:1; 83:1; 85:1–2; 91:1; 92:1 [Aramaic]) raises the possibilty that the writer's choice of the designation "sons" here bears some added significance. In Israelite wisdom literature a sage characteristically addresses prudent counsel to his literary "sons" or "son," but in the present case it is more likely that Enoch's parting words to his children are modeled on testaments such as Jacob's in Genesis 49 where the patriarch gathers his sons about him and speaks of the end of days (see especially Gen 49:1–2).[25] Use of this sapiential device fits the description of Enoch in 92:1 as "the wi]sest of mankind and the elect [one of] hum[anity]."[26] That is, here as elsewhere the ApW shows an affinity with other parts of the Epistle, since in it Enoch is presented as a wise man in the technical sense of the term—as one who imparts wisdom to the sons of righteousness and exhorts them to virtue.

*1 Enoch* 93:2b lists the sources from which Enoch drew privileged information.[27]

| *Ethiopic* | *Aramaic* |
|---|---|
| . . . according to that which appeared to me in the heavenly vision, and (which) I know from the words of the holy angels and understand from the tablets of heaven. | I have been shown [everything in a heavenly vision, and from] the word of the Watchers and Holy Ones I have known everything; [and in the heavenly tablets I] have read everything [and understoo]d.[28] |

Though the word *everything* occurs three times in Aramaic (two instances are preserved) and is absent in each case from the Ethiopic, the two versions agree that there were three sources from which Enoch derived information: a

---

[24] 4QEn^g 1 iii 20 preserves part of the word for "my sons" (*b]ny*; Milik, *The Books of Enoch*, 264). The Ethiopic version of 92:1 mentions his sons, but it is possible that the Aramaic read *Methuselah* (Milik, ibid., 260, 262).

[25] See Eva Osswald, "Zum Problem der *vaticinia ex eventu*," *ZAW* 75 (1963) 31–32. Osswald regards such *Segenssprüche* as part of the biblical background material for *vaticinia ex eventu*. Note, too that *1 Enoch* 1:1 is modeled on Deut 33:1, another of the *Segenssprüche*.

[26] 4QEn^g 1 ii 23: *ḥ]kym ꜣnwš ꜣ wbḥy[r] bny [ꜣrᶜ]* (Milik *The Books of Enoch*, 260).

[27] Rau ("Kosmologie," 350) and Dexinger (*Henochs Zehnwochenapokalypse*, 108) consider the verse redactional.

[28] Milik, *The Books of Enoch*, 264.

heavenly vision, an angelic message, and celestial tablets. All three serve a single purpose, viz., to reinforce the idea that the revelations were of heavenly origin and thus absolutely trustworthy. (Elsewhere in *1 Enoch* heavenly *books* are mentioned [e.g., 81:1–2] and they seem to be interchangeable with heavenly tablets).[29] It appears unlikely that the writer meant to distinguish rigidly between the three sources; rather, they assure the reader that Enoch did not fabricate what he said. He had learned it during his lengthy sojourn with the angels, and now he reports valid predictions to his community in order to comfort and encourage them—to hold before their despair the ultimate sovereignty of God.

Visions are familiar from the earlier written traditions in the AB and the BW as are Enoch's associations with angels who remained in God's service. Heavenly tablets, though, make their initial appearance here. They figure in just four passages in *1 Enoch*: three are in the Epistle (93:2; 103:2; 106:19) and one in an addition to the AB (81:1–2). They are also mentioned frequently in the literature of the second–temple period.[30] All of the passages in 1 Enoch indicate that the tablets were regarded as sources of data about the course of history and particularly about the end time. For example, in 103:2–4 the *mystery, tablets,* and *books* all appear to have the same contents: the future bliss of the righteous in contrast to their present afflictions. Mysteries and heavenly tablets recur at 106:19 and, as 107:1 delimits their contents, they reveal that ". . . generation upon generation will do wrong until a generation [4QEn$^c$ 5 ii 28 reads a plural] of righteousness shall arise, and sin shall depart from the earth, and everything good *shall come* upon it." 81:1–2 refer to the ". . . book of the tablets of heaven" in which Enoch reads ". . . all the deeds of men, and all who will be born of flesh on the earth for the generations of eternity." So it is understandable that the writer of the ApW would select the image of heavenly tablets as the source for Enoch's sketch of history and the *eschaton*. (The *books* from which Enoch is said to have read in the Ethiopic version of 93:1 and 93:3a are highly suspect text–critically as they do not appear in the Aramaic; on this matter, see below).

The figure of heavenly tablets implies a kind of pre-determination: that which has been inscribed will most assuredly occur. In the righteous that is supposed to arouse feelings of comfort and confidence, but, in line with the predestination thus expressed, the Epistle (and the ApW) does not exhort the

[29] See Rau, "Kosmologie," 309, 345–53, 426. Charles (*The Book of Enoch*, 91–92) has assembled the pertinent passages on this subject.

[30] Cf. Rau, "Kosmologie," 345–77; Russell, *The Method and Message of Jewish Apocalyptic*, 107–08; and F. Nötscher, "Himmlische Bücher und Schicksalsglaube in Qumran," *RevQ* 1 (1958–59) 405–11.

righteous to proselytize sinners. Fates have been sealed and are unchangeably engraved in heaven. Somewhat similar tablets are attested in other literatures—Babylonian, for instance. Here it is relevant to recall that the gods into whose presence Enmeduranki was ushered gave him a tablet that was especially suited for a diviner: "they gave him the tablet of the gods, the liver, a secret of heaven and [underworld] . . ." (K 2486.8).[31] Though the tablet is of a different kind than Enoch's, there is already in K 2486 an association between the seventh antediluvian leader and a celestial tablet. There may also be biblical or traditional Jewish influence behind the Enochic notion of such records. An interesting but only partial parallel is found in Hab 2:2-3 where the prophet is told to write on a tablet:

> And the Lord answered me:
> 'Write the vision;
> make it plain upon tablets,
> so he may run who reads it.
> For still the vision awaits its time;
> it hastens to the end—it will not lie.
> If it seem slow, wait for it;
> it will surely come, it will not delay' (cf. Isa 30:8).

A point of similarity with the tablets in *1 Enoch* is that the future is to be inscribed on Habakkuk's tablets; a difference is that the prophet himself rather than a celestial being does the writing. The Qumran commentary on this passage interprets it eschatologically: "and God told Habakkuk to write down the things that are going to come upon the last generation, but the fulfillment of the end-time he did not make known to him" (7:1-2).[32] The most likely biblical inspiration for the concept would seem to be, however, the tables of stone that the Lord gave to Moses on Mt. Sinai (Exod 24:12; 31:18; 32:15-16, 19; 34:1, 4, 28-29). Though Exodus does not say that the tablets contained an account of world history or of the sacred past, they were so understood by the writer of *Jubilees*:

> And the angel of the presence who went before the camp of Israel took the tables of the divisions of the years—from the time of creation—of the law and of the testimony of the weeks of the jubilees, according to the individual years, . . .

---

[31] Translation of Lambert, "Enmeduranki and Related Matters,"132 (he recognizes that the word *tup-pi* ["tablet"] could be plural). See, also, Hengel, *Judaism and Hellenism*, 1.200-01; Jansen, *Die Henochgestalt*, 46-47; and Collins, *The Apocalyptic Vision of the Book of Daniel*, 80.

[32] Translation of Maurya P. Horgan, *Pesharim: Qumran Interpretations of Biblical Books* (CBQMS 8; Washington: Catholic Biblical Association, 1979) 16.

from the day of the [new] creation +when+ the heavens and the earth shall be renewed. . . . (1:29)[33]

One can, therefore, point to possible biblical and extra-biblical sources or precedents for the concept of heavenly tablets in the Epistle. It is not, however, so closely modeled on any one of them so that one could specify it as the immediate source. The thinking behind it appears to have been too widely attested to allow that.

The introductory verses of the ApW in their Aramaic form show that the connection between Enochic traditions and the language of the Balaam chapters continued to be drawn. Before publication of the Aramaic fragments, Rau had maintained that there were similarities between 93:1–3a and chap. 1.[34] The Aramaic fragments have now confirmed the relation between them because in the two places in which the Ethiopic text has Enoch reading from books (93:1, 3a) 4QEn^g has the words *nsb ḥnwk mtlh* (Enoch took up his "parable")—precisely the figure of speech that appears in 1:1, 3 and which comes from the Balaam pericope.[35] That an apocalypse which contains a survey of history and a forecast follows these introductory words proves that the term *parable* could be used eschatologically in this period.

In its present form, then, the ApW is Enoch's parting report to his sons regarding information that he had learned from his celestial contacts. It is now located within an exhortation (i.e., the Epistle) which adopts some traits of wisdom literature—particularly of the testament—and which serves to encourage the righteous with the promise of an assured reversal of fortunes.

b. Dividing History into Specific Numbers of Units (Weeks): Unlike the apocalyptic visions in Daniel 7–12, which survey only the period from the exile to the author's day, the ApW begins with the antediluvian age and pursues the course of sacred history to the writer's time. The wider scope of the author's interests probably dictated his choice of Enoch as the worthy who received heavenly disclosures: he lived in primordial times and thus his predictions could begin virtually at the outset of the biblical story-line. By selecting Daniel as his hero, the writer of those visions limited the period for which he could offer *vaticinia ex eventu* because he was associated with the Babylonian exile. That is, the location of the visionary in sacred history

---

[33] Translation of Charles, *The Book of Jubilees*. The text is uncertain toward the end; but it may refer to the total course of the world's history. See Charles' notes to the text (pp. 9–10).

[34] "Kosmologie," 350–51.

[35] For the texts, see Milik, *The Books of Enoch*, 263–64. At 93:1 4QEn^g 1 iii 18 reads *nsb ḥ]nwk mtlh*, and at 93:3a (4QEn^g 1 iii 23) one finds *nsb ḥnwk mtlh*. Cf. also Knibb, *The Ethiopic Book of Enoch*, 2.223. David W. Suter ("*Māšāl* in the Similitudes of Enoch," 199–200) draws attention to several biblical *mešālîm* which, like the ApW, contrast the fate of the righteous and wicked—including the oracles of Balaam (see 200, n. 31).

determined the scope of the apocalypse granted to him.[36] Apparently accounts of the past in the straight-forward language of historical narrative fit the authors' purposes less adequately than such "predictions."

The writer of the ApW divides sacred history and the initial phases of the *eschaton* into segments of time that he labels *weeks*. He describes ten of them, and the apocalypse concludes with the prediction that these ten will be followed by "many weeks without number for ever" (91:17)—a statement which shows that the frequently used title *The Ten-Week Apocalypse* is inaccurate. Above it was argued that the first seven weeks included biblical and post-biblical history from Enoch to the author's day; weeks eight through ten then distinguish stages in the final judgment. Summaries or sketches of Israel's past are hardly unknown in biblical and apocryphal or pseudepigraphical literature. They occur in diverse kinds of texts and are put to rather different uses. One could name as examples Psalm 78, Nehemiah 9, Ezekiel 16 and 20, and Ecclesiasticus 44-49/50. But none of these earlier efforts and certainly not the major historiographical works in the Bible make the pretense of predicting the characters and events recounted in them. Moreover, no one of them subjects the past to such rigid systematization as does the ApW.

A number of extra-biblical, non-Jewish compositions show a similar interest in periodizing history, and they do so in various ways. In chap. III note was taken of the Akkadian prophecies in which a pattern of world empires is employed—a scheme that resurfaces in Greek literature and in Daniel 2 and 7.[37] The Greek poet Hesiod symbolized succeeding ages by means of different metals,[38] and Berossus, too, it has been claimed, divided his historical presentation into periods.[39] The latter two writers do not, however, claim to be predicting what will occur in these segments of time. Though scholars have been aware of these and other attempts, Iranian schematizations of history have drawn the greatest amount of favor as the nearest parallels—indeed the sources—of Jewish apocalyptic schemes. Russell, for one, finds the sources of the Jewish writers in ". . . their environment, and in particular, in the influence of Hellenistic and more especially of

[36] See Osswald, "Zum Problem der *vaticinia ex eventu*," 36-38.

[37] The four-kingdom pattern has been described and discussed very frequently; see, for example, the comments and bibliography in Collins, "Jewish Apocalyptic against its Hellenistic Near Eastern Environment," *BASOR* 220/221 (1975-76) 29. See also G. Hasel, "The Four World Empires of Daniel 2 against its Near Eastern Environment," 17-30; Hengel, *Judaism and Hellenism*, 1.181-83; and David Winston, "The Iranian Component in the Bible, Apocrypha, and Qumran: A Review of the Evidence," *HR* 5 (1966) 189-90.

[38] *Works and Days* I, 109-201.

[39] So Jansen, *Die Henochgestalt*, 78.

Persian beliefs."[40] The Iranian systems are thought to be closer parallels because they are linear rather than cyclical and culminate in an eschatological age of bliss. Hengel summarizes much of the Persian evidence thus:

> He [Theopompus, a fourth-century B.C. Greek writer who reported about Persian beliefs] speaks of several (three or four) successive periods of history, each of three thousand years, in which 'Oromazes–Zeus' and 'Ahriman–Hades' dominate in turn. For further periods of three thousand years the two fight together until, after the victory of Oromazes, Ahriman vanishes and a time of untroubled good fortune dawns for men. The later Iranian tradition records a duration of the world of twelve thousand years, which is divided into different periods of time. Various astrological themes, like the rule of certain zodiacal signs over particular millennia, are taken up, but in every case there stands at the end the victory over evil and the dawn of the time of salvation.[41]

It should be granted that there are similarities between these patterns and the Jewish ones, and it is known that Persian theology left its imprint on Judaism in other areas as well. Also, the evidence of an early writer like Theopompus circumvents the standard problem of the late dates for most surviving Iranian sources. But the marked differences ought not to be ignored. They center in this case around the issue of dualism—a doctrine that lies at the heart of the Persian systems. The ApW is not dualistic in the sense of the Iranian material, nor does it appeal to an alternating pattern of dominance by good and evil forces/beings. Less importantly, the number of periods in the Persian schemes does not coincide with those of the ApW. In commenting on the Persian arrangement into groups of three–thousand–year periods in connection with the ApW, Geo Widengren has written: "The Ethiopic Book of Enoch is *not* dominated by the idea of three periods. The ten–week scheme found in the fourth [*sic*] section of the Book would rather seem to lay stress on each single period of these thousand–year–periods [*sic*], the ten world–weeks, than on some periods of 3000 years, . . ."[42]

It is evident, therefore, that in the Hellenistic age there was a fairly common practice of dividing history into fixed periods and that some of these schemes culminated in an eschatological time of weal. In no case,

[40] *The Method and Message of Jewish Apocalyptic*, 228.

[41] *Judaism and Hellenism*, 1.193. For the report of Theopompus, see Plutarch, *Isis and Osiris* 47. See also Winston, "The Iranian Component," 197, 204; Geo Widengren, "Iran and Israel in Parthian Times with Special Regard to the Ethiopic *Book of Enoch*," *Temenos* 2 (1966) 161–63.

[42] "Iran and Israel," 163. See also Anders Hultgård, "Das Judentum in der hellenistisch-römischen Zeit und die iranische Religion—ein religionsgeschichtliches Problem" in *Aufstieg und Niedergang der römischen Welt*: II. *Principat* 19/1 (ed. H. Temporini and W. Haase; Berlin/New York: De Gruyter, 1979) 526–27.

however, including the Persian systems, can one demonstrate any direct connection with the ApW. The author wrote at a time when it was fashionable for sages to periodize their national past, but, aside from a general similarity with practices of the time, foreign influence may not have been overly strong. There are, after all, features in the ApW that betray its deep rootage in biblical traditions and which indicate that while the writer was imitating a popular international trend he nuanced that trend in a distinctively Jewish manner. His use of the term *weeks* immediately makes the point. Moreover, the fact that he divides the past into seven weeks is most suggestive: seven weeks of years constitute a kind of jubilee period[43]—a concept unusually rich in the symbolism of liberty and release.

The writer's native tradition probably inspired his particular way of periodizing. Several biblical writers showed an interest in chronology, of course, and the priestly editor of the pentateuch resorted to a series of covenants by means of which to organize the past. But the Babylonian exile seems to have provided the stimulus for a number of attempts at arranging sacred history into various periods which consist of weeks or other units with a base of seven.[44] Jeremiah stands at the beginning of this tradition. His prophecy that the exile of Judeans would continue for 70 years (25:11–12; 29:10) was later interpreted in different symbolic ways. The best known is probably Daniel's re-reading of the 70 years as 70 weeks of years or 490 years (9:2, 24–27). The writer of Daniel 9 apportioned the 70 weeks into groups of seven and 62 weeks and concludes his presentation with comments about the last week (vv 25–27). It may be that the various references in Daniel to three and one-half years—a period that coincides rather closely with the length of time that the temple was defiled by the Seleucids—should also be understood primarily against the backdrop of this pattern of weeks of years or sabbatical periods (7:25; 8:14; 9:27; 12:7,11,12).[45] 2 Chr 36:20–21 relate the 70 years of banishment to the institution of sabbaths for the land: "to fulfill the word of the Lord by the mouth of Jeremiah, until the land had enjoyed its sabbaths. All the days that it lay desolate it kept sabbath, to fulfil 70 years" (36:21; cf. Lev 26:34–35). Finally, Zech 1:12–17 (cf. 7:5) see in the 70 years the time during which the temple lay in ruins, and

---

[43] See Milik, *The Books of Enoch*, 255; Grelot, "Soixante-dix semaines d'années," *Bib* 50 (1969) 169–86.

[44] See Russell, *The Method and Message of Jewish Apocalyptic*, 195–202; Grelot, "Soixante-dix semaines d'années," 169–86; Knibb, "The Exile in the Literature of the Intertestamental Period," 253–72; and J. Licht, "twrt hᶜtym šl kt mdbr yhwdh wšl mḥšby qyṣyn ʾhrym (The Doctrine of Times of the Sect of the Desert of Judah and of Other Computers of Seasons)," *EI* 8 (1967) 63–70.

[45] So Grelot, "Soixante-dix semaines d'années," 183–84.

the Animal Apocalypse of *1 Enoch* (chaps. 85-90) divides the era from the exile to the author's time into periods of rule by 70 shepherds (*1 Enoch* 89:59-90:18, 22, 25). All of these examples show that heptads were used in segmenting sacred history, but all of them deal only with the exile or with the exilic age and beyond. The writer of the ApW is an exception: he took a heptadic scheme and applied it to all of biblical and post-biblical history. (The author of *Jubilees* also used weeks of years as historical units, but he applied them to the past explicitly and treated only the period from creation to Sinai.) It could be that he had precursors in this respect because *1 Enoch* 10:12, part of the BW, provides for a period of 70 generations (the number is confirmed by the Greek text and by 4QEn$^b$ 1 iv 10) between the first and second judgments against Shemihazah and his band; and the Testament of Levi 16 assigns 70 weeks to the time during which Levi's descendants will sin—an apostasy that leads to exile. The seventeenth and eighteenth chapters of the same work also contain some sort of apocalypse of weeks or jubilees, but the present state of the text makes interpretation precarious. It does, though, appear to refer to times before, during, and after the exile. Milik has argued that there was an earlier Jewish work in which all of history was divided into 70 ages (as suggested by *1 Enoch* 10:12) and in support of his thesis he appeals to 4Q 180 1 and 181 2.5 (where the phrase *bšbᶜym hšbwᶜ* [= in the seventy weeks] occurs). He may be correct that behind the sundry later references there lies such a composition, but the evidence that he adduces is too fragmentary to allow a reasonable degree of certainty. He also mentions a set of unpublished MSS (4Q 384-89) in which there is supposed to be an apocalypse of 10 jubilees.[46]

The ApW surveys the past in seven "weeks," and several attempts have been made to discover how long these weeks were.[47] The current view, which arose after a number of unsuccessful tries at deciphering, is that the weeks are periods of unequal length, each of which includes at least one significant person and/or event.[48] In other words, use of the same term for each unit is schematic, not strictly chronological. It should be added, though, that the

---

[46] *The Books of Enoch*, 249-55. One should also mention in this context 11QMelch 2. 6-8 which refers to the tenth jubilee, the end of which is the Day of Atonement (see also 2:18-20). For the text and commentary, see P. Kobelski, *Melchizedek and Melchireša ͨ* (CBQMS 10; Washington: Catholic Biblical Association, 1981) 5, 14-15.

[47] For some of the solutions that have been proposed, see Dexinger, *Henochs Zehnwochenapokalypse*, 119-20; Charles, *The Book of Enoch*, 228-29.

[48] Charles (*The Book of Enoch*, 228): "Rather we are to regard the ten weeks as periods of varying length, each one of which is marked, especially towards its close, by some great event . . ." Cf. also Reese, "Die Geschichte Israels," 70-72; Dexinger, *Henochs Zehnwochenapokalypse*, 120.

author took his scheme seriously and virtually invited the reader to try his hand at decoding it by referring to the ends of weeks three–eight, noting that Enoch was born seventh in the first week, and mentioning the seventh part of the tenth week. Attempts to define the length of the units are hindered by the fact that one does not know which of several possible biblical chronologies (if any of the extant ones) the author used. In addition, Jewish writers generally do not seem to have had very accurate chronological information for the post–exilic period—particularly the Persian phase of it. The MT, LXX, and Samaritan Pentateuch differ considerably in their chronologies for Genesis–Exodus, and the period of Israel's life in the land offers other possibilities for varying calculations. It is reasonable to expect, given the writer's penchant for units of seven, that he would employ a system (if he had one) in which each of his "days" would represent a number of years that is a multiple of seven. A fairly plausible result is obtained for weeks three–seven if one allows a jubilee–period for each day (whether that period is 49 or 50 years).[49] Nevertheless, the first two weeks present problems if one assumes that a "day" equals 49–50 years. Enoch was born toward the end of the first week, but according to surviving chronologies the lowest year number for his birth is 522 (the Samaritan Pentateuch and *Jubilees*)—a total that is far too high if a "week" represents 343 or 350 years. Also, the interval between Enoch's birth and the flood—an event of the second week—is too great. As a result, it is safest to say that no system which explains the duration of all the weeks has yet been uncovered.

c. "Predicting" the Past: In the ApW a Jewish writer, for reasons not fully understood, used a literary device that scholars generally term *vaticinia ex eventu* (= predictions from or on the basis of an event, that is, the event "predicted"). In other words, he makes Enoch "predict" what had already occurred.[50] Rather than following the lead of writers such as the deuteronomistic historian(s) or even Ezekiel and depicting—whether in literal or symbolic language—patterns in Israel's history and using them as the justification for his warnings and promises, the writer selected an antediluvian sage and placed on his lips a fabricated forecast. In so doing he imitated the example of others. Mention has already been made of the Akkadian prophecies attributed to Marduk and Shulgi, and many others of a similar type were written during the Hellenistic period. Egypt furnishes a number of

---

[49] K. Koch ("Die mysteriösen Zahlen der judäischen Könige und die apokalyptischen Jahrwochen," *VT* 28 [1978] 439–40) uses units of 490 years each for weeks four through seven and is able to relate these numbers to biblical givens in each case.

[50] On the phenomenon, see Osswald, "Zum Problem der *vaticinia ex eventu*," 27–44.

examples which resemble the ApW in this regard:[51] the Demotic Chronicle, the Potter's Oracle, and the Nechepso–Petosiris text, to list only some of them. Elsewhere one finds the Oracle of Hystaspes and various collections of sibylline oracles. The most famous biblical example occurs in Dan 11:1–39—a text composed just a few years after the ApW. It is noteworthy that in the Akkadian prophecies and in some of the other texts which resort to *vaticinia ex eventu* there is a polemic against Hellenistic rule and rulers (as in Daniel). In the ApW, though, native opposition to Hellenistic dominion takes the indirect form of condemning an apostate group of Jews who supported the religious and political policies of the Seleucid regime; it does not voice overt political opposition to the Hellenistic state. Another difference is that the historical scope of the ApW is larger than in most of the texts with "predictions" of the past: it confines itself to sacred history, generally leaving the nations out of consideration, but within these confines it covers the entire period from the beginning to the present and beyond.

The device of *vaticinia ex eventu* belongs in the same thought–world as the image of heavenly tablets. If such tablets recorded all that had happened and was to take place, and if they were shown to Enoch, then it is to be expected that he would be able to tell the future. In opting for this literary device the author once more reveals his awareness of current learned trends, but, as the content and language of the ApW show, his native traditions molded what he had to say and how he expressed it.

In concluding the present analysis of the ApW, note should be taken of the fact that several features which are often found in the later Jewish apocalypses are absent from it. First, the apocalypse is not mediated by an angel. Enoch is supposed to have learned its contents from angels, but the disclosures in the text come from the patriarch himself who conveys them to his sons. That is, the ApW does not relate the original experience of revelation; it now forms part of a testament—a fact which may explain why nothing is said about his reaction to the original experience. Second, there is no appeal to an interpreting angel, nor is there any suggestion that Enoch failed to understand what he had learned from his celestial sources. Third, he did not order that his words remain the secret possession of a closed group. He apparently delivers his message to a particular circle of followers, but they are not told to prevent others from having access to it. Fourth, there is no messianic figure of any sort in the eschatological section. And fifth, the

---

[51] In addition to Osswald's essay, cf. the material in C. C. McCown, "Hebrew and Egyptian Apocalyptic Literature," *HTR* 18 (1925) 387–411; Hengel, *Judaism and Hellenism*, 1.184–86; and Collins, "Jewish Apocalyptic against its Hellenistic Near Eastern Environment," 27–36; *The Sibylline Oracles of Egyptian Judaism* (SBLDS 13; Missoula: SBL, 1974) 12–15.

ApW expresses no overt political opposition to Hellenistic rule. It rather castigates renegade Jews who support pagan religious policies.

## B. The Book of Dreams

The Book of Dreams (= BD), like the Epistle, includes two apocalypses. *1 Enoch* 83:3-5 record a vision, granted to Enoch, regarding the flood and its sequel; in it one meets again the familiar practice of drawing parallels between the noachic flood and the final judgment. The second apocalypse— the so-called Animal Apocalypse (= AA; 85:1-90:42)—surveys the totality of sacred history and of the future. The first of the two apocalypses is as brief and vague as the "Methuselah" Apocalypse in *1 Enoch* 91. It requires interpretation by Mahalalel, Enoch's grandfather, whom the author here drags from his forgotten niche in the Genesis 5 genealogy for one of his rare appearances in Jewish literature. The AA resembles the ApW in scope, but it is far more detailed and resorts to different images and divisions of time in its portrayal of the sacred drama. It terms itself a vision or dream–vision (85:1, 2, 3, 9; 86:1, 3; 87:2; 89:7, 36, 70; 90:2, 8, 39, 40, 42) and is characterized by the practice of representing nations and people as animals (e.g., Israel is symbolized as sheep). The only exceptions, besides angels, are Noah (89:1) and Moses (89:36) who begin as animals (a bull and sheep respectively) but become men. Enoch conveys both of the apocalypses in the BD to Methuselah so that they have the same testamentary setting as the remainder of *1 Enoch* 72-105. The AA does differ from the shorter apocalypse in chap. 83 in that it requires no interpreter.

The BD is, like all other sections of *1 Enoch*, preserved in its entirety only in Ethiopic, but there are other, earlier witnesses to parts of the text. A Greek fragment containing 89:42-49 has survived,[52] and four Aramaic MSS offer texts that correspond to a number of passages (4QEn^c-f).[53] After the extended analysis of the ApW that was presented above, it will not be necessary to deal with all features of the AA (the largest part of the BD) since it evidences some of the same phenomena (e.g., *vaticinia ex eventu*). It will

---

[52] The fragment is reproduced in Charles, *The Book of Enoch*, 195-98 (printed parallel to his English rendering of the Ethiopic); and in Black, *Apocalypsis Henochi Graece*, 36-37. Milik ("Fragments grecs du Livre d'Hénoch," 321-43) thinks he has identified Greek fragments corresponding to 85:10-86:2 and 87:1-3, but the identification is most uncertain since only a few letters remain on each line and the rest must be restored. For similar reservations, see Knibb, *The Ethiopic Book of Enoch*, 2.196-97.

[53] For the passages with which the fragments overlap, see the chart in Milik, *The Books of Enoch*, 6. All of the fragments preserve parts of the AA (almost all of the Aramaic material is from chap. 89), but no one of them has text that comes from the first part of the BD (i.e., chaps. 83-84).

suffice to consider the date of the AA, the particular sources from which its material comes, and the information that can be gleaned from the BD about the growing biography of Enoch.

1. The Date of the AA and the BD

As the AA dominates the BD and there is no indication in the text which would suggest that the apocalypse was written by someone other than the author of the entire BD, establishing a date for the AA should reveal the date for the complete booklet.

The Aramaic MSS provide a base from which to begin a study of the date of the BD. The most ancient of them on paleographical grounds is 4QEn$^f$, of which only one small fragment has been identified and published. Milik assigns its script to the third quarter of the second century B.C.[54] 4QEn$^e$ was copied in the first half and 4QEn$^{c,d}$ in the last third of the first century B.C.[55] If one may rely on the evidence of En$^f$, the AA and presumably the whole BD was composed before B.C. 125 and perhaps well before.

Since the author of the AA resorts to *vaticinia ex eventu* followed by authentic predictions, it should be possible to locate his historical place by determining the point at which he switches from one to the other. Commentators agree that the key section is 90:6-16 and in particular the identification of the sheep or ram with a large horn in 90:9-16. There is little doubt that vv 6-7 refer to events preceding the rise of Antiochus IV (for the lambs who were born, compare *Jub.* 23:26-27)[56] and that 90:8 alludes to the removal and eventual execution of Onias III (removal from his high priestly office in 175 [2 Macc 4:1-10]; execution in ca. 171 (4:33-38]).[57] Following these events the horned animal is mentioned for the first time (90:9). In the sequel it fights against Israel's enemies (pictured as birds) and wins with divine aid. Early in the modern study of *1 Enoch* a number of prominent scholars saw in the horned ram John Hyrcanus (B.C. 134-104), the fourth Maccabean ruler.[58] Charles, however, formulated a compelling case for understanding it as a symbol for Judas Maccabeus: "The interpretation of Dillmann, Köstlin,

---

[54] *The Books of Enoch*, 5, 41, 244. The diminutive size of the fragment, which Milik reconstructs around the few preserved letters to correspond to 86:1-3, reduces the force of the argument, though there is no compelling reason to doubt that it contains part of the BD.

[55] Ibid., 5, 225 (for En$^e$); 178 (for En$^c$); cf. 217 (for En$^d$).

[56] The lambs are probably the early *ḥăsîdîm* (Charles, *The Book of Enoch*, 207; Reese, "Die Geschichte Israels," 48; Milik, *The Books of Enoch*, 43).

[57] Charles, *The Book of Enoch*, 208; Milik, *The Books of Enoch*, 43; Nickelsburg, *Jewish Literature*, 92.

[58] E.g., Beer, "Das Buch Henoch," 296 n. h (though he does grant that Judas Maccabeus could be intended). Dillmann (*Das Buch Henoch*, 277-79), among others, also defended this identification (for early views, see Charles, *The Book of Enoch*, 206-07).

Schürer, and others, which takes the 'great horn' to symbolize John Hyrcanus, does violence to the text, and meets with the insuperable objection that
thus there would not be even the faintest reference to Judas, the greatest of
the Maccabees."[59] The horned ram is the last historical figure mentioned
before the eschatological section begins, and, since he is still fighting at this
point, the AA was written, in his estimation, before B.C. 161, the date of
Judas' death.[60] Martin sided with Charles and with him believed that *Jub.* 4:19
reflected its author's knowledge of the BD.[61]

Milik has recently joined forces with advocates of the Charles–Martin
position and has maintained further that the BD was composed in B.C. 164.
". . . probably in the early months of the year, during the weeks which
followed the battle of Bethsur."[62] He finds warrant for his remarkably precise dating in the similarity between the events of 90:13–15 (a battle between
the large–horned ram and various enemies represented as eagles, vultures,
kites, ravens, and shepherds; when the ram cries for help, he receives it from
above) and 2 Macc 11:6–12 (Judas' miraculous deliverance from the Seleucid Lysias). He considers 90:16 a symbolic sketch of the situation after the
battle of Bethsur, while 90:17 marks the beginning of the *eschaton*.[63]

It is regrettable that no Aramaic or Greek text preserves the crucial
section of chap. 90 because earlier commentators saw grave problems in the
Ethiopic version—problems which would affect Milik's reconstruction. Charles, building on his and Martin's previous literary observations, argued that
vv 13–15 and 16–18 were doublets and that v 19 should be read after v 13
(which parallels v 16).[64] There certainly are similarities in the two sections,
but the hypothesis may not be necessary. Verses 13 and 16 are the closest of
the proposed parallels; both deal with attacks by gentile nations and assert
that the purpose of the attacks was to "dash the horn of that ram in pieces"
(v 13) or to "dash that horn of the ram in pieces" (v 16). But even in these
verses the attackers are not identical: v 13 includes, somewhat strangely, the
shepherds who are the guardian angels of the nations, but v 16 lacks them.
And the results are not the same: in v 13 the horned ram cries for help, but in
v 16 nothing is said about its efforts. Verses 14 and 17 are more clearly

---

[59] *The Book of Enoch*, 208.

[60] Ibid., liii. Cf. also Nickelsburg, *Jewish Literature*, 93.

[61] *Le Livre d'Hénoch*, xcvi.

[62] *The Books of Enoch*, 44.

[63] Ibid.

[64] *The Book of Enoch*, 209–11. See also Reese, "Die Geschichte Israels," 50 (he thinks
that vv 16–18 belonged to the original text but cautions that one cannot disentangle the original
text from its present form); Nickelsburg, *Jewish Literature*, 92: "We have either duplicate
versions of the same block of text or an updating of the original text of the apocalypse."

distinct. For example, in v 14 the man who records the shepherds' names in a book helps the ram and shows it that "its help was coming down"; v 17 says nothing of the sort. Finally, vv 15 and 18 are also different in significant ways. Verse 15 describes a theophany which produced panic in those enemies who saw the Lord of the sheep, but v 18 claims that the deity "took in his hand the staff of his anger and struck the earth; and the earth was split, and all the animals and birds of heaven fell from those sheep and sank in the earth, and it closed over them." The latter passage, the language of which is influenced by the story about judgment against Korah and his followers in Num 16:31–33, does appear to envisage cataclysmic events that are associated with the end, not divine intervention in a Maccabean battle. 90:19 then describes an eschatological conflict with the remaining gentiles. Whereas those of the gentiles who perished in v 18 were actually fighting Israel ("fell from those sheep"), the ones in v 19 are described differently. They are the survivors of the nations. Thus, it seems inaccurate to say that v 19 is out of place in the present arrangement.

One can agree, therefore, with Milik in considering 90:16 the end of the *vaticinia ex eventu* and 90:17 the beginning of the authentic predictions. It also appears most natural to identify the ram with the large horn as Judas. 2 Macc 11:6–12 does indeed offer an intriguing parallel to the events of 90:13–15 (cf. also 1 Macc 4:26–35); moreover, 90:16 may represent the events that are the subject of 1 Maccabees 5, i.e., attacks (apparently) from gentiles in areas corresponding to ancient Edom, Ammon, Phoenicia, Moab, and Philistia. Nevertheless, to specify the time of composition as 164 (and even as the early months of it), while possible, is overly precise. It can be concluded, though, that as Judas plays a vital role in the apocalypse and nothing is said of his death, the AA was very likely written at some time before he perished. A date in the late 160's is the most reasonable one for the AA and thus for the BD as well.[65]

### 2. Sources for the AA

The ApW and the AA have the same scope but differ significantly in many other ways. An effort at identifying sources for the latter's distinctive traits should further elucidate the bases upon which the earliest writers of apocalypses in the Enochic tradition built their works.

---

[65] Nickelsburg (*Jewish Literature*, 93) places it between B.C. 164 and 160, Reese ("Die Geschichte Israels," 21) between 166 and 160. Goldstein (*1 Maccabees*, 40–42) thinks that the description of the last period of the shepherds' rule was written in stages. His reconstruction suffers from several flaws. It does not reckon with the likelihood that 90:19 describes, not a historical, but an eschatological battle. He also reinterprets the various birds (=Israel's enemies) as officials at different administrative levels; yet, elsewhere in the AA such creatures represent nations.

a. Most obviously and most importantly the author borrows from the central biblical story-line. He begins with Adam and continues through the major characters and episodes until the beginning of the exile.[66]

b. With the exile the writer departs from the biblical narratives and turns to a scheme in which 70 shepherds pasture the sheep (Israel). The only biblical event mentioned is the rebuilding of the temple (89:72-73), but the new sanctuary is condemned because the bread placed on its altar was unclean (v 73).[67] The epoch during which the shepherds rule ends only with the final judgment (90:17-24).

c. Another section which derives from extra-biblical sources is the account of the sinful prelude to the flood (86:1-88:3). In these chapters the writer focuses upon the angels of Gen 6:1-4 whom he symbolizes as stars, but he clearly had far more information than just Genesis. There are transparent similarities with *1 Enoch* 6-11, yet the story of the stars/angels who sinned differs rather markedly from the composite tale in 6-11 (e.g., Shemihazah has no role). The two versions may be independent realizations of common traditions about the angelic Watchers.[68] A noteworthy addition is that Enoch who was absent from 6-11 now becomes the recipient of a vision that includes the Watcher story.[69] Also, his removal from earth is told within the context of the tale (87:2-4). Thus, by the time of the AA, the angelic *fall* had been brought into even closer contact with Enoch than in the BW.[70]

### 3. The Imagery in the AA

The two dominant features of the AA—representing individuals and nations by animals and dividing the exilic and post-exilic (this term is probably inappropriate for the writer of the AA) periods into times during which 70 shepherds rule Israel—call for further comment. It will be shown below

[66] This is not to say that biblical characters and episodes are always given the same significance as they have in the Bible. The time of the flood occupies a relatively large amount of space, as do the exodus and the Sinai events, but the story of Genesis 3 is omitted, the patriarchs simply mentioned, the conquest virtually ignored, and the period of the divided monarchy merely sketched. For a perceptive analysis of the historical divisions, symbols, and views in the AA, see Dimant, "History According to the Vision of the Animals (Ethiopic Enoch 85-90) [Hebrew]," *mḥqry yrwšlym bmḥšbt yśr'l* 2 (1982) 18-37.

[67] This verdict is in harmony with a series of Jewish texts in which the worship offered in the second temple is belittled. See Knibb, "The Exile in Intertestamental Literature," 203-04; Nickelsburg, *Jewish Literature*, 93-94. The words of the verse resemble Mal 1:7, 12-14.

[68] So Dimant, "The 'Fallen Angels,'" 81-87 (cf. p. 21).

[69] Dimant, ibid., 86.

[70] The comments above do not exhaust the evidence in the text that the author had access to extra-biblical texts and traditions. One could add, for example, the embellishments of the Cain-Abel story (Cain's pursuit of Abel, the name of his wife [85:4-5]) as well as the detail that Eve searched for Abel (85:6).

that both of these characteristics are closely tied to Jeremiah 25, but it should first be said that they belong to more widespread currents in biblical and post-biblical literature. For example, the writer refers to Jacob as a sheep, and all of his descendants are given the same name. This recalls those passages in which Israel is called the Lord's flock which he shepherds (e.g., Ps 78:52; 80:1; Jer 50:6-7; Ezekiel 34; Zech 9:16; 10:2-3). Another animal name for a people—wild asses for Ishmael and his offspring—derives from Gen 16:12. The other designations in the AA may have been selected to supply natural enemies for sheep, or they may have, at least in some cases, associations that have not been recorded elsewhere. Division of the time from the exile into periods of rule by 70 shepherds is rich with symbolism, as will be noted shortly, but this trait, too, joins the AA to that large number of texts (see 2.b. above) which resort to periodization based on units or multiples of seven.

The author's use of pastoral symbols and of the number 70 demonstrates the enormous importance that he (and many others) attached to the prophecy of Jeremiah for an understanding of the exile. Both the shepherd/ flock image and the number 70 come from Jeremiah 25; in fact a web of associations with terms and ideas in the chapter provided the substance and some of the form of the writer's treatment of the time from the divided monarchy to his own day.[71] A sceptic living in the second century would have condemned Jeremiah's prophecy that the exile would last 70 years as failed prediction, but for the writer it was prophecy in need of proper interpretation. The following paragraphs show the measure of his debt to Jeremiah 25.

a. In 25:3-9 Jeremiah criticizes his contemporaries for rejecting the prophets and himself and links their perversity to the impending national doom. The era of the divided monarchy is characterized in the AA as a time when Israel refused to listen to the prophets; the exile was a direct result (89:51-58; cf. also Neh 9:26-30).

b. Jer 25:11 says that the land is to be devastated and the population is to remain slaves among the nations (LXX) for 70 years.[72] These ideas were

---

[71] The hypothesis that the shepherds of the AA are related to Jeremiah's 70 years is hardly novel (cf. Charles, *The Book of Enoch*, 200-01), but the extent of the writer's use of Jeremiah 25 has been elaborated in much more detail by Carol Newsom in an unpublished Harvard seminar paper entitled "Enoch 83-90: The Historical Résumé as Biblical Exegesis," especially pp. 21-27. She relates the writer's procedure with Jeremiah 25 to the *pešer* style but quite properly does not equate them. Dimant ("History," 29) attaches some importance to Zech 10:3; 11:3-17 but as the analysis below shows, Jeremiah 25 is a more productive source. She does recognize, naturally, that the Jeremiah passage makes a contribution (see p. 35).

[72] The *RSV*, which follows the MT of 25:11, reads: "These nations shall serve the king of

combined by the writer of the AA. For him the 70 years among the nations symbolized the dominion of the 70 gentile peoples over Israel. He could have derived the number for the nations from Genesis 10, and he would have known from Deut 32:8 (LXX: cf. 4QDtq)[73] that each of the nations was associated with an angel. In the AA the shepherds are angels, as the imagery of the apocalypse suggests.[74] Consequently, they represent the rule of gentiles over Israel. These thoughts were probably also encouraged by Jer 25:17–38 in which the leaders of the nations are called shepherds under whose control Israel has been placed. The prophet refers to the kings of the nations as those who will drink the cup of divine wrath (vv 17–26), indicts the nations, and talks of a day of slaughter (27–33). Then he prophesies:

> Wail, you shepherds, and cry,
> and roll in the ashes, you lords of the flock,
> for the days of your slaughter and dispersion have come,
> and you shall fall like choice rams.
> No refuge will remain for the shepherds,
> nor escape for the lords of the flock.
> Hark, the cry of the shepherds,
> and the wail of the lords of the flock!
> For the Lord is despoiling their pasture,
> and the peaceful folds are devastated,
> because of the fierce anger of the Lord (34–37).

The same identification of gentile leaders as shepherds is made in Jer 6:3 (the shepherds of 23:1–4; Zech 13:7; and Ezekiel 34 seem to be Judean leaders).

c. The eschatological battle, which the AA depicts in 90:18–19, seems exegetically related to the universal judgment scene of Jeremiah 25 which also involves a sword sent from the Lord to slaughter the nations (25:16, 27, 29, 31, 38).

d. It is additionally possible to suggest that the book which in the AA records the excesses of the shepherds' despotic rule (89:62–64, 70–71, 76–77

Babylon seventy years." The LXX lacks the reference to the Babylonian monarch and presupposes *baggôyim* rather than *haggôyim* at the beginning of the verse.

[73] As is well known, the LXX of Deut 32:8 reflects Hebrew *bĕnê ᵓēlîm* instead of the MT's *bĕnê yiśrāᵓēl*. The LXX reading now receives some support from 4QDtq, on which see P. W. Skehan, "A Fragment of the 'Song of Moses' (Deut 32) from Qumran," *BASOR* 136 (1954) 12–15. Cf. also Nickelsburg, *Jewish Literature*, 92. Dimant ("History," 26 n. 33) opposes connecting Enoch's 70 shepherds with the 70 gentile nations. She notes that in its version of Genesis 10 the AA (89:10) lists only 14 kinds of symbolic animals, not 70. Though her observation is interesting, it does not constitute a refutation of the gentile–nation thesis. For the author the cipher of 70 shepherds could easily have embraced both the Genesis 10 notion and Jeremiah's 70 years.

[74] Charles, *The Book of Enoch*, 199–201; Beer, "Das Buch Henoch," 294 n. c.

[cf. 90:14] 90:17, 22) was inspired by Jer 25:13: "I will bring upon that land all the words which I have uttered against it, everything written in this book, which Jeremiah prophesied against all the nations."

e. Jeremiah 25 leaves one with the impression that the duration of gentile dominance is pre-determined; once it has run its course the Lord will judge the nations (note the 70 years of v 11 followed by v 12). The AA makes a similar point. In it the shepherds are not to be hindered despite their crimes; their misdeeds are simply recorded and ultimately will be repaid, but the bloodshed and violence must continue their allotted time (89:64, 75-77).

f. The excesses of the shepherds' rule may also be related to Jeremiah 25, though historical events and possibly other passages (e.g., Isa 40:2) were more direct sources. Jer 25:12 says that the Babylonian king and the Chaldeans are to be punished ". . . for their iniquity, says the Lord, making the land an everlasting waste"; and v 14 adds: "I will recompense them according to their deeds and the work of their hands."[75]

The AA, then, furnishes abundant evidence of how tightly an early apocalyptic text could be tied to a biblical prophecy. It also shows how one text could suggest numerous related ideas to a learned author. The medium through which apocalyptic information came to Enoch was mantic—a dream-vision—and its predictive nature also has a divinatory quality about it; but the contents of the AA are generally biblical and thoroughly prophetic. The biblical text has become for the wise seer another cryptic indicator of the future, a message from God whose meaning must be decoded by one endowed with special insight—much as a Babylonian *bārû* would read the marks of a liver. From inspired reading of biblical secrets such as Jeremiah's 70 years the pattern of God's work and plan in history could be perceived. Unfulfilled prophecy cannot be false prophecy; the words of God's messengers must rather be "divined" in order to discover their true meaning, i.e., their contemporary significance.

### 4. Eschatology in the AA

The writer devotes an extended section to an eschatological sequence of events (90:17-38). By distinguishing phases or stages in the *eschaton* he joins forces with the author of the ApW, but the account in the AA is much more detailed. There is no need to analyze the section in detail, but the highlights should be listed.

a. The divine warrior-judge intervenes (90:17-19).

---

[75] It may be coincidental, but the birds who represent Israel's neighbors and enemies in Maccabean times appear in biblical legislation among the fowl whose meat is prohibited for eating. E.g., the eagles, kites, vultures, and ravens are forbidden by Lev 11:13-15; Deut 14:12-14.

b. Judgment is executed on Asael, the other fallen angels, the shepherds (who are also angels), and the blind sheep (90:20-27).

c. The old house[76] is folded up and a new one brought by the Lord. Either the Lord or the sheep are said to be in it,[77] and to it the animals and birds (= the nations) come (90:28-33). Allusion is made to Enoch and Elijah at this point. It seems that the words "all those which had been destroyed and scattered" in v 33 refer to some sort of resurrection of the righteous.[78]

d. Use of the sword ends and all sheep have their eyes opened—that is, they now enjoy a proper relationship with their true shepherd and understand him and his will for them (90:34-36).[79]

e. A white bull is born, and all animals fear it (90:37). Clearly this figure is important but he is not called a messiah. Nothing in the text suggests, either, that he is davidic. The image of the bull implies rather a similarity with the antediluvian patriarchs who are also termed bulls. It is debatable whether this individual and the wild ox of v 38 are identical or whether they are perhaps two different leaders of the *eschaton*.[80]

f. All are transformed (90:38).

The important point for the present purposes is that, while the author continues the time–honored eschatological associations of Enoch, he shows that within his circle more reflection has occurred regarding the end, doubtless under the heavy impress of events during the mid–160's. The result is a fuller picture of the *eschaton* and a more concrete object of hope for the oppressed.

### 5. Enoch in the BD

The genealogy of Genesis 5 underlies the statements in the BD that Mahalalel was Enoch's grandfather (83:3, 6) and Methuselah his son (83:1, 10; 85:2). Enoch is supposed to have told Methuselah that he received both

---

[76] There is no warrant in the AA for interpreting this house as the temple in Jerusalem. In the apocalypse the word for temple is always *tower*. Nickelsburg (*Jewish Literature*, 93) understands it as the old Jerusalem.

[77] On the textual problem, see Charles, *The Book of Enoch*, 214.

[78] Cf. Nickelsburg, *Jewish Literature*, 93; Grelot, "L'eschatologie des Esséniens," 120-21 ("Bref, la résurrection corporelle semble absente des *Fragments noachiques*, du *Livre des Songes*, des *Voyages mythologiques* et du *Livre de l'Exhortation*" [121]).

[79] The motif of opened eyes is extremely important in the AA and deserves more extended study. Newsom ("Enoch 83–90," 17, 30–31) observes that it means not only obedience to the divine stipulations but also understanding of the sort of esoteric wisdom which was given to Enoch, the man whose eyes were opened. Cf. also Reese, "Die Geschichte Israels," 34–37; Dimant, "History," 25.

[80] See the discussion in Charles, *The Book of Enoch*, 215–16; Knibb, *The Ethiopic Book of Enoch*, 2.216.

visions recorded in the BD early in his life (83:2): the first when he was learning to write, the second before he married. In 85:3 his wife is named *Edna*; in *Jub*. 4:20 she is called *Edni* (in *Jub*. 4:27 Methuselah marries a certain *Edna*). Nothing more is said about her in *1 Enoch*, but *Jub*. 4.20 calls her the daughter of Dan'el—a character who has been associated with the much discussed *dn'l* of Ugarit and the Daniel of Ezek 14:14, 20.[81] If he is the same mythological figure, then the writer of *Jubilees* has managed to marry Enoch into the family of a legendary Canaanite sage.

Since Enoch saw his visions before he married,[82] he was younger than 65 years (his age when Methuselah, his first-born, entered the world [Gen 5:21; *1 Enoch* 85:3]) at the time. An implication is that Enoch had been, in the writer's estimation, singled out from others already at an early stage in his life. He was chosen before he "walked with the angels." Because the visions came before Enoch joined angelic company, his association with them has to be "predicted" in the second vision:

> And those three [celestial beings] who came out last took hold of me by my hand, and raised me from the generations of the earth, and lifted me on to a high place, and showed me a tower high above the earth, and all the hills were lower. And one said to me: "Remain here until you have seen everything which is coming upon these elephants and camels and asses [descendants of the fallen angels], and upon the stars, and upon all the bulls" (87:3-4).

His proximity to a tower is suggestive. Elsewhere in the AA the word *tower* refers to the first and second temples (89:50, 54, 56, 66, 67, 73). If the word has a similar meaning here, then one would have the first reference to Enoch's presence at a sanctuary removed from human society and ready access. The point is of some interest because in *Jub*. 4:25 Enoch officiates as a priest in a sanctuary in Eden, though he does so there only after his final removal. Regardless whether the same temple is meant, Enoch is removed from his former place while the angels and their giant offspring afflict humankind.

---

[81] For a treatment of this hypothetical connection, see Müller, "Magisch-mantische Weisheit und die Gestalt Daniels," 79-94; cf. also Collins, *The Apocalyptic Vision of the Book of Daniel*, 2-3.

[82] Some of the commentators (e.g., Beer, "Das Buch Henoch," 288 n. b.) see an ascetic tendency at work in the timing of the visions. Milik (*The Books of Enoch*, 42) disagrees but appeals to ". . . rites of incubation which demanded temporary continence." These views have no basis in the text. It seems more natural to say that the author of the BD was interested in demonstrating Enoch's unique status even before his sojourn with the angels, just as other Jewish writers created a prediluvian biography for Noah to document the scriptural assertion that he was righteous (on this see VanderKam, "The Righteousness of Noah" in *Ideal Figures in Ancient Judaism: Profiles and Paradigms* [ed. G. W. E. Nickelsburg and J. J. Collins; SCS 12; Chico, CA: Scholars, 1980] 13-32).

Locating these events within his 365 years agrees with the etymological explanation that the angels descended in the days of his father Jared.

Given the timing of his visions before his first removal from human society, the source of Enoch's apocalyptic knowledge could hardly be the heavenly tablets to which appeal was made in the ApW. The contents of the apocalypses come to him solely through dream-visions. The prayer that the youthful Enoch offers in 84:1-6 suggests that it was through his efforts that the Lord preserved a righteous remnant into the postdiluvian age. It is possible that the AA is then conceived, in its present literary position, as a further explication of the divine promise given to him that the righteous would continue to endure throughout history.[83]

## C. The Remaining Sections of the Epistle

It was convenient to analyze the two major historical apocalypses first, but now that they have been examined the relevant information in the larger part of the Epistle should be studied.

### 1. *1 Enoch* 92; 93:11-14; 94:1-105:2[84]

Two apocalypses—the "Methuselah" Apocalypse (91:1-10) and the ApW—serve as an introduction to and basis for Enoch's exhortations and warnings in the remainder of the booklet. The entire work is known as an epistle because it so designates itself in 100:6 (*epistolē* in the Greek text) and because the subscript to the Chester Beatty Papyrus also calls it one.[85] The composition does embody some epistolary formulae, particularly after 94:1,[86] but its literary dress hangs rather loosely about the body of the composition which is devoted almost exclusively to exhortations for the righteous/wise and admonitions for the sinners/fools. The prefaced apocalypses immediately

---

[83] On this issue see Reese, "Die Geschichte Israels," 22.

[84] *1 Enoch* 91 contains a little apocalypse, set in the context of Enoch's exhortation to his sons; it is rather general and vague in comparison with the AA. It does, though, provide another example of Enoch's firm association with apocalypses that survey history. *1 Enoch* 105, which had for a long time been regarded as an addition to the Epistle (Charles, *The Book of Enoch*, lii, 262; Martin, [*Le Livre d'Hénoch*, lxxxiii] called 105:2b an "element étranger"), is now attested in part by 4QEn^c 5 i 21-24 (very little is preserved; see Milik, *The Books of Enoch*, 206-08). It is clear enough that the Aramaic MS had material corresponding to 105:1, but the situation is more difficult for 105:2 which contains the textually suspect reference to God's son (see Knibb, *The Ethiopic Book of Enoch*, 2.243). The Greek MS omits chap. 105 (see Campbell Bonner, *The Last Chapters of Enoch in Greek* [SD 8; London: Christophers, 1937] 75-76). Chap. 108 is attested neither in Greek nor Aramaic and is almost certainly an addition to the Epistle as all scholars recognize (e.g., Nickelsburg, *Jewish Literature*, 151).

[85] Bonner, *The Last Chapters of Enoch in Greek*, 50-51, 86-87.

[86] Milik, *The Books of Enoch*, 51-52. He believes that in this way the writer reflects his knowledge of the BW which also includes a letter of Enoch.

place the following sections in an eschatological context, while the exhortations and warnings focus on the great reversal which will transpire at the
final judgment. Then the currently oppressed righteous will be freed to enjoy
bliss, but the presently wealthy sinners will suffer the deserved penalties of
their oppression. Consequently the Epistle does not offer simple, practical
instructions for every-day living; rather, it commands a life of patient hope
in the firm confidence, bolstered by revelation, that an eschatological transformation lies in the near future. Nickelsburg has shown that, in its non-
apocalyptic sections, the Epistle exhibits a balanced organization as the
writer alternately exhorts the righteous and admonishes the sinners.[87] It has
been argued above that there is no need to identify the righteous with the
Pharisees or the sinners with Sadducees. Other compelling evidence pointing
to a late-second or early-first-century dating of these parts of the Epistle is
also lacking. An earlier, perhaps even pre-Maccabean date for the entire
booklet is quite possible and indeed probable.

For the purposes of this study it will be useful to comment only on the
data in the Epistle for the biography of Enoch and on the roles that the
writer has him play.

a. Enoch's Biographical Situation: The patriarch, who is pictured as
the recipient of revelation and teacher of the righteous, is living in that short
interval between his 300-year stay with the angels and his final removal from
humankind. During those days he reports to his children (e.g., 91:1-3, 18;
92:1; 93:2; 94:1), who are the righteous (compare 94:1 with 94:3, for example), what he had learned from the angels and other celestial sources. On the
basis of that information he utters his exhortations and woes. The same
situation was presupposed in the AB (and perhaps the BD), but it receives
greater elaboration in *1 Enoch* 81:5-10—part of an addition to the original
AB which shows several points of contact with the Epistle. According to
81:6, the angels who had returned Enoch to his kin allowed him one year in
which to instruct his children. The chronology of his life, which is the same
in the MT, LXX, Samaritan Pentateuch, and *Jubilees*, could tolerate only a
brief homecoming for him. He was 65 years of age when he became the
father of Methuselah; he then spent 300 years with the angels; and he was
365 when God took him (Gen 5:21-24). Thus only a part of a year was
available for his pedagogical labors. The result is that the Epistle assumes the
testamentary setting that proved quite popular elsewhere in Jewish literature
(e.g., Genesis 49; the Testaments of the 12 Patriarchs; the final speeches of
Noah, Abraham, and Isaac in *Jubilees*, etc.).

---

[87] *Resurrection, Immortality, and Eternal Life,* 112-29; "The Apocalyptic Message of
*1 Enoch* 92-105," *CBQ* 39 (1977) 309-28; "Riches, the Rich, and God's Judgment in 1 Enoch
92-105 and the Gospel According to Luke," *NTS* 25 (1979) 326-32.

b. Enoch's Roles: The ancient patriarch wears the mantle of both prophet and wise man as he looks to the day of judgment, exhorts the righteous, and warns the sinners. He provides a clear example of how these two professions or functions were more closely fused in the Hellenistic age than they had been previously.[88] Jansen observed that Enoch's imitation of the prophetic role was apparent from his nurturing and warning, his use of woe-oracles, and his choice of phrases such as "in that day."[89] One could add that the fundamental outline of the Epistle's eschatology is a development of prophetic eschatology. It seems, though, that the traits which one regularly associates with sapiential literature and sages are more strongly to the fore in these chapters. Jansen suggested as characteristics of wisdom that figure here Enoch's words of comfort and consolation to the righteous, the theodicy of chap. 103, the virtual absence of *torah*, and the formula "my sons" as a designation for the audience.[90] R. Coughenour has, in contrast to Jansen's view, argued that the many woe-oracles in the Epistle (all but two of the 32 are in chaps. 94-100), as their context shows, ". . . constitute one of the wisdom elements in the Book of Enoch."[91] Comparison of his statement with Jansen's classification of the woe-oracles indicates that one cannot always neatly disentangle prophetic and sapiential influences, but it is safe to say that both are present. The kinds of wisdom influences that are evident are, however, not mantic. Instead, one encounters the more familiar and traditional sorts of wisdom that dominate books such as Proverbs, Ben Sira, and, to some extent, Job. All of it is, nevertheless, transposed into an eschatological key.

Other features of the Epistle can also be included among its debts to traditional Israelite wisdom or as modified reflections of it. The writer contrasts two ways[92]—that of the righteous wise and that of the foolish sinners (see 91:19; 94:1-4)—and develops the theme that Enoch's words are truly wise as are those who heed them (cf. also 82:2-3). He himself is described as "the wisest of men" (92:1 [Aramaic; 4QEn⁀ 1 ii 23]).[93] In this respect 93:11-14, which in the Ethiopic version follow the account of the seventh week of the

[88] Jansen, *Die Henochgestalt*, 62-63; Hengel, *Judaism and Hellenism*, 1.206-07.

[89] *Die Henochgestalt*, 62-63. Regarding the transformation of the prophetic "day of the Lord" into the apocalyptic day of judgment, see Russell, *The Method and Message of Jewish Apocalyptic*, 92-96.

[90] *Die Henochgestalt*, 62-66.

[91] "The Woe-Oracles in Ethiopic Enoch," *JSJ* 9 (1978) 197; cf. also Nickelsburg, "The Apocalyptic Message of *1 Enoch* 92-105," 326-28.

[92] Coughenour, "The Woe-Oracles in Ethiopic Enoch," 195-96.

[93] Milik, *The Books of Enoch*, 260. On the differences between the Aramaic and Ethiopic versions here, see the comments below.

ApW—attracted there perhaps by the reference to "sevenfold instruction concerning his whole creation" in 93:10[94]—provide an interesting twist on a traditional sapiential motif. Verses 11-14 consist of a series of questions which inquire about the possibility of humankind's gaining complete knowledge of the creation.[95] Such questions, as they function in, say, Job 38, presuppose a negative reply, but here the presumed response is positive because Enoch had learned all this through his travels and heavenly contacts. Such knowledge is an eschatological gift now made available to the last generations through the chosen sage Enoch.[96] On the day of judgment it is the wise who will perceive and grasp the truth contained in his Letter (100:6); those who accept his words will be blessed (99:10; cf. 91:10).[97] Whereas Enoch's writings embody the truth (104:11-13; 105:1), the sinners, whose precedessors (93:8) as well as they themselves (98:3, 9; 99:7-8) err through their folly, deny his words of wisdom (94:5; 98:9, 14-15), alter the words of truth (104:9), and concoct their own writings (104:10). In other words, the claims made for the Enochic literature (including at least the Epistle and Enoch's cosmological teachings) have become extraordinarily bold: his teachings are special disclosures for the end of the ages and by their response to them people are divided into two eschatological camps.[98] The use of wisdom motifs is thus frequent and wide-ranging in the Epistle. Enoch is a sage who teaches to the last generations the way of righteousness in critical times and exhorts his community to patient hope in the final hours of the world.

One last note should be appended to the present section. The Ethiopic version of 92:1 reads: "Written by Enoch the scribe—this complete wisdom teaching, praised by all men and a judge of the whole earth. . . ." Here it is Enoch's sapiential instruction (*temherta*[99] *ṭebab*) which is universally acclaim-

---

[94] 4QEn^g 1 iv 13 mentions "wisdom and knowledge" (*ḥkmh wmd^c*) where the Ethiopic reads "teaching concerning his whole creation" (Milik, *The Books of Enoch*, 265). The Ethiopic seems a result of interpretation within the tradition, since the questions in 93:11-14 (which follow the entire ApW in Aramaic; more text of a similar nature may also have been present [see Milik, ibid., 270]) do refer to the creation.

[95] Cf. Stone, "Lists of Revealed Things," 423-26. As Stone observes, this is one more instance in apocalyptic literature of the re-use of wisdom material (see also 438).

[96] Ibid., 425.

[97] The Ethiopic text of 91:10 reads in part: ". . . the righteous will rise from sleep, and wisdom will rise and will be given to them." Milik (*The Books of Enoch*, 260-61) reconstructs the Aramaic to agree with the Ethiopic, but Black ("The Apocalypse of Weeks," 466-67) argues for a restoration on the basis of 92:3 which would remove the reference to wisdom.

[98] For an analysis of the claims of revelation in the Epistle, see Nickelsburg, "The Apocalyptic Message of *1 Enoch* 92-105," 315-26.

[99] Milik (*The Books of Enoch*, 261) takes *te^merta* (= sign, etc.) as the Ethiopic reading and criticizes the translators who give *doctrine* or *teaching* as the meaning. He seems unaware that these translators have preferred the reading *temherta* (= teaching) which is better attested.

ed and acts as judge of the entire earth (*makʷannena kʷellu medr*). Part of the verse is preserved in 4QEnᵍ 1 ii 22–24. The Aramaic text shows that the Ethiopic reading is the result of alterations at some point in the textual transmission of the book. Of special interest are the words of 1. 23: *ḥ]kym ᵓnwšᵓ wbḥ.*[.¹⁰⁰ The word *ḥkym* is a masculine adjective that grammatically could not modify the feminine noun *ḥokmāᵓ* which the Ethiopic suggests should be restored in this context. It could, though, refer to a word for *teaching* (e.g., *maddaᶜ*). But with *ᵓnwšᵓ* (humankind) following, it is unlikely that *ḥkym* modifies either a word for wisdom or teaching. It seems rather to refer to Enoch. If so, it would imply that what the Ethiopic text says about his teaching originally was said about the patriarch himself. That is, he would be named the wisest of men and perhaps (no Aramaic is preserved for this part of the verse) a/the judge of the whole earth. Milik interprets the verse in this way and correctly observes that in *Jub.* 4:23 one also finds Enoch in a judicial role (after his final removal).¹⁰¹

### 2. *1 Enoch* 106–07

Commentators have generally regarded chaps. 106–07 as an addition to the Epistle (or to the entire book of *1 Enoch*) and have usually assigned them, with several other passages, to a hypothetical Book or Apocalypse of Noah.¹⁰² There are at least two issues involved in such claims: whether 106–07 are independent of the remainder of the Epistle, and, if so, whether they have been drawn from a Book of Noah from which other parts of *1 Enoch* derive. Regarding the first, one can readily grant that the two chapters differ in several respects from the other sections of the Epistle and that they are placed in a different setting in Enoch's career. Here he is with the angels and can be reached only at the ends of the earth (106:7–8), where Methuselah finds him and asks him about the paternity of the infant Noah. It may be that these chapters did not originally belong to the Epistle, but the apocalyptic speech of Enoch in 106:13–107:1 resembles the "Methuselah" Apocalypse of chap. 91 structurally (evil–flood–greater evil–judgment); and in 106:19 reference is made to the heavenly tablets—a term used elsewhere in the Epistle. At least as it is arranged in the Aramaic, the Epistle begins and ends with

---

¹⁰⁰ Ibid., 260.

¹⁰¹ Ibid., 263.

¹⁰² Charles, *The Book of Enoch*, 264, xlvi–xlvii (dated no later than B.C. 161 [lii]); Beer, "Das Buch Henoch," 229; Martin, *Le Livre d'Hénoch*, lxxxviii, xcviii. See also, Russell, *The Method and Message of Jewish Apocalyptic*, 51; Bousset-Gressmann, *Die Religion des Judentums*, 13; Nickelsburg, *Jewish Literature*, 151. Parts of chaps. 106–07 are preserved in 4QEnᶜ 5 i, ii, a fact which indicates that if they have been added to the Epistle, they are a very ancient supplement (for the fragments, see Milik, *The Books of Enoch*, 206–10). It is interesting that chap. 106 is separated from 105 by one and one-half spaces at 4QEnᶜ 5 i 24–25.

similar apocalypses which Enoch narrates to Methuselah. In other words, they constitute a literary *inclusio* for the booklet.

The Genesis Apocryphon proves, however, that the story of Noah's birth was used in other literary contexts. Cols. 2–5, of which only col. 2 is preserved to any appreciable extent, tell largely the same story but present it as a first-person narrative of Lamech and his wife Bathenosh. The presence of essentially the same tale in two places shows that it did circulate independently, but where it belonged originally cannot be discerned at present. Whether the story ever formed part of a larger, unified cycle of Noah material also cannot be answered conclusively, but Dimant has fashioned a compelling argument that the various segments of *1 Enoch* which scholars have often attributed to a single Book of Noah are not unified and hardly belonged to the same composition.[103]

The picture of Enoch in chaps. 106–07 offers an intriguing and convincing example of the ongoing influence of Mesopotamian mythology on Enochic circles and writings. As a number of scholars have noted, the description of Enoch and his place of residence in 106–07 is closely modeled on the story of the ultimate fate of the Mesopotamian flood hero who, after surviving the deluge, was removed to the ends of the earth, "in the distance, at the mouth of the rivers" (Gilgamesh XI.195–96).[104] There, at the ends of the earth, he lived far from human habitation and enjoyed the comfortable life of the gods. Yet, he remained accessible to visitors, though they had to undergo exhausting struggles, exertions, and travels, as Gilgamesh learned. Moreover from Utnapishtim Gilgamesh sought information not available to humans— how he had attained immortality and how Gilgamesh, too, could gain it. Methuselah, like Gilgamesh, went to the ends of the earth to learn from Enoch the answer to his immediate question (who was Noah's father) but he also heard from him what would be the general course of the future. Thus one sees here in transparent form the efforts of a Jewish writer (or his tradition) to transfer some traits of the flood hero to Enoch rather than to Noah—a process that is significant for assessing Enoch's position in the tradition.[105]

---

[103] "The 'Fallen Angels,'" 122–28.

[104] Translation of A. Heidel, *The Gilgamesh Epic and Old Testament Parallels* (2nd ed.; Chicago: University of Chicago, 1949).

[105] Cf. Bousset-Gressmann, *Die Religion des Judentums*, 491; and especially Grelot, "La légende," 9–24 (though, as explained in chap. I, one can improve on his explanation for transferring this motif from the flood hero to Enoch). Regarding the remarkable description of the newborn Noah in 106:2–3, 5–6, 10–11, which Fitzmyer ("The Aramaic 'Elect of God' Text from Qumran Cave IV," *CBQ* 27 [1965] 348–72) and, following him, Milik (*The Books of Enoch*, 55–56) relate to other texts from Quman, Hultgård ("Das Judentum in der hellenistisch-römischen Zeit," 551) writes: "Die Geburtslegende Noahs ist in gewissen Einzelheiten direkt parallel mit der Erzählung von der Geburt Zarathustras."

Why would a writer describe Enoch in terms and images drawn from the mythology of the Mesopotamian flood hero when Judaism could boast its own pious survivor of the deluge? Indeed, why would he do so in a story about Noah's birth? After all, Noah, like Enoch, walked with the *ʾĕlōhîm* (Gen 6:9), and he was the first man to be called righteous (6:9; 7:1). Perhaps a definitive solution to the problem is now beyond reach, but a suggestion can be offered. The scholars who compiled the different books of Enoch were obviously conversant with the mythologies of their neighbors, and they incorporated aspects of them into their system(s) with appropriate changes. The flood hero, however, posed a special difficulty because in the Mesopotamian traditions he was not only granted immortality but was also removed to the company of the gods.[106] The priestly writer of Gen 9:1–17 transformed the hero's immortality into an eternal agreement between God and Noah, but the authors of *1 Enoch* 106–07 and the Genesis Apocryphon approached the issue differently. They dealt with the question of Noah's nature (quasi-divine like Utnapishtim or human) through a debate about his paternity. When it was suspected that the miraculous child had been fathered by one of the angels, Enoch delivered an authoritative denial of the supernatural origin of the flood hero.[107] Yet, the concept of a man who lives among divine beings, who has access to their choicest secrets, but who nevertheless remains somewhat accessible was too precious to sacrifice to the dictates of monotheism. As a result, these valuable traits were attached to Enoch who also associated with celestial beings according to the tradition but about whose paternity there could be no question. The writer managed to have it both ways: he retained the idea of an accessible human being in divine company but avoided any danger that his readers would infer a divine status for the Jewish survivor of the flood.

It may appear that chaps. 106–07 relate a tale which belongs after Enoch's ultimate assumption by God. He is removed from human company, is with the angels (106:7), and dwells at the ends of the earth (106:8). In addition, if the episode takes place after his second removal, it would parallel Utnapishtim's situation more precisely. It also seems that one can defend this conclusion from chronological data, since the story deals with the biblically dated birth of Noah. In the MT Enoch was 65 years of age at Methuselah's

---

[106] Gilgamesh XI.189–96. Cf. the Sumerian Deluge VI.255–60; Berossus, *Babyloniaca*. This fate is not attributed to Deucalion in the Greek myth of the flood in Apollodorus' *Library* I. vii. 2 nor in the curious hybrid form of the tale in Lucian's *de dea Syria* 12–13.

[107] See Wacholder, "Pseudo-Eupolemus' Two Greek Fragments on the Life of Abraham," 90–91. In the Animal Apocalypse Noah with Moses is the only biblical character who becomes a man—a symbol that represents angels (89:1, 9).

birth (Gen 5:21), Methuselah was 187 when Lamech was born (5:25), and Lamech had reached 182 years when Noah arrived (5:28). The sum of these figures is 434 years, but Enoch lived only 365 (5:23). Therefore, Noah was born some 69 years after Enoch's final removal. One could also argue that the place of the story in the last phase of Enoch's career led someone to add it to the end of the book of *1 Enoch*.

This line of reasoning may be correct, but there are problems connected with it. Since Enoch sojourned with the angels twice—both during and after his 365 years (Gen 5:22, 24)—the story in chaps. 106–07 could theoretically belong to either phase in his biography. If one calculates the chronological position of the story according to the figures found in the Samaritan Pentateuch and *Jubilees*, then one learns that Noah was born during Enoch's 365 years. *Jub.* 4:16 dates Enoch's birth to the year of the world 522, Methuselah's is placed in 587 (4:20), Lamech's in 652 (4:27), and Noah's in some year within the sabbatical period 701–707 (4:28). Consequently, in this system Enoch was approximately 180 years of age when Noah was born—an age when he was enjoying his first stay with the angels (it lasted from his 65th to his 365th year). As no other episode in the AB, BW, or the Epistle (and BD) happens after his 365th year, it can be argued that this story, too, is to be located within his 365 years.[108] Thus, both options seem possible at present.

In concluding this chapter, a few points should be underscored. The Enoch of the AB and the BW showed interest in cosmological matters primarily and eschatological issues secondarily (not at all in the original AB). The authors of the Epistle of Enoch and the BD chose this figure, who was surrounded by mantic associations, as the seer of apocalyptic visions that claim to predict the essential patterns of sacred history and of the *eschaton*. The critical events involving the hellenizing of Judaism during the reign of Antiochus IV appear to form the immediate background for this new turn in Enochic traditions. In a literary or formal sense the apocalypses evidence similarities with features of some kinds of contemporary Hellenistic literature in the Near East (e.g., *vaticinia ex eventu*), but more profoundly they betray a heavy dependence on biblical and extra–biblical Jewish traditions which their authors reinterpreted to fit the great needs of their age.

With his unparalleled knowledge of the cosmos, history, and the *eschaton*, Enoch was the ideal preacher of hope, comfort, and warning to the last generations. While his words echo the language of ancient prophecy, Enoch appears preeminently as the supreme Jewish sage whose wisdom knows no bounds and whose message rests on unfailing divine revelation. In harmony with the literary experience of other ancient heroes, his biography experien-

---

[108] So Beer, "Das Buch Henoch," 234; Grelot, "La géographie mythique d'Hénoch," 44–45.

ces some development. One learns that he did not have to wait until his first stay with the angels to receive disclosures from above; already before his marriage to Edna he had been selected by God as the one who was to be told what would happen to the farthest generations and beyond. While the Enochic traditions show heavy indebtedness to native literature and beliefs, chaps. 106–07 provide evidence that Mesopotamian mythology continued to exercise a profound influence on writers of these booklets.

VII

## AN EPILOGUE AND A SUMMARY

### A. *Enoch in the Book of* Jubilees

Jewish speculation about Enoch did not cease with the close of the Antiochan crisis. The sources indicate that it continued to grow while at the same time older traditions were reproduced, revised, and pressed into service in new contexts. The present study is not concerned with later compositions such as the Book of Giants,[1] the Similitudes (*1 Enoch* 37–71), or *2* and *3 Enoch*, but it will be fitting to conclude the investigation with a study of the short paragraph which *Jubilees* devotes to the patriarch (4:16–25) and which was cited in full in chap. I. It furnishes both a partial summary of much that was told about Enoch before the author's time and confirmation that there were more legends about him than those now recorded in the AB, the BW, the BD, or the Epistle. In a limited sense the *Jubilees* material forms a précis of the sections of *1 Enoch* known to the writer because he acknowledges his familiarity with Enochic *books* (4:17, 18, 19, 21; also 21:10) which, from the terse descriptions that he gives of them, certainly appear to be parts of *1 Enoch*. But *Jub.* 4:16–25 are unmistakably more than just a summary of most of *1 Enoch*. They constitute a new, partly independent portrait of the sage and incorporate themes which cannot be documented either in Gen 5:21–24 or in the four older booklets of *1 Enoch*. Whether the new material in *Jubilees* was created by the author or was inherited from now lost sources is not certain. The elements in 4:16–25 that are innovations *vis-à-vis 1 Enoch* will be the focus of the following paragraphs.

### 1. The Character of *Jub.* 4:16–25

*Jubilees* 4 reproduces the genealogy of Genesis 5 and edits and supplements it with notices that are typical of *Jubilees* (e.g., expressing dates in its cumbersome way, adding names of wives and relatives). In the section about Enoch one finds, as indicated in chap. I, a large-scale expansion of the biblical framework. The writer packs additional biographical information

---

[1] For information about this newly identified Enochic work, see Milik, *The Books of Enoch*, 298–339. It has been left out of consideration because so little of the text is available and therefore not much is known about it.

179

between the several formulaic lines drawn from Gen 5:21-24, and it is these addenda which betray his wide knowledge of Enochic literature and lore. The genealogical skeleton dictates that the sage's career and achievements be treated in chronological order. A happy result is that one is spared questions about the precise location of the various episodes in his eventful life.

2. The Enochic Booklets Mentioned

A question that has exercised scholars is the identity of the Enochic books to which the writer refers in 4:17, 18, 19, and 21. He considered the compositions authoritative for the subjects with which they dealt—a view shared at a later time by the sectaries at Qumran. The *Jubilees* pericope is—at least in part—the product of reflection on earlier and highly regarded books of Enoch.

There appears to be general agreement that the writer, in addition to the other Enochic material with which he was familiar, refers to the AB, the BW, and the BD. Charles, Milik, and Grelot have arrived at this conclusion, though they differ somewhat regarding which sections of these booklets he knew.[2] There is sufficient warrant for believing that he alludes to these three, but it is also quite possible, as indicated in chap. VI above, that he refers to the Epistle as well. One must be cautious about including the Epistle in the roster of Enochic works mentioned by the writer of *Jubilees*, but he does give some indication that he was acquainted with its framework.[3] His knowledge of the BD entails that *Jubilees* was not composed before ca. B.C. 165-160.

3. New Features of the Enochic Legend

The most interesting sections of *Jub.* 4:16-25 are the ones in which one finds hitherto unattested data about the patriarch. There are two principal supplements that should be examined: Enoch as culture hero and Enoch in the Garden of Eden.

a. Enoch as Culture Hero: Verses 17-18 highlight the fact that Enoch was the first man to learn or do several things:

[17] And he was the first [*prōtos*][4] among men that are born on earth who learnt

---

[2] Charles, *The Book of Jubilees*, xliv, lxviii-lxix (*1 Enoch* 6-16; 23-36; 72-90); Milik, *The Books of Enoch*, 11, 24-25, 45 (the AB, BW, and BD); and Grelot, "Hénoch et ses écritures," *RB* 82 (1975) 484-88 (agrees with Milik but excepts chaps. 1-5).

[3] For a fuller discussion and documentation, see VanderKam, "Enoch Traditions in Jubilees and Other Second-Century Sources," 231-41.

[4] A small Hebrew fragment of *Jubilees*—11QJub M 3.2—preserves the first two words of the verse: zh ry²š[wn (this one was the first). See Milik, "A propos de 11QJub," *Bib* 54 (1973) 78; VanderKam, *Textual and Historical Studies in the Book of Jubilees*, 29-30 (where the Ethiopic, Greek, and Syriac evidence is also cited). The Greek terms in brackets are from a citation of *Jubilees* by George Cedrenus; for the text, see Denis, *Fragmenta Pseudepigraphorum Graeca* (PVTG 3; Leiden: Brill, 1970) 83; cf. also Charles, *The Book of Jubilees*, 37.

writing [*grammata*] and knowledge and wisdom and who wrote down the signs of heaven according to the order of their months in a book, that men might know the seasons of the years according to the order of their separate months. [18] And he was the first to write a testimony, and he testified to the sons of men among the generations of the earth, and recounted the weeks of the jubilees, and made known to them the days of the years, and set in order the months and recounted the Sabbaths of the years as we made (them) known to him.[5]

In these verses the Enochic "firsts" are: learning writing, knowledge, and wisdom; recording and systematizing astronomical/calendrical data; and writing a testimony. All of these activities can be documented in more ancient Enochic literature, but *Jubilees* itself scores a "first" by claiming that Enoch was the pioneer in each area.

Enoch's "firsts" include contributions that constitute the basis of civilized life, and in this respect they resemble other ancient traditions about mythological culture-bringers or culture heroes. Such tales were popular in the Hellenistic world; examples can be cited for many places, including Mesopotamia, Phoenicia, Egypt, and Greece. Though the various culture-hero stories involve individual peculiarities, they share several ingredients which also figure in the *Jubilees* list for Enoch.

Perhaps the earliest examples are the *apkallūs* who have come into consideration at a number of points in this study. Berossus reported that Oannes, the first *apkallū*, was credited with introducing to savage humankind all that was needed for human culture.

It gave to men the knowledge of letters [*grammatōn*] and sciences [*mathēmatōn*] and crafts of all types. It also taught them how to found cities, establish temples, introduce laws and measure land. It also revealed to them seeds and the gathering of fruits, and in general it gave men everything which is connected with the civilized life.

Elsewhere astronomical compositions are also attributed to this primeval sage.[6]

A second and intriguing example comes from Phoenicia—a land that may have played a more significant part in the transmission and modification of Mesopotamian lore to Israel than can now be determined because of the paucity of evidence that has survived. The culture hero in question is the Taautos of Philo of Byblos' *Phoenician History*.[7] Philo, who wrote in the

---

[5] Translation of Charles, ibid. It is noteworthy that as in the BD *Jubilees* places Enoch's learning to write before his marriage which is not mentioned until 4:20.

[6] See chap. II, n. 84.

[7] Virtually all extant fragments of the *Phoenician History* come from Eusebius' *Preparation for the Gospel*. The quotations (English and Greek) from Philo's book are from the very

first century A.D., named as his source the writings of a certain Sanchunia-thon who in turn was supposed to have drawn his material from the compo-sitions of Taautos. How much truth underlies such claims is disputed,[8] but for the present concerns the important feature is Philo's description of Taau-tos. He explains why it was that Sanchuniathon relied on the writings of Taautos in these words:

> He did this since he realized that Taautos was the first [*prōtos*] person under the sun who thought of the invention of writing [*grammatōn*] and who began to compose records, thereby laying the foundation, as it were, of learning. The Egyptians call him Thouth and the Alexandrians Thoth and the Greeks trans-lated his name as Hermes.[9]

His discovery of writing is noted elsewhere in the *Phoenician History* (1.10, 14) as is the claim that he composed sacred books (1.10, 47), including a cosmogony (1.10, 5). Philo adds in another passage that

> Taautos . . . was outstanding in wisdom among the Phoenicians. He was the first [*prōtos*] in religious matters to abandon the ignorance of common folk and to introduce scientific discipline. Following his lead, many generations later a god Sourmoubelos and Thouro who took the name Chousarthis, brought to light the hidden [*kekrymmenēn*] and allegorically obscured theology of Taautos (1.10, 43).

Taautos, therefore, introduced writing, wrote sacred compositions, excelled in wisdom, brought about religious reform, and wrote obscure works which subsequently required expert decoding. Similarities with Enoch and the *ap-kallū* are obvious, and, like them, Taautos belonged to primeval times.

As Philo wrote, the Egyptians called Taautos Thouth and the Alexan-drians Thoth. If one examines the traits of this Egyptian god, it becomes apparent that he, too, functioned as a culture-bringer. He was considered the gods' scribe and inventor of the arts and sciences.[10] J. Ebach writes regarding the identification of Taautos-Thoth in the *Phoenician History*:

> Diese Charakterisierung stimmt mit den Funktionen des Thot in Ägypten über-ein. Er ist der Gott der Weisheit, er gibt den Dingen Namen, ist Erfinder und

---

convenient new edition by H. W. Attridge and R. A. Oden, *Philo of Byblos* The Phoenician History (CBQMS 9; Washington: Catholic Biblical Association, 1981). All of the fragments of the work that deal with Taautos have been assembled and discussed by J. Ebach, *Weltent-stehung und Kulturentwicklung bei Philo von Byblos* (BWANT 108; Stuttgart: Kohlhammer, 1979) 60–71, 223–34.

[8] See the discussion in Attridge and Oden, *Philo of Byblos*, 3–9.

[9] Ibid., 29 (= 1.9, 24).

[10] E. A. Wallis Budge, *The Egyptian Book of the Dead* (reprinted; New York: Dover, 1967) cxviii.

Schützer der Schrift, Schreiber der Götter und Berater des Königs. Schon in Ägypten gilt er als Verfasser von Büchern. Dieser Zug wird in hellenistischer Zeit ausgebaut. Von Hermes—wo wird Thot in der interpretatio Graeca genannt—berichtet Seleukos, er habe 20000, Manetho gar, er habe 36525 Bücher verfasst. Als Hermes trismegistos wird er in späthellenistischer Zeit zum mystischen Allgott, dem Künder der heiligen Offenbarung schlechthin.[11]

There is also a tradition that Thoth was a god who had reigned for an astonishingly long time in primeval days.[12]

Philo extended the Taautos–Thoth equation by adding that the Greeks rendered his name as Hermes. At least as he was depicted in Hellenistic times Hermes does bear resemblance to the culture heroes mentioned above and thus to Enoch. Diodorus Siculus' picture of him makes the point well. In his *Library of History*, which dates to approximately the middle of the first century B.C., he begins his survey with Egypt (1.9, 6) and deals with the Egyptian gods and the myths attached to them.[13] In the section that deals with Osiris he comes to that god's favorite Hermes ". . . who was endowed with unusual ingenuity for devising things capable of improving the social life of man" (1.15, 9). The next paragraphs he devotes to Hermes:

> It was by Hermes, for instance, according to them, that the common language of mankind was first further articulated, and that many objects which were still nameless received an appellation, that the alphabet [*grammatōn*] was invented, and that ordinances regarding the honours and offerings due to the gods were duly established; he was the first also to observe the orderly arrangement of the stars and the harmony of the musical sounds and their nature, . . . He also made a lyre and gave it three strings, imitating the seasons of the year; . . . The Greeks also were taught by him how to expound (*hermeneia*) their thoughts, and it was for this reason that he was given the name Hermes. In a word, Osiris, taking him for his priestly scribe, communicated with him on every matter and used his counsel above that of all others (1. 16, 1-2).

Parallels with *Jubilees'* presentation of Enoch are again strongly in evidence: invention of letters, orderly arrangement of the stars, a priestly scribe of a god who consults with him (for offerings due the gods compare *Jub.* 21.10).

Finally, mention should be made of Prometheus, the classical bringer of culture, although his achievements bear a negative stamp—recalling the fallen

---

[11] *Weltentstehung*, 67–68. Note that the number of books given by Manetho is related to the length of the solar year. See also Hengel, *Judaism and Hellenism*, 1.215, for the remarkable parallels between Enoch and the Hermes of the later Kore Kosmu.

[12] *Weltentstehung*, 69.

[13] The quotations below from the *Library of History* are from C. H. Oldfather, *Diodorus of Sicily I* (LCL; Cambridge: Harvard University/London: Heinemann, 1933). For Diodorus' dates, see vii–xv.

angels of *1 Enoch* 6–11 (cf. 69:8–11) and perhaps the Cainite genealogy of
Gen 4:17–24. Though his most notorious gift to humankind was fire, classical tradition holds that he supplied much more. According to Aeschylus'
*Prometheus Bound*,[14] he was surpassingly wise (1. 330; cf. the play on his
name in 11. 85–87; see also 887) and his present of fire allowed mortals to
learn many arts (1. 256; cf. 108–10). Like Oannes and Taautos, he confronted a barbarous human population and gave them the ingredients necessary for civilized living (442–506): he taught them to determine the rising
and setting of stars, numbers, combining letters (*grammatōn te syntheseis*
[460]), harnassing animals, medicines, etc. Or, as 11. 505–06 put it: "Hear
the sum of the whole matter in the compass of one brief word—every art
possessed by man comes from Prometheus." He also had knowledge of
the future: "All that will be I know full well and in advance, nor shall
any affliction come upon me unforeseen" (101–03). His foreknowledge of
one who would dethrone Zeus provides much of the drama in the larger
story of Prometheus. Not surprisingly, then, he was also considered the
one who introduced divinatory arts, a number of which are detailed in the
play (484–99).

The purpose for adducing these Hellenistic parallels to *Jubilees'* portrait
of Enoch is surely not to claim that the writer copied or closely based his
work on any one of them. It is rather to show that in this instance, as in
many passages in *1 Enoch*, a Jewish writer followed contemporary international trends. He fashioned his Enoch as a Jewish counterpart to the legendary or mythical culture heroes of other peoples. His native traditions clearly
furnished the contents of his portrait of Enoch, but the language with which
he nuanced the picture belongs to the literature of culture-bringers. It was
not surprising perhaps to find a pre-Maccabean writer such as Pseudo-Eupolemus equating Enoch with the Greek Atlas, but it is unexpected to meet
this sort of Hellenistic literary device in Jubilees—a work that is not exactly
characterized by a broad openness to the gentile world.

b. Enoch in Eden: Verses 23–25 enlarge the Enochic legend with an
account of his life after the angels removed him permanently from his family.
Moses, the recipient of the information now recorded in *Jubilees*, was able to
learn about this phase of Enoch's career because one of the angels who
conducted him to the Garden of Eden also revealed *Jubilees*.

> 23 And he was taken from amongst the children of men, and we conducted him
> into the Garden of Eden in majesty and honour, and behold there he writes
> down the condemnation and judgment of the world, and all the wickedness of
> the children of men.

---

[14] Citations from *Prometheus Bound* are taken from H. W. Smyth, *Aeschylus I* (LCL;
Cambridge: Harvard University/London: Heinemann, 1922).

<sup>24</sup> And on account of [him the waters of the flood did not come] upon all the land of Eden; for there he was set as a sign and that he should testify against all the children of men, that he should recount all the deeds of the generations until the day of condemnation. <sup>25</sup> And he burnt the incense of the sanctuary, (even) sweet spices acceptable before the Lord on the Mount.<sup>15</sup>

The writer does not explain whether he thought that Enoch had lived in Eden during his first removal; he mentions the name of the place only in connection with his second assumption. His placing Enoch in Eden may have something of an exegetical basis, since, according to Gen 5:24, *God* took him and in Ezek 28:13 Eden is identified as the garden of God. *Jub.* 8:19 considers the garden God's residence. Hence the writer inferred that God had brought the righteous patriarch to his home. The text makes it clear that Eden is conceived as a place on earth: 8:19 locates it in the eastern portion of Shem's patrimony; 4:26 lists it as one of four holy places on earth; and 4:24 indicates that, though the flood could have reached Eden (here called the land of Eden within which lies the garden; cf. Gen 2:8), it did not for the sake of Enoch.<sup>16</sup> It was believed to be situated at some remove from the normal centers of human habitation but a part of the earth nevertheless.

In Eden Enoch continued to perform several kinds of duties with which he had been associated during his 365 years. He remains a scribe although now as the recorder of all human misdeeds. He is slated to continue executing this task until the day of judgment (4:24; cf. 10:17). It seems likely that the older traditions that the patriarch had written the divine indictment of the Watchers (*1 Enoch* 12–16), that he had read from the heavenly tablets on which all human actions—past, present, and future—were inscribed, and possibly that he had invented writing combined to create the image of him as God's recorder of all that people do. In this instance he performs another duty that in other ancient cultures was assigned to one of the gods (e.g., Nabu, Thoth). To be sure, the writer carefully nuances the motif of a divine scribe and also relates it to Jewish eschatological expectations, but the fact remains that he uses the notion. Enoch's record of human wickedness will, it seems, serve as the basis for God's verdicts at the final judgment (cf. the reference in *1 Enoch* 92:1 [Aramaic] to Enoch as judge of the world).<sup>17</sup>

Besides writing, Enoch is portrayed as offering sacrifices on a mountain.

<sup>15</sup> Translation of Charles, *The Book of Jubilees*. See chap. I, n. 27 for an explanation of the words in brackets.

<sup>16</sup> See Bowker, *The Targums and Rabbinic Literature*, 170 for references in rabbinic writings to the claim that the dove in the flood story got its olive branch from the Garden of Eden.

<sup>17</sup> For later developments of the motif and for references, see Milik, *The Books of Enoch*, 103–07, 127–31.

Mention of the mountain then triggers a listing of the four holy places that belong to the Lord: the Garden of Eden (in the Ethiopic version), the mountain of the east, Mt. Sinai, and Mt. Zion (4:26). The motif of Enoch as priest is a curious one, and, other than the prayer that he offered in the BD, this sort of mediatorial function is not attested for him prior to *Jubilees*. Making Enoch a priest does, however, fit a larger pattern in *Jubilees* which posits that all ancient worthies in the Sethite line were priests who transmitted sacerdotal legislation from father to son. Enoch as a link in this chain is mentioned in 7:38–39 and 21:10. In both passages the author credits him with giving halakhic instructions about priestly concerns.[18]

The patriarch offers sacrifices on a mountain, perhaps in a sanctuary.[19] There are several text-critical problems in vv 25 and 26, and, as some of them bear directly on present issues, they should be considered. At the end of v 25 the best Ethiopic reading is *ba–dabra qatr*.[20] Both Dillmann and E. Littmann translated *qatr* as *south*, but the word means *noon*.[21] Charles[22] emended *qatr* to *qetārē* ("sweet spices") and rearranged the word–order to yield "sweet spices (acceptable before the Lord) on the Mount." However, he lacked MS support both for his emendation and for the change in word–order. His only warrant for omitting a word after *dabr(a)* (mountain) was MS A, but the reading of A can better be explained as omission by homoioteleuton.[23]

A Syriac citation of the verse, which was unavailable to Dillmann, Littmann, and Charles, reads *ṭwr² dṭymn²* (mountain of the south, or of Teiman) at the end of v 25, thus seemingly confirming the view of Dillmann and Littmann.[24] The Ethiopic MS tradition is solid that *qatr* follows *dabra*, while the Syriac citation offers *ṭymn²* not only here but also in v 26 where the Ethiopic reads (mountain of) the east (see Gen 10:30). The Syriac in both instances can be regarded as interpretations by the translator rather than

---

[18] Cf. Milik, ibid., 114–15; and VanderKam, "The Righteousness of Noah," 21.

[19] A Syriac citation of *Jub.* 4:25–26 reads the word *first* (*qdmy²*) instead of a term for sanctuary, thus making Enoch's sacrificing another of his "firsts." For the text see E. Tisserant, "Fragments syriaques du Livre des Jubilés," *RB* 30 (1921) 73–75. He proposed that Ethiopic *maqdas* (sanctuary) be corrected to read *qadāmi* (first).

[20] For the Ethiopic readings, see Charles, *Maṣḥafa Kufālē*. The MSS that have become available since Charles' edition but which remain unpublished verify this reading.

[21] Dillmann, "Das Buch der Jubiläen oder die kleine Genesis," *Jahrbücher der Biblischen wissenschaft* 2 (1850) 241; E. Littmann, "Das Buch der Jubiläen" in *Die Apokryphen und Pseudepigraphen des Alten Testaments* (2 vols.; ed. E. Kautzsch; Tübingen: Freiburg/Leipzig: Mohr, 1900), 2.47.

[22] *The Book of Jubilees*, 39.

[23] So Tisserant, "Fragments syriaques," 75.

[24] Ibid., 73.

reflections of the original readings,[25] and the Ethiopic terms enjoy the text-critical advantage of greater variation. Consequently, the Ethiopic ought to be retained in both cases. It may be that *qatr* is not the Ethiopic term for *noon* but rather a transcription, now somewhat corrupted, of an original Hebrew form of *qtrt* (incense) which a translator misunderstood as the name of the mountain.[26] This suggestion would produce Charles' understanding of the text without resort to his emendation. "Mount of incense" is, therefore, probably the original meaning.

The Syriac citation may, nevertheless, preserve an original reading in v 26 where the Ethiopic would then be corrupt. The first of the four sacred locations is given as the Garden of Eden in Ethiopic, but in the Syriac it is called *ṭwr³ dprdys³* (the mountain of paradise).[27] In favor of the Syriac reading one can argue that the list of places otherwise includes only mountains—appropriate locations for descents of the heavenly God. Also, the Ethiopic reading could be explained as an assimilation to the much more familiar phrase *Garden of Eden*. Furthermore, if one read *mountain* rather than *garden*, it would result in a more logical connection with v 25 which concludes with a reference to a mountain in Eden. An implication of accepting the Syriac here would be that the old question whether the mountain of v 25 is to be identified with the mountain of the east in v 26 would be answered negatively.[28]

The presence of a mountain in Eden may seem puzzling since Genesis 2–3 mention no mountain either in the garden itself or in the larger region named Eden. The author of *Jubilees* did, however, build upon a biblical foundation. His geography of Eden combines the givens of Genesis 2–3 with Ezek 28:11–19—the prophet's lament on the Tyrian king. There one reads that the monarch was in Eden, the garden of God (28:13), and several terms in the paragraph are reminiscent of the Genesis 2–3 story (cherub, blamelessness, creation in vv 13–15, expulsion by a cherub in v 16). Ezek 28:14 adds that God had set the king on his holy mountain—a lofty residence from which he has now been removed (v 16). While Ezek 28:11–19 raises many exegetical problems, it is sufficient for a study of *Jub.* 4:25 to have established that Ezekiel's Tyrian lament locates God's sacred mountain in a garden of Eden. This mythological theme, which reflects motifs known

---

[25] Ibid., 76–77.

[26] Cf. ibid., 77.

[27] Ibid., 73.

[28] If the text-critical argument is acceptable, it would require that the same change be made at 8:19, where the Garden of Eden, Mt. Sinai, and Mt. Zion are listed as God's holy places.

from Ugaritic literature,[29] was used by the writer of *Jubilees* to enrich his account of Enoch's post–assumption labors.[30]

The picture of Enoch that emerges from *Jubilees* confirms a thesis that was advanced in the earlier chapters on the BW, the Epistle, and the BD, viz., that the seventh patriarch, who was already surrounded by mythical associations of Mesopotamian origin, was chosen by learned Jewish writers as the figure upon whom they concentrated valuable mythological motifs or traits that were current in the Hellenistic world. There is no mistaking the fact that he remains a Jewish hero, but the scholars behind the Enochic literature and the circles whose views they articulated had no scruples against incorporating (with some changes) pagan mythological material into their books in order to proclaim more forcefully and colorfully the theological convictions that motivated them.

### B. A Summary Statement

In the preceding chapters it has been maintained that the biblical and Jewish Enoch was originally fashioned in the likeness of the seventh Mesopotamian king Enmeduranki. Both occupied seventh position in antediluvian lists, enjoyed the society of celestial beings, received instructions from them and information about the future or how to learn what it held in store, and, in their respective ways, bore solar associations. It was seen that Enmeduranki was regarded as the founder of the *bārûtum* and that the Jewish Enoch displayed clear mantic traits.

The divinatory connection proved to be a rich source for interpreting several prominent features of the Enochic traditions. Mesopotamian divination, like other forms of manticism, included two fundamental elements: observation of natural objects, etc. and predictions based upon the particular character of what was observed. The belief that the gods communicated advance information about the future through forms and configurations of the most diverse sorts of phenomena led to a primitive kind of scientific

---

[29] See Clifford, *The Cosmic Mountain in Canaan and the Old Testament*, 168–73 (and 102–03). In light of the textual problem mentioned above in n. 19, it is interesting that Ezek 28:18 refers to sanctuaries, presumably in Eden, that the king had defiled.

[30] See also Grelot, "La géographie mythique d'Hénoch," 45–47. He finds problems with the statements in *Jubilees* about Eden. For the author there is just one Garden of Eden, but it must serve as the divine residence, the place where Adam was tested, and Enoch's location after his removal. He explains the difficulties that the texts raise by arguing that the writer somewhat confusingly attempted to reduce the two Edens of *1 Enoch* (the divine residence in the northwest; the primitive Eden, which is a replica of the divine one, in the east) to one (46–47). His two–Eden theory for *1 Enoch* remains questionable, though, despite any problems that may attach to *Jubilees*' geography.

listing and classification. It seemed reasonable to understand Enoch's early associations with "scientific" revelations (particularly astronomical ones) against this divinatory background. Parallels between early Babylonian astronomical texts and aspects of the AB bolstered the thesis. A noteworthy difference was, however, that in the original AB no predictions were based upon natural phenomena. The similarities between the AB and Babylonian astrological texts do raise the question whether it was composed in the eastern diaspora.

In the later Enochic booklets that were studied (the BW, the Epistle, and the BD) Enoch's divinatory characteristics never faded from view but they did take on some new forms. While Gen 5:21-24 and the AB, the most ancient extant sources regarding Enoch, showed strong connections with Mesopotamian lore, the late compositions built upon their oriental base and added material that reflects influence from biblical and Hellenistic models. That is, the well educated authors of these later works nuanced their powerful biblical, Jewish heritage with mythological notions and motifs that were popular in the Hellenistic world. They enlivened the remarkable person of Enoch with a variety of mythological traits and thus created for Judaism a primeval hero who outshone the legendary supermen or even divinities of any other people. Attributing these characteristics to a person to whom tradition ascribed a unique familiarity with the angels also furnished an absolutely authoritative and reliable source of information about the universe and about the past, present, and future. Thus Enoch, who is introduced to the reader in language drawn from the Numbers chapters about the diviner Balaam, sees a theophanic vision of the final judgment and condemns the Prometheus–like angels who transgressed the boundaries of flesh and spirit, heaven and earth, and rebelliously taught cultural secrets to humankind. Moreover, he travels with angels throughout a world that is patterned along lines which are roughly analogous to some Greek and Babylonian geographical conceptions.

Eschatology does indeed play a leading part in the BW, but it is only in the Enochic texts which were written during the hellenizing crisis in Judea (the Epistle and the BD) that it assumes overwhelming significance. Like any good diviner, Enoch learned of the future from dreams that were expressed in coded language, but his nocturnal visions surveyed the full expanse of history and culminated in predictions of the *eschaton*. Though they are dominated by biblical views and data, the major Enochic apocalypses (the ApW and the AA) also employ the popular Hellenistic devices of periodizing history and placing *vaticinia ex eventu* on the lips of ancient national worthies. It is of particular interest that the Akkadian prophecies, which borrow extensively from the language of divination, attest a parallel development: from mantic (and other) roots grow surveys of history which "predict" the past and look to restoration of national good after times of trouble. Enoch transmitted his revealed wisdom—whether about the universe or history and the future—to his son Methuselah, much as the ancient *bārûs* passed their secrets from father to son.

The Enochic traditions that have been examined in this book confirm the thesis of Müller that mantic wisdom lies behind the phenomenon of Jewish apocalypticism. The literture that was associated with that other sage Daniel makes the same point. It is necessary to add, however, that the scholars who produced the earliest Jewish apocalypses raided more sources than just divinatory ones. Divination supplied a thought-world and suggested certain media for revelations about the future, but a wide range of biblical, Jewish, and Hellenistic materials enriched the mantic base. It would be simplistic to claim that "apocalyptic" derives either from "wisdom" (of whatever kind) or "prophecy." The Jewish writers of apocalyptic works drew on both and much more. Apocalyptists were essentially interpreters[31]—whether of scriptural texts, dreams, history, or the phenomenal world. All revealed the work, character, and purpose of God to the inspired exegete who called upon every resource at his disposal in order to disengage the appropriate messages from their sources. And, in articulating those messages, he did not hesitate to borrow literary devices and themes that were familiar to a person of his erudition from gentile writings and traditions. Enoch, a figure surrounded by a rich and diverse traditional aura, was a natural choice as hero for the writings of these Jewish scholars. Like Dante centuries later and others, they wedded pagan and biblical themes into a creative union.

[31] Von Rad, *Old Testament Theology*, 2.308.

# BIBLIOGRAPHY

Albright, W. F. "The Babylonian Matter in the Predeuteronomic Primeval History (JE) in Gen 1–11," *JBL* 58 (1939) 91–103.

———. "Balaam: Critical View," *Encyclopaedia Judaica* 4.121-23.

Alt, A. "Die Weisheit Salomos," *TLZ* 76 (1951) cols. 139–44.

Attridge, H. W. and Oden, R. A. *Philo of Byblos*, The Phoenician History. CBQMS 9, Washington: Catholic Biblical Association, 1981.

Avigad, N. and Yadin Y. *A Genesis Apocryphon: A Scroll from the Wilderness of Judaea.* Jerusalem: Magnes/Heikhal ha-Sefer, 1956.

Barr, J. "Jewish Apocalyptic in Recent Scholarly Study," *BJRL* 58 (1975) 9–35.

Bartelmus, R. *Heroentum in Israel und seiner Umwelt.* ATANT 65. Zurich: Theologischer, 1979.

Beer, G. "Das Buch Henoch." In *Die Apokryphen und Pseudepigraphen des Alten Testaments.* Ed. E. Kautzsch; 2 vols. Tübingen: Freiburg/Leipzig: Mohr, 1900.

Betz, H. D. "Zum religionsgeschichtlichen Verständnisses der Apokalyptik," *ZTK* 63 (1966) 391–409.

Beyerlin, W., ed. *Near Eastern Religious Texts Relating to the Old Testament.* Old Testament Library; London: SCM, 1978.

Bezold, C. and Boll, F. *Sternglaube und Sterndeutung: Die Geschichte und das Wesen der Astrologie.* Aus Natur und Geisteswelt 638. Leipzig/Berlin: Teubner, 1918.

Bietenhard, H. *Die himmlische Welt in Urchristentum und Spätjudentum.* WUNT 2. Tübingen: Mohr, 1951.

Biggs, R. "More Babylonian 'Prophecies,'" *Iraq* 29 (1967) 117–32.

Black, M. *Apocalypsis Henochi Graece.* PVTG 3; Leiden: Brill, 1970.

———. "The Fragments of the Aramaic Enoch from Qumran." In *La littérature juive entre Tenach et Mischna. Quelques problèmes.* Ed. W. C. van Unnik. RechBib 9; Leiden: Brill, 1974, 15–28.

———. "The Throne-Theophany Prophetic Commission and the 'Son of Man': A Study in Tradition-History." In *Jews, Greeks and Christians: Religious Cultures in Late Antiquity.* W. D. Davies Festschrift. Ed. R. Hamerton-Kelly and R. Scroggs; SJLA 21; Leiden: Brill, 1976, 57–73.

————— . "The Apocalypse of Weeks in the Light of 4Q En^G," *VT* 28 (1978) 464–69.

Bonner, C. *The Last Chapters of Enoch in Greek.* SD 8. London: Christophers, 1937.

Borger, R. "Gott Marduk und Gott-König Šulgi als Propheten: Zwei prophetische Texte," *BO* 28 (1971) 3–24.

————— . "Die Beschwörungsserie BĪT MĒSERI und die Himmelfahrt Henochs," *JNES* 33 (1974) 183-96.

Bousset, D. W. and Gressmann, H. *Die Religion des Judentums im späthellenistischen Zeitalter.* 4th ed. HAT 21; Tübingen: Mohr, 1966.

Bowker, J. *The Targums and Rabbinic Literature.* Cambridge: University, 1969.

Brock, S. "A Fragment of Enoch in Syriac," *JTS* 19 (1968) 626–31.

Budge, E. A. Wallis. *The Egyptian Book of the Dead.* Reprinted; New York: Dover, 1967.

Burstein, S. *The Babyloniaca of Berossus.* Sources and Monographs, Sources from the Ancient Near East 1, 5. Malibu: Undena, 1978.

Cagni, L. *The Poem of Erra.* Sources and Monographs, Sources from the Ancient Near East 1, 3. Malibu: Undena, 1977.

Caquot, A. "Sur les quatre bêtes de Daniel VII," *Sem* 5 (1955) 5–13.

————— , and Leibovici, M., ed. *La divination.* 2 vols. Paris: Presses Universitaires de France, 1968.

————— . "La divination dans l'Ancien Israël." In *La divination,* 1.83–113.

Carmignac, J. "Qu'est-ce que l'apocalyptique? Son emploi à Qumrân," *RevQ* 10 (1979) 3–33.

Cassuto, U. *Commentary on the Book of Genesis,* Part 1: *From Adam to Noah.* Jerusalem: Magnes, 1961.

Charles, R. H. *The Book of Enoch.* Oxford: Clarendon, 1893.

————— . Maṣḥafa Kufālē *or the Ethiopic Version of the Hebrew Book of Jubilees.* Anecdota Oxoniensia; Oxford: Clarendon, 1895.

————— . *The Book of Jubilees or the Little Genesis.* London: Black, 1902.

————— . *The Ethiopic Version of the Book of Enoch.* Anecdota Oxoniensia; Oxford: Clarendon, 1906.

————— . *The Book of Enoch or 1 Enoch.* Oxford: Clarendon, 1912.

————— . *Eschatology: The Doctrine of a Future Life in Israel, Judaism, and Christianity: A Critical History.* Reprinted; New York: Schocken, 1963.

Clifford, R. J. *The Cosmic Mountain in Canaan and the Old Testament.* HSM 4. Cambridge: Harvard University, 1972.

Collins, J. J. *The Sibylline Oracles of Egyptian Judaism.* SBLDS 13. Missoula: Society of Biblical Literature, 1974.

————— . "Apocalyptic Eschatology as the Transcendence of Death," *CBQ* 36 (1974) 21–43.

_____ . "The Court-Tales in Daniel and the Development of Apocalyptic," *JBL* 94 (1975) 218–34.

_____ . "Jewish Apocalyptic against its Hellenistic Near Eastern Environment," *BASOR* 220/221 (1975–76) 27–36.

_____ . *The Apocalyptic Vision of the Book of Daniel.* HSM 16. Missoula: Scholars, 1977.

_____ . "Cosmos and Salvation: Jewish Wisdom and Apocalyptic in the Hellenistic Age," *HR* 17 (1977–78) 121–42.

_____ , ed. *Apocalypse: The Morphology of a Genre. Semeia* 14. Missoula: Scholars, 1979.

_____ . "The Apocalyptic Technique: Setting and Function in the Book of Watchers," *CBQ* 44 (1982) 91–111.

Coughenour, R. "The Woe-Oracles in Ethiopic Enoch," *JSJ* 9 (1978) 192–97.

Cross, F. M. "The Development of the Jewish Scripts." In *The Bible and the Ancient Near East.* Ed. G. E. Wright. Garden City: Doubleday, 1965 170–264.

_____ . *Canaanite Myth and Hebrew Epic.* Cambridge: Harvard, 1973.

Cumont, F. "La plus ancienne géographie astrologique," *Klio* 9 (1909) 263–73.

Daiches, S. "Balaam—a Babylonian *bārū*: The episode of Num 22, 2–24, 24 and some Babylonian Parallels." In *Hilprecht Anniversary Volume: Studies in Assyriology and Archaeology.* Leipzig: Hinrichs, 1909, 60–70.

Delcor, M. "Le mythe de la chute des anges et de l'origine des géants comme explication du mal dans le monde dans l'apocalyptique juive: Histoire des traditions," *RHR* 190 (1976) 3–53.

_____ , ed. *Qumran: Sa piété, sa théologie et son milieu.* BETL 46; Paris-Gembloux: Editions Duculot/Leuven: University, 1978.

Denis, A. M. *Fragmenta Pseudepigraphorum Graeca.* PVTG 3, Leiden: Brill, 1970.

_____ . *Introduction aux pseudépigraphes grecs d'Ancien Testament.* SVTP 1. Leiden: Brill, 1970.

Dexinger, F. *Henochs Zehnwochenapokalypse und offene Probleme der Apokalyptikforschung.* SPB 29. Leiden: Brill, 1977.

Dieterich, A. *Nekyia: Beiträge zur Erklärung der neuentdeckten Petrusapokalypse.* 2nd ed. Leipzig/Berlin: Teubner, 1913.

Dijk, J. van. *La sagesse suméro-accadienne.* Commentationes orientales 1. Leiden: Brill, 1953.

_____ . "Die Inschriftenfunde." In Lenzen, H. J. *XVIII. vorläufiger Bericht über die von dem Deutschen Archäologischen Institut und der Deutschen Orientgesellschaft aus Mitteln der Deutschen Forschungsgemeinschaft unternommenen Ausgrabungen in Uruk-Warka.* Berlin: Mann, 1962, 39–62.

Dillmann, A. "Das Buch der Jubiläen oder die kleine Genesis," *Jahrbücher der Biblischen wissenschaft* 2 (1850) 230–56; 3 (1851) 1–96.

———. *Das Buch Henoch Uebersetzt und erklärt*. Leipzig: Vogel, 1853.

———. "Pseudepigraphen des Alten Testaments," *RE*, 2ed., 12.341–67.

———. *Lexicon Linguae Aethiopicae*. Reprinted; New York: Ungar, 1955.

Dimant, D. "The 'Fallen Angels' in the Dead Sea Scrolls and in the Apocryphal and Pseudepigraphic Books Related to Them." Unpublished Ph. D. dissertation, Hebrew University, Jerusalem, 1974 (Hebrew).

———. "History According to the Vision of the Animals (Ethiopic Enoch 85-90) [Hebrew]," *mḥqry yrwšlym bmḥšbt yśr'l* 2 (1982) 18–37.

Driver, S. R. *Deuteronomy*. ICC; 3rd ed. Edinburgh: Clark, 1902.

———. *An Introduction to the Literature of the Old Testament*. Reprinted; New York: Meridian, 1957.

Ebach, J. *Weltentstehung und Kulturentwicklung bei Philo von Byblos*. BWANT 108. Stuttgart: Kohlhammer, 1979.

Ebeling, E. *Keilschrifttexte aus Assur religiösen Inhalts*. Leipzig: Hinrichs, 1920.

Ehrlich, E. L. *Der Traum im Alten Testament*. BZAW 73. Berlin: Töpelmann, 1953.

Eissfeldt, O. *The Old Testament: An Introduction*. New York/Evanston: Harper and Row, 1965.

———. "Wahrsagung im Alten Testament." In *La divination en Mésopotamie ancienne et dans les régions voisines*. Rencontre assyriologique internationale 14. Bibliothèque des Centres d'Études supérieures spécialisées; Paris: Presses Universitaires de France, 1966, 141–46.

Finkelstein, J. J. "The Antediluvian Kings: A University of California Tablet," *JCS* 17 (1963) 39–51.

Fitzmyer, J. "The Aramaic 'Elect of God' Text from Qumran Cave IV," *CBQ* 27 (1965) 348–72.

———. *The Genesis Apocryphon of Qumran Cave 1*. BibOr 18A. Rome: Biblical Institute, 1971.

Fohrer, G. "Prophetie und Magie," *ZAW* 78 (1966) 25–47.

Freudenthal, J. *Hellenistische Studien 1 & 2: Alexander Polyhistor und die von ihm erhaltenen Reste judäischer und samaritanischer Geschichtswerke*. Breslau: Skutsch, 1875.

Gadd, C. J. *Ideas of Divine Rule in the Ancient East*. Schweich Lectures 1945. London: Oxford, 1948.

Gil, M. "ḥnwk b'rṣ hḥyym [Enoch in the Land of Life]," *Tarbiz* 38 (1968-69) 322–37.

Glasson, T. F. *Greek Influence in Jewish Eschatology*. London: SPCK, 1961.

Goetze, A. "An Old Babylonian Prayer of the Divination Priest," *JCS* 22 (1968) 25–29.

Goldstein, J. *1 Maccabees*. AB 41. Garden City: Doubleday, 1976.

Gray, G. *Numbers*. ICC; Edinburgh: Clark, 1903.

Grayson, A. K. and Lambert, W. "Akkadian Prophecies," *JCS* 18 (1964) 7–30.

Grayson, A. K. "Divination and the Babylonian Chronicles." In *La Divination en Mésopotamie*, 69–76.

————. *Babylonian Historical-Literary Texts*. Toronto Semitic Texts and Studies 3. Toronto/Buffalo: University of Toronto, 1975.

————. "Assyria and Babylonia," *Or* 49 (1980) 140–94.

Greenfield, J. C. and Stone, M. E. "The Book of Enoch and the Traditions of Enoch," *Numen* 26 (1979) 89–103.

Grelot, P. "L'eschatologie des Esséniens et le livre d'Hénoch," *RevQ* 1 (1958–59) 113–31.

————. "La géographie mythique d'Hénoch et ses sources orientales," *RB* 65 (1958) 33–69.

————. "La légende d'Hénoch dans les apocryphes et dans la Bible: origine et signification," *RSR* 46 (1958) 5–26, 181–220.

————. "Soixante-dix semaines d'années," *Bib* 50 (1969) 169–86.

————. "Hénoch et ses écritures," *RB* 82 (1975) 481–500.

Grintz, Y. M. "Balaam: In the Aggadah," *Encyclopaedia Judaica* 4.123–24.

Gruenwald, I. *Apocalyptic and Merkavah Mysticism*. AGJU 14. Leiden/Cologne: Brill, 1980.

Gunkel, H. "Der Schreiberengel Nabû im A. T. und in Judentum," *ARW* 1 (1898) 294–300.

————. *Genesis*. 9th ed. = 3rd ed. Göttingen: Vandenhoeck & Ruprecht, 1977 (1910).

Hallo, W. W. "On the Antiquity of Sumerian Literature," *JAOS* 83 (1963) 167–76.

————. "Akkadian Apocalypses," *IEJ* 16 (1966) 231–42.

————. "Antediluvian Cities," *JCS* 23 (1970) 57–67.

Hanson, P. D. *The Dawn of Apocalyptic: The Historical and Sociological Roots of Jewish Apocalyptic Eschatology*. Philadelphia: Fortress, 1975.

————. "Apocalypticism," *IDBSup* 28–34.

————. "Prolegomena to the Study of Jewish Apocalyptic." In *Magnalia Dei: The Mighty Acts of God*. Ed. F. M. Cross, W. E. Lemke, and P. D. Miller; Garden City: Doubleday, 1976, 389–413.

————. "Rebellion in Heaven, Azazel, and Euhemeristic Heroes in 1 Enoch 6–11," *JBL* 96 (1977) 197–233.

Hartman, L. *Prophecy Interpreted: The Formation of Some Jewish Apocalyptic Texts and of the Eschatological Discourse Mark 13 Par*. ConB 1, Lund: Gleerup, 1966.

————. *Asking for a Meaning: A Study of 1 Enoch 1–5.* ConB 12. Lund: Gleerup, 1979.

Hartman, T. "Some Thoughts on the Sumerian King List and Genesis 5 and 11B," *JBL* 91 (1972) 25–32.

Hasel, G. "The Four World Empires of Daniel 2 Against Its Near Eastern Environment," *JSOT* 12 (1979) 17–30.

Heidel, A. *The Gilgamesh Epic and Old Testament Parallels.* 2nd ed. Chicago: University of Chicago, 1949.

————. *The Babylonian Genesis.* 2nd ed. Chicago/London: University of Chicago, 1951.

Helfmeyer, F. J. "Hālakh," *TDOT* 3.388–403.

Hengel, M. *Judaism and Hellenism.* 2 vols. Philadelphia: Fortress, 1974.

Hoftijzer, J. and Kooij, G. van der. *Aramaic Texts from Deir ʿAllā.* Documenta et Monumenta Orientis Antiqui 19. Leiden: Brill, 1976.

Horgan, M. P. *Pesharim: Qumran Interpretations of Biblical Books.* CBQMS 8. Washington: Catholic Biblical Association, 1979.

Hultgård, A. "Das Judentum in der hellenistisch-römischen Zeit und die iranische Religion—ein religionsgeschichtliches Problem." In *Aufstieg und Niedergang der römischen Welt:* II. *Principat* 19/1. ed. H. Temporini and W. Haase; Berlin/New York: DeGruyter, 1979, 512–90.

Hunger, H. *XXVI/XXVII. vorläufiger Bericht über die von dem Deutschen Archäologischen Institut und der Deutschen Orientgesellschaft aus Mitteln der Deutschen Forschungsgemeinschaft unternommenen Ausgrabungen in Uruk-Warka.* Berlin: Mann, 1972.

Jacobsen, T. *The Sumerian King List.* Oriental Institute of the University of Chicago, Assyriological Studies 11. Chicago: University of Chicago, 1939.

————. *The Treasures of Darkness: A History of Mesopotamian Religion.* New Haven/London: Yale, 1976.

Jacoby, F. *Die Fragmente der griechischen Historiker.* 3 vols. Leiden: Brill, 1923-.

Jansen. H. L. *Die Henochgestalt: Eine vergleichende religionsgeschichtliche Untersuchung.* Norske Videnskaps-Akademi i Oslo II. Hist.-Filos. Klasse 1. Oslo: Dybwad, 1939.

Jastrow, M. *The Civilization of Babylonia and Assyria.* Reprinted; New York: Blom, 1971.

Johnson, A. R. "*Māšāl*" in *Wisdom in Israel and in the Ancient Near East.* VTSup 3. ed. M. Noth and D. W. Thomas; Leiden: Brill, 1960, 162–69.

Knibb, M. "The Exile in the Literature of the Intertestamental Period," *HeyJ* 17 (1976) 253–72.

————. *The Ethiopic Book of Enoch: A new edition in the light of the Aramaic Dead Sea Fragments.* 2 vols. Oxford: Clarendon, 1978.

Kobelski, P. *Melchizedek and Melchireša<sup>c</sup>*. CBQMS 10. Washington: Catholic Biblical Association, 1981.

Koch, K. *The Rediscovery of Apocalyptic*. SBT 2/22. Naperville: Allenson, 1970.

———. "Die mysteriösen Zahlen der judäischen Könige und die apokalyptischen Jahrwochen," *VT* 28 (1978) 433–41.

Komoróczy, G. "Berosos and the Mesopotamian Literature," *Acta Antiqua* 21 (1973) 125–52.

Kraus, F. R. "Zur Liste der älteren Könige von Babylonien," *ZA* 16 (1952) 29–60.

Lambdin, T. O. "Egyptian Loan Words in the Old Testament," *JAOS* 73 (1953) 145-55.

Lambert, W. *Babylonian Wisdom Literature*. Oxford: Clarendon, 1960.

———. "A Catalogue of Texts and Authors," *JCS* 16 (1962) 59–77.

———. "A New Look at the Babylonian Background of Genesis," *JTS* 16 (1965) 287–300.

———. "Enmeduranki and Related Matters," *JCS* 21 (1967) 126–38.

———. "History and the Gods: A Review Article," *Or* 39 (1970) 170–77.

———. "A New Fragment from a List of Antediluvian Kings and Marduk's Chariot." In *Symbolae Biblicae et Mesopotamicae Francisco Mario Theodoro de Liagre Böhl Dedicatae*. Ed. M. A. Beek, A. A. Kampman, C. Nijland, and J. Ryckmans; Leiden: Brill, 1973, 271–80.

———. "The Seed of Kingship." In *Le palais et la royauté: archéologie et civilisation*. Ed. P. Garelli. XIXe Rencontre Assyriologique Internationale, 1971; Paris: Geuthner, 1974, 427–40.

———. "Berossus and Babylonian Eschatology," *Iraq* 38 (1974) 171–73.

———. "Babylonien und Israel," *Theologische Realenzyklopädie* (ed. G. Krause and G. Müller; New York/Berlin: DeGruyter, 1977—), 5.67–79.

Landsberger, B. and Tadmor, H. "Fragments of Clay Liver Models from Hazor," *IEJ* 14 (1964) 201–17.

Langdon, S. "An Assyrian Royal Inscription from a Series of Poems," *JRAS* (1932) 33–41.

Largement, R. "Les oracles de Bile<sup>c</sup>am et la mantique suméro-akkadienne." In *Ecole des langues orientales anciennes de l'Institut Catholique de Paris: Mémorial du cinquantenaire 1914–1964*. Travaux de l'Institut Catholique de Paris 10. Paris: Bloud et Gay, 1964, 37–50.

Leichty, E. "Teratological Omens." In *La divination en Mésopotamie*, 131–39.

———. *The Omen Series Šumma Izbu*. Texts from Cuneiform Sources IV, Locust Valley: J. J. Augustin, 1970.

Levine, B. "The Deir <sup>c</sup>Alla Plaster Inscriptions," *JAOS* 101 (1981) 195–205.

Licht, J. "twrt hᶜtym šl kt mdbr yhwdh wšl mḥšby qyṣyn ᵓḥrym [The Doctrine of Times of the Sect of the Desert of Judah and of Other Computers of Seasons]," *EI* 8 (1967) 63–70.

Littmann, E. "Das Buch der Jubiläen." In *Die Apokryphen und Pseudepigraphen des Alten Testaments.* 2 vols. Ed. E. Kautzsch; Tübingen: Freiburg/Leipzig: Mohr, 1900, 2.31–119.

Long, B. "The Effect of Divination upon Israelite Literature," *JBL* 92 (1973) 489–97.

———. "Divination," *IDBSup* 241–43.

McCown, C. C. "Hebrew and Egyptian Apocalyptic Literature," *HTR* 18 (1925) 387–411.

McKane, W. *Prophets and Wise Men.* SBT 44. London: SCM, 1965.

Malamat, A. "King Lists of the Old Babylonian Period and Biblical Genealogies," *JAOS* 88 (1968) 163–73.

Martin, F. *Le livre d'Hénoch.* Paris: Letouzey et Ané, 1906.

Mendelsohn, I. "Divination," *IDB* 1.856–58.

Milik, J. T. "Hénoch au pays des aromates (ch. XXVII à XXXII): Fragments araméens de la grotte 4 de Qumran," *RB* 65 (1958) 70–77.

———. "Fragments grecs du livre d'Hénoch (P. Oxy. xvii 2069)," *Chronique d'Égypte* 46 (1971) 321–43.

———. "A propos de 11QJub," *Bib* 54 (1973) 77–78.

———. *The Books of Enoch: Aramaic Fragments of Qumrân Cave 4.* Oxford: Clarendon, 1976.

Müller, H. P. "Magisch-mantische Weisheit und die Gestalt Daniels," *UF* 1 (1969) 79–94.

———. "Mantische Weisheit und Apokalyptik," *Congress Volume, Uppsala 1971.* VTSup 22. Leiden: Brill, 1972, 268–93.

Neugebauer, O. "The History of Ancient Astronomy: Problems and Methods," *JNES* 4 (1945) 1–38.

———. "Studies in Ancient Astronomy. VIII. The Water Clock in Babylonian Astronomy," *Isis* 37 (1947) 37–43.

———. *Astronomical Cuneiform Texts.* 3 vols. London: Lund Humphreys, 1955.

———. *The Exact Sciences in Antiquity.* 2nd ed. Providence: Brown, 1957.

———. "Notes on Ethiopic Astronomy," *Or* 33 (1964) 49–71.

———. *A History of Ancient Mathematical Astronomy.* Studies in the History of Mathematical and Physical Sciences 1. 3 vols. Berlin/Heidelberg/New York: Springer, 1975.

_____ . *Ethiopic Astronomy and Computus*. Österreiche Akademie der Wissenschaften, Philosophisch-Historische Klasse, Sitzungsberichte 347. Veröffentlichungen der Kommission für Geschichte der Mathematik, Naturwissenschaften und Medizin, Heft 22. Vienna: Akademie der Wissenschaften, 1979.

_____ . *The 'Astronomical' Chapters of the Ethiopic Book of Enoch (72–82)*: *Translation and Commentary, With Additional Notes on the Aramaic Fragments* by Matthew Black. Det Kongelige Danske Videnskabernes Selskab Matematisk–fysiske Meddelelser, 40:10. Copenhagen: Munksgaard, 1981.

Newsom, C. "Enoch 83–90: The Historical Résumé as Biblical Exegesis" (unpublished seminar paper, Harvard, 1975).

_____ . "The Development of *1 Enoch* 6–19: Cosmology and Judgment," *CBQ* 42 (1980) 310–29.

Nickelsburg, G. W. E. *Resurrection, Immortality, and Eternal Life in Intertestamental Judaism*. HTS 26. Cambridge: Harvard University, 1972.

_____ . "Apocalyptic and Myth in 1 Enoch 6–11," *JBL* 96 (1977) 383–405.

_____ . "The Apocalyptic Message of *1 Enoch* 92–105," *CBQ* 39 (1977) 309–28.

_____ . Review of Milik, *The Books of Enoch* in *CBQ* 40 (1978) 411–19.

_____ . "Riches, the Rich, and God's Judgment in 1 Enoch 92–105 and the Gospel According to Luke," *NTS* 25 (1979) 324–44.

_____ . *Jewish Literature Between the Bible and the Mishnah*. Philadelphia: Fortress, 1981.

Notscher, F. "Himmlische Bücher und Schicksalsglaube in Qumran," *RevQ* 1 (1958-59) 405–11.

Noth, M. *Numbers*. Old Testament Library; Philadelphia: Westminster, 1968.

Nougayrol, J. "Trente ans de recherches sur la divination babylonienne (1935-1965)." In *La divination en Mésopotamie*, 5–19.

_____ . "La divination babylonienne." In *La divination*, 1.25–81.

Oldfather, C. H. *Diodorus of Sicily*. LCL; Cambridge: Harvard University/ London: Heinemann, 1933.

Oppenheim, A. L. *The Interpretation of Dreams in the Ancient Near East, with a Translation of an Assyrian Dream-Book*. Transactions of the American Philosophical Society 46/3. Philadelphia: American Philosophical Society, 1956.

_____ . "Divination and Celestial Observation in the Latest Assyrian Empire," *Centaurus* 14 (1969) 97–135.

_____ . *Ancient Mesopotamia: Portrait of a Dead Civilization*. Rev. ed. completed by E. Reiner; Chicago/London: University of Chicago, 1977.

Osswald, E. "Zum Problem der *vaticinia ex eventu*," *ZAW* 75 (1963) 27–44.

Osten-Sacken, P. von der. *Die Apokalyptik in ihrem Verhältnis zu Prophetie und Weisheit*. Theologische Existenz Heute 157, Munich: Kaiser, 1969.

Parpola, S. *Letters from Assyrian Scholars to the Kings Esarhaddon and Assurbanipal, Part I: Texts*. AOAT 5/1. Kevelaer: Butzon & Bercker/ Neukirchen-Vluyn: Neukirchener, 1970.

Pettinato, G. "Zur Überlieferungsgeschichte der aB-Ölomentexte und einige Erwägungen zur Stellung der Ölwahrsagung in der Religionsgeschichte." In *La divination en Mésopotamie*, 95–107.

Rad, G. von. "Hiob xxxviii und die altägyptische Weisheit." In *Wisdom in Israel and in the Ancient Near East*. VTSup 3. Ed. M. Noth and D. W. Thomas; Leiden: Brill, 1960, 293–301.

———. *Genesis*. Old Testament Library; Philadelphia: Westminster, 1961.

———. *Old Testament Theology*. 2 vols. Edinburgh: Oliver and Boyd, 1962.

———. *Deuteronomy*. Old Testament Library; Philadelphia: Westminster, 1966.

———. *Theologie des Alten Testaments*, vol. 2: *Die Theologie der prophetischen Überlieferungen Israels*. Einführung in die evangelische Theologie 1, 5th ed. Munich: Kaiser, 1968.

———. *Wisdom in Israel*. Nashville/New York: Abingdon, 1972.

Rau, E. "Kosmologie, Eschatologie und die Lehrautorität Henochs: Traditions- und formgeschichtliche Untersuchungen zum äth. Henochbuch und zu verwandten Schriften." Unpublished Ph. D. dissertation, University of.Hamburg, Hamburg, 1974.

Rawlinson, H. C. *et al. The Cuneiform Inscriptions of Western Asia*. Vol. 2. London: Bowler, 1866.

Reese, G. "Die Geschichte Israels in der Auffassung des frühen Judentums: Eine Untersuchung der Tiervision und der Zehnwochenapokalypse des äthiopischen Henochbuches, der Geschichtsdarstellung der Assumptio Mosis und der des 4 Esrabuches." Unpublished Ph. D. dissertation, Ruprecht-Karl-Universität, Heidelberg, 1967.

Reiner, E. "Fortune-Telling in Mesopotamia," *JNES* 19 (1960) 23–35.

———. "The Etiological Myth of the 'Seven Sages'," *Or* 30 (1961) 1–11.

———, with Pingree, D. *Babylonian Planetary Omens, Part One: Enūma Anu Enlil Tablet 63: The Venus Tablet of Ammiṣaduqa*. Bibliotheca Mesopotamica 2/1. Malibu: Undena, 1975.

Rowley, H. H. *The Relevance of Apocalyptic*. 2nd ed. London/Redhill: Lutterworth, 1947.

Russell, D. S. *The Method and Message of Jewish Apocalyptic*. Old Testament Library; Philadelphia: Westminster, 1964.

Rutten, M. "Trente-deux modèles de foies in argile provenant de Tell-Hariri," *RA* 35 (1938) 36–70.

Saggs, H. W. F. *The Greatness That Was Babylon.* New York/Scarborough: New American Library, 1968.

Sasson, J. M. "Word-Play in Gen 6:8-9," *CBQ* 37 (1975) 165-66.

————. "Generation, Seventh," *IDBSup* 354-56.

————. "A Genealogical 'Convention' in Biblical Chronography?" *ZAW* 90 (1978) 171-85.

Schmidt, A. "Die Angaben über Henoch Gen 5, 21-24 in der LXX." In *Wort, Lied und Gottesspruch: Beiträge zur Septuaginta.* Festschrift für Joseph Ziegler. Ed. J. Schreiner; Forschung zur Bibel 1. Würzburg: Echter, 1972, 161-69.

Schmidt, J. M. *Die jüdische Apokalyptik: die Geschichte ihrer Erforschung von den Anfängen bis zu den Textfunden von Qumran.* 2nd ed. Neukirchen-Vluyn: Neukirchener, 1976.

Schnabel, P. *Berossos und die babylonisch-hellenistische Literatur.* Leipzig/Berlin, Teubner, 1923; reprinted Hildesheim: Olms, 1968.

Schott, A. and Schaumberger, J. "Vier Briefe Mâr-Ištars an Asarhaddon über Himmelserscheinungen der Jahre—670/668," *ZA* 47 (1942) 89-130.

Schrader, E. *Die Keilinschriften und das Alte Testament.* 2 vols. 3rd ed. Ed. H. Zimmern and H. Winckler; Berlin: Reuther & Reichard, 1902-03.

Skehan, P. W. "A Fragment of the 'Song of Moses' (Deut 32) from Qumran," *BASOR* 136 (1954) 12-15.

Skinner, J. *Genesis.* 2nd ed. ICC; Edinburgh: Clark, 1930.

Smyth, H. W. *Aeschylus I.* LCL; Cambridge: Harvard University/London: Heinemann, 1922.

Speiser, E. *Genesis.* 2nd ed. AB 1, Garden City: Doubleday, 1964.

Stern, M. *Greek and Latin Authors on Jews and Judaism,* vol. 1: *From Herodotus to Plutarch.* Jerusalem: Israel Academy of Sciences and Humanities, 1976.

Stone, M. "Lists of Revealed Things in the Apocalyptic Literature." In *Magnalia Dei: The Mighty Acts of God.* Ed. F. M. Cross, W. E. Lemke, and P. D. Miller; Garden City: Doubleday, 1976, 414-52.

————. "The Book of Enoch and Judaism in the Third Century B.C.E.," *CBQ* 40 (1978) 479-92.

Strugnell, J. "The Angelic Liturgy at Qumran: 4QSerek Šîrôt ᶜÔlat Haššabbāt." *Congress Volume, Oxford, 1959.* VTSup 7. Leiden: Brill, 1960, 318-45.

Suter, D. W. "*MĀŠĀL* in the Similitudes of Enoch," *JBL* 100 (1981) 193-212.

Thackeray, H. St. J. *Josephus IV: Jewish Antiquities Book I-IV.* LCL; Cambridge: Harvard University/London: Heinemann, 1930.

Tisserant. E. "Fragments syriaques du Livre des Jubilés," *RB* 30 (1921) 55-86, 206-32.

202     *Enoch and the Growth of an Apocalyptic Tradition*

Ullendorff, E. and Knibb, M. Review of Milik, *The Books of Enoch* in *BSO(A)S* 40 (1977) 601–02.

VanderKam, J. "The Theophany of Enoch i, 3b-7, 9," *VT* 23 (1973) 129–50.

———. *Textual and Historical Studies in the Book of Jubilees.* HSM 14, Missoula: Scholars, 1977.

———. "Enoch Traditions in Jubilees and Other Second-Century Sources," SBLASP (1978), 1.229–51.

———. "The Origin, Character, and Early History of the 364-Day Calendar: A Reassessment of Jaubert's Hypotheses," *CBQ* 41 (1979) 390–411.

———. "The Righteousness of Noah." In *Ideal Figures in Ancient Judaism: Profiles and Paradigms.* Ed. G. W. E. Nickelsburg and J. J. Collins; SCS 12. Chico, CA: Scholars, 1980, 13–32.

———. "2 Maccabees 6,7a and Calendrical Change in Jerusalem," *JSJ* 12 (1981) 52–74.

———. "1 Enoch 77, 3 and a Babylonian Map of the World," *RevQ* 11 (1983) 271–78.

Wacholder, B. Z. *Eupolemus: A Study of Judaeo-Greek Literature.* Monographs of the Hebrew Union College 3. Cincinnati/New York/Los Angeles/Jerusalem: HUC, 1974.

———. *Essays on Jewish Chronology and Chronography.* New York: KTAV, 1976.

Waerden, B. L. van der. *Die Anfänge der Astronomie.* Erwachende Wissenschaft 2. Groningen: Noordhoff, 1965.

Wehr, H. *A Dictionary of Modern Written Arabic.* Ed. J. M. Cowan; 3rd ed. Ithaca, NY: Spoken Language Services, 1976.

Weidner, E. "Babylonisches im Buche Henoch," *OLZ* 19 (1916) cols. 74–75.

———. "Die astrologische Serie Enûma Anu Enlil," *AfO* 14 (1941-44) 172-95, 308–18; 17 (1954-56) 71–89; 22 (1968-69) 65–75.

———. "Astrologische Geographie im Alten Orient," *AfO* 20 (1963) 117–21.

Westermann, C. *Isaiah 40-66* Old Testament Library; Philadelphia: Westminster, 1969.

———. *Genesis.* BK I/1. Neukirchen-Vluyn: Neukirchener, 1974.

Widengren. G. "Iran and Israel in Parthian Times with Special Regard to the Ethiopic *Book of Enoch*," *Temenos* 2 (1966) 139–77.

Wildberger, H. *Jesaja.* BK X/1. Neukirchen-Vluyn: Neukirchener, 1972.

Wilson, R. "The Old Testament Genealogies in Recent Research," *JBL* 94 (1975) 175–88.

———. *Genealogy and History in the Biblical World.* Yale Near Eastern Researches 7, New Haven/London: Yale University, 1977.

Winston, D. "The Iranian Component in the Bible, Apocrypha, and Qumran: A Review of the Evidence," *HR* 5 (1966) 183–216.

Yadin, Y. *The Scroll of the War of the Sons of Light Against the Sons of Darkness.* Oxford: Oxford University, 1962.

Zimmern, H. *Beiträge zur Kenntnis der babylonischen Religion:Die Beschwörungstafeln Šurpu, Ritualtafeln für den Wahrsager, Beschwörer und Sänger.* Assyriologische Bibliothek 12. Leipzig: Hinrichs, 1901.

_____ . "Zu den 'Keilschrifttexten aus Assur religiösen Inhalts'," *ZA* 30 (1915/16) 184–229.

_____ . "Die sieben Weisen Babyloniens," *ZA* 35 (1924) 151–54.

(See also Schrader, E.)

# SUBJECT INDEX

# INDEX OF SCRIPTURAL PASSAGES

# INDEX OF PSEUDEPIGRAPHICAL PASSAGES

| 2 Enoch | | 4 Esdras | |
|---|---|---|---|
| 22–23 (B) | 85 n.42 | 14:49 | 33 n.40 |
| 2 Baruch | | | |
| 59:5-11 | 5 | | |